© Laura Wilson

SKIP HOLLANDSWORTH is an award-winning journalist, screenwriter, and executive editor of *Texas Monthly* magazine. His work was included in the 2002, 2003, 2006, and 2010 editions of *Best American Crime Writing*, and he has won a National Magazine Award for feature writing. Hollandsworth cowrote the acclaimed screenplay *Bernie* with director Richard Linklater. He lives in Dallas with his wife and daughter.

Additional Praise for *The Midnight Assassin*

"Skip Hollandsworth knows his way around a crime scene. . . . This is true crime of high quality. . . . Mr. Hollandsworth handles gruesome details with a smart, restrained touch. . . . Chilling."
—John Williams, *The New York Times*

"Hollandsworth immerses the reader in the time and place with meticulously researched detail." —Talia Lavin, *The New Yorker*

"This riveting—and frankly, terrifying—true story of a pre–Jack the Ripper serial killer in 1880s Austin reads like a crime thriller and makes a widespread panic from more than one hundred years ago feel palpable." —*Entertainment Weekly*

"A lucid, lurid . . . page-turner that evokes a simpler time, when Texas was young and its cities were on the rise . . . [Hollandsworth's] book has its tragic charm." —Matt Damsker, *USA Today*

"A thoroughly researched, excitingly written history . . . Does a fine job of setting the crimes in the context of a growing metropolis in the midst of an economic boom . . . Absorbing."
—Tom Nolan, *The Wall Street Journal*

"Fans of Erik Larson's *Devil in the White City* will relish this gripping and atmospheric account of a horrific series of murders in late-nineteenth-century Texas. . . . With a novelist's eye for detail, the author brings the reader inside the reign of terror that gripped Austin, Texas. . . . This true-crime page-turner is a balanced and insightful examination of one of the most stirring serial killing sprees in American history, and certainly one of the least well-known."
—*Publishers Weekly* (starred review)

"Skip Hollandsworth has long entertained and enlightened—and perhaps appalled—readers of *Texas Monthly* with his compellingly lurid dispatches from the rich underworld of Lone Star crime. We fans of his have wondered when he would expand his range and deliver a book. He has now done so, and it was worth waiting. . . . Hollandsworth spent more than a decade pulling this tale together and shows himself to be a master storyteller working at the top of his form."

—*The Dallas Morning News*

"It's clear from the narrative polish that true crime is one of the author's fortes; he provides just the right amount of subtle hinting at a suspect and the accumulation of details left out until the perfect moment. . . . An engaging true-crime tale." —*Kirkus Reviews*

"In *The Midnight Assassin*, *Texas Monthly* editor Skip Hollandsworth tells the little-known story in riveting fashion, presenting this historical page-turner in spellbinding detail. . . . Hollandsworth balances the grim realities . . . with unexpected humor." —*BookPage*

"Hollandsworth spins a spine-tingling tale set in the context of Austin's transformation from a tiny outpost into a young city."

—*Alcade* magazine

"Hollandsworth skillfully blends a disturbing murder mystery with the history of the Lone Star State when it was just forty years into statehood. . . . *The Midnight Assassin* captures the lawlessness and ribaldry of frontier life—you can almost hear the tinny piano, the laughter, the squeals, the breaking glass and boot heels on wooden planks as a saloon fistfight spills into the street. . . . Hollandsworth has delivered— for lovers of true-crime stories, American history, and underappreciated Texana—an irresistible spellbinder."

—*The National Book Review*

"Skip Hollandsworth has a terrific new book about how Austin was home to America's first serial killer, and it's a must-read for fans of local history. . . . Lively and lurid." —*Austin American Statesman*

"[*The Midnight Assassin*] should stand among the genre's greats. . . . What makes *The Midnight Assassin* every bit as addictive as *Making a Murderer* is that Hollandsworth perfectly captures the terror that gripped Austin." —*Men's Journal*

"A well-deserved new feather in Hollandsworth's well-feathered hat . . . His rendering of time and place is sublime; as much as the assassin remains opaque, the city of Austin is etched in high relief, and becomes the key character of the book." —*Minneapolis Star Tribune*

"A ridiculously entertaining, page-turning history . . . Hollandsworth's prodigious, dogged research provides an engaging history of Austin's development." —*Lone Star Literary Review*

"Before Hollandsworth can tear apart circa-1880s Austin, he first has to build it. The way he manages to do both proves just how gifted a storyteller the longtime *Texas Monthly* writer really is. . . . Strip away the crimes, and *The Midnight Assassin* functions as an adroit chronicle of Austin's first toddling steps toward the city we know today. Ignore the scenery, and it's still a page-turning true-crime thriller." —*D* Magazine

"What makes *The Midnight Assassin* a fascinating read over much of your typical true-crime fare is the portrait of a city. . . . *The Midnight Assassin* is most compelling not in the moments of crime, but in the way that the community leaders in Austin try to quash the problem and save their city from self-destructing. . . . An incredible story." —*American Microreviews*

"Skip Hollandsworth has achieved a literary miracle with *The Midnight Assassin*. With haunting granularity, Hollandsworth breathes vivid life into a forgotten, century-old tale of the hunt for America's first diabolical serial murderer—set in, of all places, the quaint but upwardly mobile town of Austin, Texas. To read *The Midnight Assassin* is to experience the lost innocence of a nineteenth-century capital city set on edge by the unseen monster in its midst." —Robert Draper, *The New York Times Magazine* and author of *Dead Certain*

THE MIDNIGHT ASSASSIN

THE HUNT FOR AMERICA'S FIRST SERIAL KILLER

SKIP HOLLANDSWORTH

PICADOR   HENRY HOLT AND COMPANY   NEW YORK

For Shannon, Hailey, and Tyler, with all my love

picadorusa.com • picadorbookroom.tumblr.com
twitter.com/picadorusa • facebook.com/picadorusa

Picador® is a U.S. registered trademark and is used by Macmillan Publishing Group, LLC, under license from Pan Books Limited.

For book club information, please visit facebook.com/picadorbookclub or e-mail marketing@picadorusa.com.

Designed by Kelly S. Too

The Library of Congress has cataloged the Henry Holt edition as follows:

Hollandsworth, Skip.
The midnight assassin : panic, scandal, and the hunt for America's first serial killer / Skip Hollandsworth.
p. cm.
Includes bibliographical references and index.
ISBN 978-0-8050-9767-2 (hardcover)
ISBN 978-0-8050-9768-9 (e-book)
1. Serial murders—Texas—Austin—History—19th century.
2. Serial murderers—Texas—Austin—History—19th century.
I. Title.
HV6534.A8H65 2016
364.152'32092—dc23   2015024689

Picador Paperback ISBN 978-1-250-11849-3

Our books may be purchased in bulk for promotional, educational, or business use. Please contact your local bookseller or the Macmillan Corporate and Premium Sales Department at 1-800-221-7945, extension 5442, or by e-mail at MacmillanSpecialMarkets@macmillan.com.

First published by Henry Holt and Company, LLC

First Picador Edition: April 2017

10 9 8 7 6

"The crimes still remain a mystery. They are abnormal and unnatural, as compared with ordinary crimes among men. No one, not even the expert, skilled in the detection of crime, can find a plausible motive. The mutilated bodies of the victims are always found in parts of the city where crime is not expected or anticipated, and beyond the fact of the murders we have never been able to penetrate."

—John W. Robertson, Mayor of Austin, Texas, November 10, 1885

CONTENTS

THE
MIDNIGHT
ASSASSIN

A panoramic view of Austin, Texas, in the 1880s

PROLOGUE

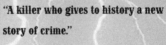

"A killer who gives to history a new story of crime."

PROLOGUE

I **first read about him when I was shown a pamphlet, the pages**
umber with age, titled "Leather Apron; or, the Horrors of Whitechapel." Published in the year 1888, the pamphlet chronicled a series of
murders that were then taking place in London. An unknown killer,
who was being called Jack the Ripper, had attacked five prostitutes in
the city's East End over a three-month period, slitting their throats and
mutilating their bodies. On page 10, the author mentioned that London
police officials were speculating that the Ripper was the same man who
had committed a series of similar murders three years earlier in "a small
city in Texas."

Why is it that certain sensational events in history are remembered
and others, just as dramatic, are completely forgotten? Jack the Ripper
has haunted the imagination of the public like no other killer in Western civilization. He is universally considered to be the prototype of
the modern-day criminal monster, his exploits the subject of at least a
hundred books and dozens of films and plays.

But beginning in December 1884, Austin, Texas, was terrorized by someone equally as vicious and, in some ways, far more diabolical than London's Ripper. For almost exactly one year, the Austin killer criss-crossed the entire city, striking on moonlit nights, using axes, knives, and long steel rods to rip apart women. On Christmas Eve of 1885, almost exactly one year after the killings began, he brought Austin to the brink of chaos when, in the space of an hour, he slaughtered two prominent women in separate neighborhoods, cutting up their bodies in their backyards before vanishing in the briefest imaginable time.

The story was treated as one of the great American murder mysteries of the late nineteenth century, a blood-curdling whodunit chronicled on the front pages of newspapers from New York to Chicago to San Francisco. Joseph Pulitzer, the famous publisher of the *New York World*, was so fascinated by what was happening that he commissioned a reporter to produce a 7,000-word article under the headline "Why These Assassinations? The Extraordinary Series of Similar Murders in a Texas City." Several journalists proclaimed in their articles that the murders were nothing less than an Edgar Allan Poe tale of terror come to life. One reporter nicknamed the killer "the Midnight Assassin . . . who strides at will over Austin's sacred soil."

For the first time on record, an American city was forced to confront a brilliant, brutal monster who for some unknown reason was driven to murder, in almost ritualistic fashion, one woman after another—"a killer who gives to history a new story of crime," the *New York World* declared. Baffled Austin police officers sat around a table, attempting to predict what circumstances would make this Midnight Assassin strike again. Anxious citizens came up with increasingly desperate proposals to stop the murders. (One citizen suggested that every woman in Austin be given a large guard dog. Another wanted the city to be lit with newly invented electric "arc lamps" so that the killer would have no place at night to hide.) Self-proclaimed "private eyes" arrived in Austin to begin their own investigations in hopes of finding the killer so that they could claim the sizable reward money being offered by the city's businessmen and by the governor of Texas himself. Even a group of distinguished medical doctors in New York City who were known as "alienists," experts in the study of mentally troubled minds, gathered in the lecture hall at the New York Academy of Medicine, just across the street from Bryant Park, to discuss the methods of the Midnight Assassin, hoping that they too might somehow uncover his identity.

Before it was all over, at least a dozen men would be arrested in connection with the murders. There would be three murder trials of three different suspects, all of whom would vehemently proclaim their innocence. Along the way, the murders would expose what a newspaper described as "the most extensive and profound scandal ever known in Austin," one that ruined the careers of several prominent Austin men and set off sensational allegations that one of the state's most well-known politicians was himself the Midnight Assassin. And yes, when Jack the Ripper began his attacks in 1888, London police investigators did wonder if the killer from Austin had crossed the ocean to terrorize their own city.

Who was the Midnight Assassin, and why did he go on such a rampage? Was he a crazed, itinerant outlaw? Was he, as many Austin residents believed, a deranged black man? Or was he well known in Austin society—someone who lived respectably, dressed neatly, and who periodically felt the need to slip out of his house to slaughter a woman? Was it also true, as rumor had it, that he was quietly caught and then put away by city officials who were determined to avoid more public scandal?

It has taken me years to put the story together, looking for facts hidden away in faded newspaper articles and in old scrapbooks, in the crumbling pages of diaries and letters, in long-forgotten records boxed up in the back storage rooms of libraries and government offices, and in files at the state's former lunatic asylum, the once-imposing limestone fortress that loomed over the northern edge of Austin. Some details about the killings were discovered in abandoned sections of cemeteries, the tombstones nearly covered by time. Others were provided by grandchildren and great-grandchildren of residents involved in the

Midnight Assassin's murder spree. And then there were records that should have been readily available but had curiously—tantalizingly—disappeared.

As the journalists once wrote, it is a story worthy of Edgar Allan Poe, a multilayered Gothic saga of madness and intrigue, panic and paranoia, beautiful women and baying bloodhounds, and flabbergasting plot twists and sensational courtroom drama. In fact, a well-regarded New York mystery writer, Kenward Philp, was commissioned by his publisher to produce a short story, filled with shivery Poe-like prose, based on the Austin murders. The publisher then attempted to sell the story, which was titled "The Texas Vendetta," to newspapers around the country.

But only a handful of editors ran the story. Apparently, they concluded, the truth needed no embellishment.

The truth, they said, was scary enough.

PART ONE

DECEMBER
1884 – APRIL 1885

"Doctor Steiner reports a woman lying
near Ravy's."

CHAPTER ONE

A few days before the first murder, the telegraph lines began buzzing with news about a storm making its way south from the Canadian Rockies. A Western Union operator in Sioux City, Iowa, punched out the words "13 degrees at 2 p.m. . . . ice . . . trains slowing."

It was a blue norther, people were saying, the oncoming clouds low and dark blue along the horizon. The storm swooped through the Great Plains, where the cattle turned their rumps against the wind, and then it rushed into Texas, moving so quickly that a cowboy, traveling on horseback across a treeless stretch of land near the town of Archer City, froze to death before he could find shelter. According to a newspaper account, when the cowboy was finally found, he was slumped on the ground, a rim of ice covering his mustache, his eyelids, and the edges of his hat.

When the norther reached the city of Austin, the capital of Texas, in the early morning hours of December 31, 1884—New Year's Eve—it was still cold enough to drop thermometers there by another thirty degrees. The wind knifed through the cracks in the houses, rattling coffee cups laid out on kitchen tables. Ice bounced off the roofs like dried peas. A young man named Tom Chalmers, who was lying in bed at the home of his brother-in-law on the western edge of the city, heard a knocking sound at the front door. Chalmers then heard the voice of a man.

"Help me."

Chalmers and his wife, who lived outside Austin on a small ranch, had come to the city earlier that week to celebrate the holidays. They were the only ones at the home that evening. Chalmers's brother-in-law William Hall, an insurance agent, was with his wife in the coastal city of Galveston, where they had once lived, visiting friends.

The knocking at the door persisted. "Help me," the man shouted again.

Chalmers was not an easy man to intimidate. A former member of the Texas Rangers, the state's police force, he had once been featured in the *Austin Daily Statesman* after he had been thrown by his horse, face-first, onto the ground, breaking all of his front teeth. The article had congratulated Chalmers on his fortitude, noting that he had spit out his broken teeth, returned to his horse, and kept riding.

On this frigid evening, however, he was not all that eager to leave his warm bed. Then he heard the front door open.

The home of Chalmers's brother-in-law was one of Austin's nicer residences, more than 2,000 square feet in size, with two chimneys and ten-foot ceilings. The master bedroom was toward the back of the house. Chalmers rose, crept to the bedroom doorway, and peered down the hall. He had no weapon: his gun was sitting in another part of the house. In the deep gloom of the foyer, he saw a man move past the draperies and stagger over the wooden floors. Based on what Chalmers later told police and newspaper reporters, the man said, "Mr. Tom, Mr. Tom, for God's sakes, do something to help me! Somebody has nearly killed me!"

Chalmers lit a match and held it before him. The light flickered across the face of Walter Spencer, a twenty-nine-year-old black man who worked as a laborer at Butler's Brick Yard. Spencer was also the boyfriend of Mollie Smith, who worked as a cook and maid at the

Halls' home. Mollie was a pretty young woman, about twenty-three years of age. She was known as a "yellow girl," a phrase used by white people in those years to describe a light-skinned black person. She worked six days a week in return for a monthly salary of ten to twelve dollars and a free place to live, which consisted of a tiny one-room servants' quarters—a shack, really, that was in the backyard.

Spencer was barefoot, clad only in a nightshirt. Blood was oozing from several gashes in his head. He was wobbling, as if he was having trouble keeping his balance. He told Chalmers that someone must have attacked him while he had been asleep in bed next to Mollie, hitting him over the head and knocking him unconscious. And the person who attacked him, he said, must have done something with Mollie. She was nowhere to be found.

Spencer seemed terrified, his breaths coming in gasps. He said he had looked for Mollie in the back and front yard, and that he had searched for her up and down the street. Without a lantern, however, he could see nothing: the sky was as black as a skillet. The blood from Spencer's head wound was still flowing down his face and pouring into his mouth, making it difficult to breathe. He had trouble keeping his head up.

"Mr. Tom, please . . . ," Spencer pleaded.

But Chalmers had no intention of walking outside in such weather and looking for a black man's missing girlfriend. That was a matter, of course, that could wait until daylight. What Spencer needed to do, Chalmers said, was wrap a bandage around his head before he bled to death. Chalmers escorted Spencer out of the house, shut the front door, cleaned the blood off the floor, and returned to bed.

CHAPTER TWO

By the time the sun rose at 7:28 that morning, the norther had passed on to the south, but there was still a stinging cold. Only a handful of Austin's 17,000 citizens dared to step outside. It was the kind of morning, a newspaper reporter would later write, "when the average Austin man prefers to lie still . . . and let his wife get up and make the fires."

A little after nine o'clock, the telephone began ringing in the Austin Police Department. The department was located in a large room on the second floor of city hall. It contained a few chairs and tables, a potbellied stove, and a couple of tarnished brass cuspidors for the officers to use whenever they needed to spit out their chewing tobacco. On a wall was the telephone: a walnut box with a hole in the middle, a trumpet-like receiver on one side, and a crank on the other. The department's day clerk, Bart Delong, picked up the receiver, turned the crank, and shouted "Police!" into the hole.

There was static over the phone—after a storm, the telephone wires hanging above the streets would usually get tangled, causing heavier

Congress Avenue, the main boulevard of Austin in the 1880s

static than usual—and then came the voice of a Hello Girl from the downtown telephone exchange. She told Delong that she was patching through a call from the phone box at Ravy's Grocery in the western part of the city.

After some more static, Delong heard the voice of Dr. Ralph Steiner, a surgeon who had been working in Austin for more than twenty years. Steiner kept his remarks brief. All that Delong wrote on the daily police log was the following:

> Doctor Steiner reports a woman lying near Ravy's store and wishes an officer sent out to take charge.

The Austin Police Department consisted of twelve men. Only a few of them were in the office that morning. Grooms Lee, the city's young marshal (chief of police), was home in bed, suffering from dengue fever, a virulent form of the flu. The number two man in the department, Sergeant John Chenneville, was taking the morning off; he would be working the streets later that evening, keeping watch over the New Year's Eve revelers. Delong pointed to William Howe, a young officer who was in his midtwenties, and ordered him to Ravy's to find out what had happened.

Howe mostly did patrol work, spending his shifts on the downtown streets, handing out tickets to citizens who left horses unhitched in front of businesses or who drove their carriages faster than a "slow trot." He arrested vagrants, gun toters, sneak thieves (shoplifters), and moll buzzers (pickpockets who specialized in robbing women). He collared drunks who urinated in the alleys behind the saloons and prostitutes who wandered outside the boundaries of Guy Town, the city's vice district in the southwest corner of downtown.

One thing Howe did not do was investigate the four or five murders that occurred in Austin every year. Those were left to Sergeant Chenneville, who handled all the major criminal investigations. Nevertheless, because Dr. Steiner had said nothing in his phone call about foul play, there was no reason to think the woman's death was due to anything but an accident. Perhaps she had slipped on some ice during the previous night's storm and succumbed to exposure—the kind of death that would require a minor police investigation, if that. Surely, if the woman had been murdered, Steiner would have mentioned that fact to the police.

Howe put on his department-issued Stetson hat and double-breasted gray overcoat with two vertical rows of buttons and a tin police badge pinned to the lapel. He walked down the iron stairs leading to the first floor and headed for the police department's stable behind the city hall building. He mounted a horse and rode toward Ravy's, which was a half mile from downtown. When he arrived, he was directed across the street to the home of the young insurance man William Hall.

Tom Chalmers and Dr. Steiner, who lived a couple of houses away, were waiting for him. A few other men from the neighborhood were also standing around. Chalmers told Howe about Walter Spencer coming to the house, looking for his girlfriend, Mollie Smith, and begging for help. Steiner mentioned that Spencer had come to his home after leaving the Hall residence, where Steiner bandaged his head and sent him on his way. Chalmers then said that just after daylight, a black man who worked for one of the Halls' neighbors had stepped into the back alley to collect some firewood. The man had looked down the alley and seen a "strange-looking object" lying on the ground behind the Halls' outhouse. At first, he thought it was a dead animal. But after taking a closer look, he had seen the scrap of a nightdress. He realized there were legs coming out of that dress: human legs, grotesquely bent. Then he had started screaming.

Chalmers told Howe that he, Steiner, and others had come out of their homes, hurried over to the outhouse, and looked at what the black man had found. Steiner had volunteered to walk over to Ravy's to call the police. Perhaps because he didn't want to offend the sensibilities of the Hello Girl, whom he suspected would be listening in on the phone call, he had decided to say very little to Delong, the police clerk, about what he'd seen.

Howe walked into the servants' quarters. He noticed that two or three pieces of furniture in the small room had been upended and a mirror knocked to the floor and broken. On the bed, the sheets and pillows were saturated in blood. Blood had dripped off one side of the bed and formed a puddle on the floor. At the foot of the bed was a bloodstained ax. On the wall by the door leading into the backyard was a bloody handprint showing what the police in those years called "finger marks."

Howe opened the door and followed a trail of blood for more than fifty feet, got to the outhouse, and stopped.

Mollie Smith was on her back. Her head had been nearly split in two and she had been stabbed repeatedly in the chest and abdomen. Some of the gashes were deep enough to expose her organs. Her legs and arms were also slashed. Blood was everywhere—bright red lung blood and nearly black gut blood. So much blood was around her, filling up the ruts in the alley, that she seemed to be floating in a pool of it.

There is no police record indicating what exactly happened next, but the most probable scenario is that young Howe headed back to Ravy's, called Delong at the police department, and, trying to keep his voice calm, told him he needed help. Soon, other officers arrived at the Halls'. Sergeant Chenneville eventually showed up on his big bay horse. Trotting behind the horse were his bloodhounds, two slobbering dogs of unknown origin that lived in Chenneville's backyard when they weren't tracking criminals on the run.

Chenneville was in his late thirties. He was built like an upright piano through the shoulders, and had a thick mustache that drooped over his upper lip. Whenever he walked into city hall, the employees didn't have to look up from their desks to know he had arrived because of the heavy thud his boots made across the floor. Some of those employees, especially the less muscular men who worked in accounting, had no particular desire to make eye contact with him, perhaps fearing that he might walk over, thrust forward his gun hand, and say hello. According to local gossip, Chenneville's handshake was strong enough to crack corn.

Most citizens fondly called Chenneville "Ronnie O Johnnie." Raised in New Orleans, where he spent his teenage years working as a cabin boy on a Confederate ship that traversed the Mississippi River during the Civil War, Chenneville had come to Austin in the mid-1870s, joined the police department, and quickly became known, in the words of the *Daily Statesman*, as Austin's "most industrious officer." He was often seen barrel-assing down the dirt streets, chasing after troublemakers, his holstered gun slapping against his thigh, and at night he didn't hesitate to push his way into the saloons to break up the brawls among the cowboys who had ridden into town to "hell around," as the police officers wrote in their reports. Because his voice was so loud and commanding, he even had agreed in those years to be the auctioneer at the city market held on Saturday mornings in front of city hall, selling off everything from dry goods to sides of beef.

Now, a decade later, there was very little about Ronnie O Johnnie that had changed. To let the city's rogues and riffraff know that he was still in charge, he continued to work the dirt streets, riding through downtown at least once in the morning and once in the afternoon, always keeping his back perfectly straight—"straight as a bull's dick" was the phrase some men used in those days to describe horsemen with good posture. He also maintained a network of "pals" throughout Austin: informers who, in return for a handful of coins, kept him abreast of the activities of the city's more disreputable characters.

Chenneville was so devoted to his job that he had traveled to San Antonio in November, less than two months earlier, just to get a look at all the thieves working the horse races there. He said he had wanted to memorize their faces in case they decided to come up to Austin's annual fair in December. When the fair passed without a single crime taking place, the *Daily Statesman* had praised Chenneville for his "untiring vigilance" at watching over "the visiting crooks."

Chenneville walked into the Halls' backyard and headed to the outhouse to take a look at Mollie Smith. Unlike young Officer Howe, he had seen his share of dead bodies. He had seen men who had been shot

A prominent white Austin family posing with their "servant girl" and her daughter

or stabbed. He had watched murderers and horse thieves, black hoods over their heads, hanged from scaffolding behind the county courthouse, their feet continuing to kick even after the rope had snapped their necks. He had come across a lonely prostitute known as Buzzard Liz, named for the smallpox scars across her face, who had "suicided" from a morphine overdose in an alley.

But he had never seen anything like this. Mollie Smith had been ripped open like a calf at a slaughterhouse.

Despite all the years Chenneville had spent chasing criminals, the truth was that he was not exactly an experienced homicide detective. Almost all the murders he had investigated had taken place in Austin's saloons and poorer neighborhoods, where small, drunken insults had escalated into deadly brawls and personal scores had been settled with knives or guns. None of the killings had been carefully planned out, and more often than not they were carried out in front of at least one eyewitness. Rarely did a killer even try to flee. All Chenneville had to do was ride up on his horse, remove the smoking gun or bloody knife from the killer's hand, and drag him to the calaboose—the local jail, which was just down the hall from the police department.

But on this morning, Chenneville had no killer waiting to be arrested. Nor did he have any eyewitnesses or "pals" to tell him who the killer was. What's more, he had no forensic tools to help him study the murder scene. In 1884, the science of criminology had not yet been invented. Police officers had no idea that the way blood dripped across the floor or spattered against the wall could help them decipher how a murder took place. They didn't know that hairs or fibers found on a victim could possibly help identify a killer. Through a microscope, they could distinguish the blood of human beings from that of other animals, but so far, no system of blood typing had been created to distinguish one human being's blood from another's. Although a scientist, Dr. Henry Faulds, had published a paper in 1880 suggesting that finger marks were so unique to a person that they could be used for identification, no procedure had been devised so that police could accurately record or store those prints.

As part of their standard murder investigations, police officers did look for footprints or shoeprints around a body. Sometimes they would have those prints measured and replicated on a sheet of paper or a piece of wood, or even dug out of the earth and preserved with plaster of Paris, hoping they could later be matched with the prints of a murder suspect. But if there were any prints close to Mollie's body, they had already been obliterated by the boots of Chalmers, Steiner, and other men from the neighborhood who had come into the backyard to look at her.

The only real investigative tools Chenneville had at his disposal this New Year's Eve morning were his two bloodhounds. Baying at the top of their lungs, their strange harmonic chorus as complex as part singing, they were led to Mollie's body and then to Mollie's room, where they dropped their heads, their nostrils flaring as they smelled the floor, the bed covers, the wall with the finger marks, and the ax.

Like their owner, however, the dogs had never before encountered such a scene. All that they seemed to be able to smell was Mollie's blood. They didn't pick up any other scent, nor did they take a single trail.

III

From the road came the clatter of hoofbeats and the squeak of carriage wheels. The newspaper reporters were arriving: one from the *Daily Statesman*, another from the *Austin Daily Sun* (a poorly funded newspaper that had opened earlier that year and was already preparing to close), and a few more from the Galveston, Dallas, Houston, and Fort Worth papers, all of which maintained bureaus in Austin to report the political news coming out of the state's government offices. One of the Hello Girls most likely had let the newspapermen know that there had been a call to the police department about a dead woman, and because there was little else going on that New Year's Eve day, they had decided to check out the story for themselves.

The reporters were a cocky, jabbery bunch. They wore their hats at jaunty angles and chewed on cigars. A few of them drank too much, tipping from pocket flasks throughout the day. They ate their lunches at one of the cheap chili con carne stands on the downtown streets, and they spent much of their free time at the shabby Austin Press Club, above the Horseshoe Saloon, where they played heated games of penny ante poker, argued over the merits of their own prose, and debated the literary talent of the former western newspaperman Mark Twain, whose newest novel, *The Adventures of Huckleberry Finn*, was being excerpted that very month in *Century* magazine.

For once, however, they were silent. To keep his stomach from buckling, one of the reporters moved to another part of the Halls' yard. ("A brief glance at the sickening sight was sufficient," he would later write.) The reporters knew all about the way the Comanche Indians had once attacked Texas's frontier settlers. Articles about the old "Indian depredations," as they were called, were still being published in the state's newspapers: horrifying (but highly read) accounts of settlers in the 1830s and 1840s being tortured and mutilated, stabbed over and over, their scalps ruthlessly torn from their bleeding heads. Standing in the Halls' yard, their hands buried deep in the pockets of their coats and their breaths making jets of smoke in the frozen morning air, the reporters must have wondered: was it possible that this was some sort of Indian killing?

But there hadn't been a report of any kind of Indian attack anywhere in Texas in more than a decade. The last of the Comanches were now huddled away on a reservation in Fort Sill, Oklahoma, their food and blankets doled out by federal employees. The idea that some rogue Indian would have slipped off the reservation and come to Austin to commit this gruesome attack was preposterous.

Maybe, said someone in the backyard, Mollie's boyfriend—this Walter Spencer fellow—had invented the entire story about waking up to find her missing. Maybe the two had gotten into an argument and he had taken after her with his knife and ax—and then afterward he had hit himself in the head and face with the back of the ax to make people think that he too had been attacked.

Yet those who knew Spencer couldn't imagine him carrying out such an act. Except for an arrest back in 1881 for disturbing the peace at a black saloon, he had no criminal record whatsoever, and at Butler's Brick Yard he was considered an excellent worker, carrying five hundred bricks a day to the wagons waiting outside. It was an excruciating job: if a black laborer didn't get his five hundred bricks loaded on the wagons for any reason whatsoever, including illness or injury, he did not receive his daily pay of seventy-five cents. Rarely, however, did Spencer not make his quota.

The case for Spencer's innocence was bolstered when Nancy Anderson, a black woman who worked part-time as a nurse in the Hall home, told the police and reporters that Spencer had maintained a "peaceful relationship" with Mollie. She said that Spencer "generally did everything Mollie requested." The couple was on "the best of terms," the nurse insisted.

And, Chalmers had to admit, Spencer certainly hadn't acted the previous evening like a man who had just committed a murder. He had to have known the risk he was taking when he walked unannounced into the Hall home. If Chalmers had shot him between the eyes, there would have been no arrest and no questions asked. "Protection of home from Negro burglar," a judge would have declared without a second thought. Yet instead of fleeing like any normal killer would have, Spencer had seemed genuinely concerned about Mollie's fate.

Then a story circulated through the Halls' yard about an ex-boyfriend of Mollie's named William "Lem" Brooks. He worked behind the bar at one of the city's downtown saloons, washing and drying glasses, and on his nights off he was the "prompter" at the city's black dances, calling "the figures" for the Peacock, the Chicken Wing, and the Cakewalk. Brooks had first gotten to know Mollie in Waco, a town about a hundred miles north of Austin, where they were both born. As a teenager, Mollie had been romantically involved with another black man and given birth to a son. At some point after her son's birth she had broken up with that man and taken up with Brooks. But when Mollie's son died at the age of six from an untreated disease, she had decided the time had come to start a new life, and she had moved to Austin. Brooks later followed her there, hoping to rekindle the romance. By then, however, Mollie was already involved with Walter Spencer. Brooks was supposedly so upset that he had tried to start a fight with Spencer when the two of them had recently run across each other.

When Chenneville and his officers heard that story, they jumped on their horses and headed downtown, looking for Brooks. They found him asleep in the shanty of his new girlfriend, Rosa Brown.

Brooks stammered out his alibi—he had spent the evening prompting a dance at Sand Hill, a black meeting hall on the city's east side, a full two miles from the Hall residence.

For Chenneville, however, Brooks was the only decent suspect he had: a jealous ex-lover, someone who at least had some motive to harm Spencer and do away with Mollie. He decided to arrest Brooks for "suspicion of murder," which under the criminal code of that era was not the same as being arrested for murder. It only meant that the police wanted to keep a suspect in custody while the investigation continued. Brooks was escorted to the calaboose and thrown into the main holding tank with the other prisoners.

III

By then, it was early afternoon, the temperature still below freezing. Ice-lined branches in the trees made cracking noises. Smoke from the chimneys of the nearby homes rose into the air, black against the iron-colored sky. A black man who volunteered as the undertaker for the city's black community arrived at the Halls' in his wagon to collect Mollie and take her to the "dead room" of the City-County Hospital for an autopsy.

In those days, black undertakers used certain hopeful phrases whenever they lifted a dead person from the spot where he or she died. "Here you come, my child," the undertakers would sometimes say, "coming to Jesus." But it is doubtful those were the words this undertaker used. According to one newspaperman's account, when the undertaker tried to place her into a crude wooden casket, the body did not "hold together."

Eventually, after regaining his composure, the undertaker tried again. He scooped up all of Mollie and her body parts, placed them in the casket, and loaded the casket back onto the wagon. The undertaker called out to his horse and the horse trudged forward, disappearing into the distance, the *clip-clop* of the horse's hooves like a metronome's ticks on the frozen streets.

Meanwhile, Tom Chalmers began cleaning the blood off the walls and the floor of Mollie's quarters. He threw out her clothes and discarded the broken mirror on her wall. Chalmers wanted everything to be perfectly spotless by the time his brother-in-law returned to Austin. He wanted everything to look as if nothing at all had happened there—absolutely nothing at all.

CHAPTER THREE

The hospital's dead room was in the basement, down a series of stone steps. In the middle of the room was a sturdy wooden table where Mollie's body was placed. The smell of her blood, combined with the odors wafting from the bottles of chemicals on a shelf, would have been as choking as a wooden spoon pushed down a throat.

Dr. William Burt, the hospital's staff physician, walked in to do the autopsy. On a sheet of paper, he recorded Mollie's height and weight. He looked at her hands, her fingernails, her wrists, and the insides of her upper arms. Then he examined Mollie's wounds. She looked like the victim of some horrific amateur medical operation—an experiment in anatomy. Not sure what else to do, Burt took a few more notes, pulled a sheet over Mollie's body, walked out of the dead room, shut the door, and headed up the stone steps.

Soon dusk began to descend over Austin. Holding a long wooden pole with a dangling wick, a black man named Henry Stamps, the city's lamplighter, walked up and down Austin's two main downtown boulevards, Congress Avenue and Pecan Street, lighting the gas lamps, twenty-five in all. The proprietors of the saloons and restaurants shoved logs into their fireplaces and cast-iron stoves, and they scraped the ice off the wooden sidewalks in front of their doors. A few of the more progressive store owners flicked on their new, electrically powered, "incandescent light bulbs." The filaments in the bulbs, guaranteed to last for six hours, sputtered and hissed, and the white light poured out of the windows and almost reached the other side of the street.

By seven o'clock that evening, Austin's residents were heading downtown. Some of them came on horseback, some in leather-topped buggies, and some in horse-drawn hacks (taxis). The wealthier citizens had reservations at the city's finest restaurant, Simon and Billeisen's, where the chef was preparing a dinner of quail, venison, "fine chops," and "Berwick Bay oysters." Others made their way to Millett's Opera House to watch *The Banker's Daughter*, a comedy put on by a traveling theatrical troupe about a young woman who announces that she will be marrying a man old enough to be her father. Still others paid a twenty-five-cent admission to attend a "Dancing and Roller Skating Carnival" at Turner Hall, with music provided by the fourteen-piece Manning Rifle Band. Couples swooshed in a giant circle around the wooden floor on their metal skates, the women giggling and whooping, trying to maintain their balance in thick skirts that swept around their legs. At intermission, there was a half-mile race for the men, with the winner receiving a basket of apples.

Throughout the night, the saloons were packed with customers—men only, of course. The Gold Room held a raffle for a gold-plated shotgun worth $125, and the Crystal Saloon featured billiards on its three felt-covered tables, which had been shipped down from New York City. Over at Austin's oldest saloon, the Iron Front, which had an oak bar as long as a railroad car and a buffalo head on the wall the size of a cast-iron bathtub, the bartenders were offering Budweiser, a new beer from St. Louis, for just five cents a draw, and upstairs in the Iron Front's gambling den, dealers were offering games of monte, chuck-a-luck, stud poker, and keno.

Another view of downtown Austin in the 1880s

The biggest party of the night, by far, was the New Year's Eve Phantom Ball at the Brunswick Hotel. The scene there was like something straight out of a Henry James novel. Women in evening gowns and black masquerade masks swept into the ballroom, followed by their husbands wearing black capes and bearing wooden swords. Waiters stood by the doors, offering flutes of champagne and glasses of lemonade for the prohibitionists. In the center of the ballroom, water poured out of the top of the hotel's famous five-foot-tall "rustic fountain" and flowed downward through an array of fake foliage before landing in a tub filled with shiny rocks. A small band began playing, and couples walked out to the dance floor to dance the "German," the men slipping their hands down to the women's waists.

At the stroke of midnight, everyone raised their glasses and made toasts to the future. Outside on the streets, kids shot off Roman candles and sent "sky lanterns"—hot-air balloons made of paper, with small candles suspended at the bottom—into the night sky. A couple of men, filled up with liquor, staggered out of the saloons and fired their pistols, holding them straight above their heads. People cheered. Men and women kissed. The sky lanterns fluttered back to earth, the candles still flickering underneath the paper.

Mayor John Robertson, Austin's leading "boomer"

III

Strolling the streets that night, Austin's mayor, the Honorable John W. Robertson, must have been swelling with pride. Since his election the previous June, he had been telling just about anyone who would listen that the city was on the verge of a golden new era—and if this New Year's Eve didn't prove that the new era was here, what did? Theater and roller skating! A gold-plated shotgun at the Gold Room, a masquerade ball at the Brunswick, and fireworks at midnight! Despite the cold, his constituents were having the time of their lives.

A forty-four-year-old real estate lawyer by trade, Robertson was an ambitious man who, according to the *Daily Statesman*, wanted to be known as the politician who led Austin "beyond the good old days of rawhide and chile con carne." To give himself a more distinguished appearance, he often wore a beautiful black frock coat that he kept buttoned from top to bottom, and in his city hall office he passed around cigars to his most important out-of-town visitors as he talked on and on about all his plans for Austin: graded streets, sewer lines, more schools, and even a magnificent new waterworks plant.

"No city has the promise of a more healthful prosperity!" Robertson loved to proclaim in his speeches. "Austin's development is strong and vigorous, and its public improvements will advance along with its wealth and population!"

Like other mayors in small cities who wanted to attract more residents and thus increase the property tax base, Robertson was a highly skilled "boomer." But the fact was that when he talked about all the changes taking place in Austin, he wasn't exaggerating at all. Just a half century earlier, Austin had been nothing more than a primitive settlement on what was then regarded as the edge of the American frontier, populated by a handful of traders and subsistence farmers, along with their families. Few people even knew about the settlement, which was called Waterloo, until 1838, when Mirabeau B. Lamar, the vice president of the newly formed Republic of Texas, stopped there during a buffalo hunt and was so impressed with its natural beauty that he reportedly exclaimed, "This will one day be the seat of future empire!"

Later that year, when Lamar was elected president of the republic, he announced that the territory's future lay in westward expansion. He persuaded the Texas Congress to move the capital from Houston (which was named after his rival and predecessor as president, the famous General Sam Houston, who had led the Texas Army in its revolutionary war against Mexico) and place it in Waterloo, 165 miles to the west. Crude log buildings were erected to serve as government offices, a newspaper was started, a church was opened by a group of Presbyterians, and Waterloo itself was renamed Austin, in honor of Stephen F. Austin, the beloved "Father of Texas" who had helped bring many of the first white settlers to the region.

Built on a small hill next to the Colorado River, surrounded by a rampart of other hills, Austin was indeed a picturesque place. The sunsets were particularly beautiful, the violet light bouncing off the clouds and hills, catching the panes of glass of the homes and buildings, and then vanishing like a bright, shimmering liquid sucked into the earth. Yet life at the new capital was hardly easy. Aside from the Comanche

Indians periodically staging attacks on the residents, outlaws in masks showed up to rob the town's stores and the stagecoaches going to and from San Antonio. Hogs slept on the downtown streets, which after rainstorms would get so muddy that none of the wagons could move.

When Sam Houston regained the presidency of the republic in 1841, he tried to relocate the capital back to Houston. A group of his supporters came to Austin in the dead of night to take back the government's archives. But one of the town's more devoted female loyalists, an innkeeper named Angelina Eberly, fired a six-pound cannon at the interlopers. Other gun-wielding Austinites recovered the archives and returned them to the General Land Office. Barely, Austin was saved.

Nevertheless, even after Texas was annexed by the United States in 1845, becoming the twenty-eighth state in the union, Austin remained a dusty cow town with a sagging, wood-framed capitol building where the state legislature met every two years. In the aftermath of the Civil War, Austin's population was only 3,546 residents. There was practically no industry at all except for a sawmill. About the only businesses that prospered were the saloons, the gambling dens—the city directory listed twenty "professional gamblers"—and the brothels. When the fence that surrounded the governor's mansion fell down, there was no money to put it back up, and cattle wandered in to eat the shrubs. "Jayhawkers, bandits and bush-wackers had everything their own way," wrote Elizabeth Custer, who accompanied her husband, General George Armstrong Custer, to Austin after the war. (He had been sent there to command a division of the U.S. Cavalry to prevent the possibility of a Confederate resurgence.) "The lawlessness was terrible."

In 1871, railroad tracks were laid that connected Austin to the rest of Texas, and the city begin to grow. But two years later, the Texas economy went into free fall when the price of cotton, the state's biggest commodity, collapsed from thirty cents to thirteen cents a pound. Land values fell, incomes plummeted, and the state government nearly went bankrupt. In 1876, the state's four-hundred-pound governor, Richard B. Hubbard, who was described by one historian as being "fat almost to the point of being pitiable," desperately slashed state expenditures. It didn't help. Within a year, the state's debt had risen from three million to four million dollars. Half of the state remained unsettled, undeveloped, and unpoliced. Wrote another historian, Texas seemed to be "headed straight for hell."

By 1880, however, the price of cotton was rising again. Cotton production in the state doubled, cattle money brought in more revenue, and soon, a full-fledged economic boom was under way that, according to yet another historian, would eventually transform "nearly every facet of Texas society."

And nowhere was that boom more pronounced than in Austin. That year, the state legislature, its tax coffers filling up, agreed to fund the building of the long-planned state university in Austin, a four-story Gothic-style building that would be called the University of Texas, and one year later, in 1881, the legislature voted to build a massive new state capitol building just north of downtown that would be 566 feet across, 289 feet long, and 316 feet high—larger than the German Reichstag and the English Parliament buildings and, by some estimates, 31 feet taller than the U.S. Capitol itself.

Passenger trains began chuffing into the Union Depot to drop off new residents: lawyers and doctors, bookkeepers and clerks, Jewish merchants and Yankee spielers, Chinese laundrymen and the sons of patrician Old South families, hoping to find fame and fortune of their own. The pounding of hammers and heehawing of saws could be heard everywhere as builders threw up homes, boardinghouses, offices, schools, factories, churches, restaurants, hotels, and more saloons. A few doors down from J. C. Petmecky's Gunsmiths, which offered the finest in "Winchester repeating arms" and Bowie knives, Mrs. Doris Barker, a self-described "artist and art instructor," opened a studio to teach portrait and landscape painting to the ladies of Austin society, and around the corner from Lewis and Peacock's leather goods store, which featured fine "horse saddles" and "cowman's boots," an enterprising businessman named Julien Prade opened an ice-cream parlor, complete with a steam engine that blew air over blocks of ice in order to "air-cool" the parlor in the summers.

One entrepreneur, Gus Barnett, even built a roller coaster, a modern marvel of flight and speed that he claimed was exactly like the one at New York's Coney Island. He had his customers walk up a long flight of steps to the top of a tower, climb inside tiny open-air railroad cars, and race down an undulating 500-foot-long track in an exhilarating sixteen seconds. As the cars tilted sideways on the curves, everyone squealed with delight, making sure to keep their faces inclined "slightly downward and forward," as Mr. Barnett had advised them, to avoid insects hitting their faces.

Now, at the dawn of 1885, Austin was four square miles in size, and Mayor Robertson and other city leaders were predicting the population would soar to at least 20,000 within another year. Compared to such eastern metropolitan centers as New York City, which was already twenty-two square miles in size and filled with more than a million people, Austin still looked like a small western town. On a road just east of Austin, herds of bawling Longhorn cattle sometimes could be seen making their way from south Texas ranches to the Fort Worth or Kansas cattle markets, pushed along by cowboys on horseback.

But what no one could deny was that the city was changing, in the words of one reporter, as quickly "as the turn of a kaleidoscope," hurtling from its sepia-toned past into America's glittery new Gilded Age. Every afternoon except on Sunday, Congress Avenue, the city's main boulevard, was teeming with brightly painted, mule-driven streetcars and livery wagons, the drivers pulling at their reins to miss children swerving gleefully past them on velocipedes (also known as bicycles). The members of Austin society—the men dressed in their best suits and Stetsons, and the women in feathered hats and freshly ironed dresses with wiggling two-inch bustles—promenaded up and down the Avenue's wooden sidewalks past Mexican immigrants selling tamales out of carts. Unmarried Texas farmgirls who had come to Austin to get their first taste of "urban life" slowed before shop windows to admire the bedecked mannequins beckoning with gloved hands while businessmen stood outside Fatty's Barber Shop, where they had just had their mustaches twirled, to discuss the latest prices on the commodities exchanges.

On the Avenue's street corners, shoeshine boys whistled off-key, hotel drummers shouted the names of the hotels they were being paid to advertise, and traveling salesman hawked everything from medicines to Opera Puff cigarettes—"guaranteed," they said, not to stick to one's lips. An Italian organ grinder named Berninzo performed with his monkey, which turned backflips, and a woman who called herself "Madame Stanley, the Gypsy Fortune Teller" offered customers the chance to sit at her table while she flipped tarot cards and unveiled their futures.

And always walking the sidewalks was Professor Damos, an elderly, befuddled man who wore numerous tattered overcoats that flapped behind him like the tails of a kite and who stopped beside the gas lamp posts to deliver orations on such subjects as shipwrecks and the end of the world.

"Beware!" cried Professor Damos. "Beware!"

One young man who had moved to Austin in 1884—William Sydney Porter, a wry, mustachioed North Carolina native who had dreams of being a writer—was so fascinated by what he saw that he sometimes slipped out of Harrell's Cigar Store, where he worked, just to wander the streets. A couple of decades later, after the young Porter had moved to New York, changed his name to O. Henry, and become the most popular American short story writer of the late nineteenth century, literary scholars would study his fiction, wondering just how much of it was based on what he had experienced during his Austin days.

And how could they not? For a young writer—any writer, for that matter—Austin in that era was a feast for the imagination. On Saturday afternoons, there were chess tournaments sponsored by the Austin Chess Club, rope-jumping contests sponsored by the Austin Athletic Association, and horse races on the downtown streets. Out at the fairgrounds, the city's semi-professional baseball team, the Austins, faced off against semi-professional teams from other Texas cities, with as many as fifty runs being scored each game due to a lively ball, extraordinarily small gloves for the players, and absolutely horrendous pitching. One weekend, two midget sisters from Chicago came to Austin to perform musical duets, and on another weekend, the great boxer John L. Sullivan put on an exhibition at Millett's Opera House, decking a group of hopeful Austin men who stepped into the ring, one by one, to challenge him. The circus owner Mollie Bailey occasionally paraded down the Avenue with her clowns, sword swallowers, painted ladies, trained canaries, camels, and an elephant that deposited droppings the size of cannonballs, and a young man named William Iry, known in the newspapers as the "Boy Rope Walker," also showed up on the Avenue to string a rope between the roofs of two downtown buildings and walk serenely back and forth, thirty feet in the air, waving at the cheering crowds below him.

III

In the months and years to come, when newspaper reporters would arrive from around the country to ask Austin's residents if they sensed anything—absolutely anything—going wrong in their city during those last days of 1884, the residents would just shake their heads. They truly believed, as Mayor Robertson kept telling them, that they were on the verge of a golden new era. Even the old-timers could feel the excitement: grizzled men in buckskin jackets and battered hats whose eyes would widen in wonder when they talked into the new telephones, or when they watched the electric lights hissing through the night, or when they stood in front of Mr. Barnett's Austin Roller Coaster as it swooped up and down the tracks.

And on New Year's Day 1885, as Austin came one year closer to the twentieth century, its citizens were determined to celebrate their good fortune. That morning there were at least a couple of dozen "calling parties" at homes throughout the city. The wealthier couples were shuttled from one house to another by what were known as "the blacks and bays": black boys who drove carriages pulled by chestnut-colored mares. Standing at the front doors to greet the guests were young unmarried women, wearing velvet gowns that had been ordered months in advance from the city's couture clothier, Phil Hatzfield, who had been described by one Austin diarist as "the dictator of fashion in Austin who makes two visits each year to Paris in his efforts to keep his customers up to the minute in fashions and styles." The men handed their calling cards, which were six inches long and two and one-half inches wide, to the young ladies, who folded their gloved hands over the cards and led the men inside toward the tables covered with candies and cordials.

Later in the afternoon, the state's governor, John Ireland, hosted his annual New Year's Day open house at the two-storied, white-columned Greek Revival governor's mansion—at 6,000 square feet in size, the biggest governor's mansion in the country, built on a small hill overlooking the city. Ireland was a good-looking man, slender, with a high forehead, a broad-ridged nose, deep lines in his face tracking outward from his eyes, and a Lincolnesque beard, his whiskers as stiff as quills. He had once been described as being "a great favorite with the ladies." Just two months earlier, he had been reelected to another two-year term as governor, and there was already talk among his supporters that he would be running for the U.S. Senate in 1886.

On this New Year's Day, the governor was in an ebullient mood. Earlier that morning, he had gone to his office and signed pardons for a handful of convicts at the state prison over in the town of Huntsville who he believed had served enough time. He graciously had met with Reverend Abraham Grant, the pastor of Austin's all-black African Methodist Episcopal Church, to listen to his complaints about the railroads in Texas ordering black citizens to buy first-class fares but forcing them to ride in second-class cars, and he had met with a delegation of sightless children from the state's Institute for the Blind, who presented him with brooms they had made in the institute's broom factory.

Now, standing in the foyer of the governor's mansion with his wife, Anna, who was dressed in a black silk gown with lace trimmings, he greeted all of his guests, including members of the state legislature, judges from the state's supreme court, and valued members of his administration. At some point that afternoon, the man who wanted to replace Ireland as governor made an appearance at the mansion. Six feet, six inches tall and as big as an oak wardrobe, William Swain was the state's comptroller, in charge of revenues and taxes. In November, he had been reelected to his office by more than 240,000 votes, the largest majority of votes ever cast in favor of any candidate for public office in Texas his-

Before the murders began, Governor John Ireland (left) was considered to be the favorite as Texas's next United States senator. Comptroller William J. Swain (right) was an overwhelming favorite to be the next governor.

tory, and almost all of the state's newspapers were predicting a gubernatorial victory for Swain in the 1886 elections.

According to the newspapers, Swain, a Democrat, was "a modern financial Moses," the kind of leader that Texas needed in order to prepare for the complexities of the twentieth century. He possessed "a strong personal magnetism" and "immense intelligence" that captivated just about everyone who met him. One newspaper, the *Fort Worth Gazette*, went so far as to write that Swain had "that dignity of intellect and personal bearing which would make him a leader of men anywhere."

Throughout the afternoon, Swain, Ireland, and the other great men of Texas downed their cordials, spoke grandly to one another about the possibilities of the future, and occasionally shot glances across the room at the young women in their gowns that showed off their décolletage. The sweet scent of Magnolia Charm Balm for the Skin hung in the air, as did the oily smoke of cigars, and the delicious wafting smell of roasted pigs and turkey. The fires leapt and snapped in the fireplaces, and the oil paintings, some of which depicted great heroes of Texas history, glimmered on the walls.

When the open house came to an end, the governor's guests made their last toasts, gathered up their coats, and walked out the front door. Standing on the mansion's vast front porch, waiting for their carriages to come up the drive, they were not only able to look eastward and get a full view of the twenty-two-acre grounds where the new state capitol was being built, they could turn to the south and gaze upon all the new buildings of downtown.

By then, the sun was setting. Henry Stamps, the lamplighter, was already back on the streets, lighting the gas lamps, each light casting off the color of burnished gold. At the far end of downtown, a freight train was pulling into the depot, sparks flying like red insects from the funnel-stacked locomotive. The train sat there for several minutes, exhaling steam, while goods were unloaded: sewing machines, pianos, fine clothing, "hardwood carpets" (linoleum floors), boxes of telephones, and pallets of lightbulbs. Then the engineer clanged the bell, a whistle blew twice, and the train took off, the cars lurching and jangling and the locomotive tossing another plume of cinders above the treetops.

It was such a beautiful evening, everyone said to one another, and indeed it was. At that very moment, Austin looked like a small, fabled kingdom—shiny and unsullied and so full of promise. If someone at that moment would have walked onto the porch and told the guests that their young city was about to descend into chaos, they would have laughed out loud.

CHAPTER FOUR

At Governor Ireland's open house and the other calling parties, Mollie Smith's murder was no doubt a topic of at least some conversation. The story of her killing, after all, had been splashed on the top of page 3, the page devoted to local news, of the *Daily Statesman*, which newspaper boys on horseback had tossed onto the residents' front lawns. Right beside an advertisement for Madame E. F. Duke's new vapor baths (designed to relieve women of their monthly menstrual pain) was the headline: "Bloody Work! A Fearful Midnight Murder on West Pecan—Mystery and Crime. A Colored Woman Killed Outright, and Her Lover Almost Done For!"

The *Daily Statesman*'s reporter—in those years in American journalism, newspaper reporters were rarely given bylines—went through the details of the killing, calling it "a deed almost unparalleled in the atrocity of its execution" and "one of the most horrible murders that ever a reporter was called on to chronicle." He described Mollie's mutilated body as "a ghastly object to behold," and he added that "a horrible hole on the side of her head" was the cause of her death.

The headline in the *Austin Daily Statesman* after the first murder.

The reporter then mentioned that he had conducted an interview with Walter Spencer, whom he had found at his brother's apartment above Newton's Restaurant, in the heart of downtown. (Spencer's brother worked at the restaurant as a cook.) Spencer was in severe pain, with five deep gashes in his head and a puncture under the eye that had fractured the orbital bone. In a halting voice, he had told the reporter that after Tom Chalmers and Dr. Steiner had pushed him out of their homes, he had staggered around the neighborhood, still looking for Mollie, before he finally decided to make his way to his brother's apartment.

When asked about Lem Brooks, Spencer did say that he and his romantic rival had had a confrontation in October, but no punches had been thrown. Nor, interestingly, would Spencer suggest that Brooks had killed Mollie. "I don't know who did it," Spencer told the reporter.

"But anybody could have got into Mollie's room easily through the door connecting it with the kitchen."

The reporter also informed his readers that he had gone to the calaboose to interview Brooks. The young black man said that he liked both Mollie and Spencer and that he had never harbored any ill feelings toward Mollie for leaving him. "I'm innocent of the murder, and can prove by any number of witnesses that I was at a ball at Sand Hill till four o'clock in the morning and was the prompter," Brooks told the reporter. "They've got hold of the wrong man, for sure."

Was Brooks lying when he said he liked both Mollie and Spencer? It was hard to tell. But according to a handful of other black men the *Daily Statesman* reporter had interviewed, Brooks definitely had been at the Sand Hill dance until four o'clock, which was around the time that Tom Chalmers said he had been awakened by Spencer. If those men were telling the truth, the reporter surmised, then Brooks would have had to have run the two miles from Sand Hill to the Halls' home "at almost lightning speed" in order to have knocked Spencer unconscious and slashed Mollie nearly to pieces.

And there was one other thing. If Brooks was the killer, why didn't he murder Spencer? Why did Brooks take the time to rip apart his ex-girlfriend but only knock Spencer unconscious?

The reporter did point out that there had been speculation that Spencer himself could be the killer. But he added that there was no way of telling for sure. "The reader is left to draw his own conclusions," he concluded. "Whether slain by her lover, or some party from the outside, is as yet a mystery that envelops as foul a deed as was ever done in Austin."

III

In those years in Texas, before the establishment of medical examiner's offices, a justice of the peace was required to conduct an inquest into any death that was deemed unusual, unexplainable, or suspicious. The inquest was held before "a jury of inquest": six male jurors who were required to listen to statements from eyewitnesses, police officers, or doctors regarding the way the deceased met his or her end. At the end of the testimony, the jurors were required to declare what they believed was the official cause of death. If the death was due to murder, the jurors had the additional responsibility of declaring who they believed had committed the murder, and the justice of the peace would issue a warrant for that person's arrest, if he or she hadn't been arrested already. If the jurors couldn't find enough evidence pointing to a particular killer, they were required to rule that the murder had taken place "at the hands of a person or persons unknown."

Mollie Smith's inquest was conducted in private, which was then perfectly legal. Standing in the hallway outside the courtroom, the newspaper reporters tried to pick up some scraps of new information about her murder. They learned that no one who testified could come up with the name of anyone other than Brooks who might have had any reason to harm Mollie. They also learned that there was some testimony (probably coming from Sergeant Chenneville) suggesting that Brooks could very well have gone to the Halls' *before* the dance to commit his murder. After a brief deliberation in a back room of the courthouse, the inquest jurors returned to the courtroom and the foreman read the verdict. "We, the jury of inquest over the remains of Mollie Smith find that she came to her death between ten o'clock p.m. and three o'clock a.m. on the night of December 30th from injuries on her head inflicted with an ax, and we believe that said injuries were inflicted by one Lem, alias William Brooks."

Why didn't Brooks kill Spencer? Well, the jurors speculated, perhaps Brooks kept him alive because he wanted the police to believe Spencer was the culprit. Or maybe Brooks planned to go back to the servants' quarters and use the ax he had left there to do away with Spencer—and then was scared off by something, perhaps a noise.

The black undertaker returned to the hospital's dead room, gathered up Mollie's body, put her back in the casket, loaded it into his wagon, and headed for Colored Ground, the black section of the city cemetery. Located at the bottom of a hill, Colored Ground was the most beautiful part of the cemetery except when the rains arrived and flooded all of the graves. A few of Mollie's friends came to witness her burial, shivering in their threadbare coats, their faces squinting in the cold.

After singing some spirituals, they headed back to their own little homes and shanties, completely at a loss to explain what had happened.

Later that day, the cemetery's elderly sexton, Charles Nitschke, walked into his office by the front gates and opened a beautifully bound ledger that listed everyone who had been buried at the cemetery. In one column, he wrote down Mollie's name. In another column, he wrote that her birthplace was Waco.

The kindly sexton decided, however, that it would serve no purpose to go into the details of her murder. Under the column in the ledger that asked for the cause of death, Nitschke simply wrote that Mollie Smith had died from "a broken skull."

III

And that seemed to be that. A few days after Mollie's burial, a hundred or so of Austin's more prominent white citizens headed up to the University of Texas to hear Dr. M. W. Humphreys, the chin-whiskered professor of ancient languages, speak in the university's lecture hall on "The Debt We Owe to the Ancient Athenians." ("Surely he is one of the most accomplished Greek scholars of modern times," trumpeted the *Daily Statesman*.) A week later, more than six hundred citizens packed into the Millett's Opera House to watch the acclaimed New York actress Clara Morris, who had arrived in Austin in her private railroad car attached to the back of an International and Great Northern passenger train, perform the lead role in the melodrama *Miss Multon*. Renowned among New York drama critics for her "spectacular depictions" of death-bed scenes, Miss Morris portrayed a disgraced, brokenhearted wife who had returned to her home in disguise to care for her own children. As the play came to an end, with Miss Morris dying in her bed, the theatergoers wept. They stood and shouted "Bravo!" as she came out for her curtain calls. Some were so enraptured by her performance that they went to the railroad depot the next day to call out her name and wave as she left in her private railroad car.

Then the state's cattlemen arrived for their annual convention, throwing raucous parties for four consecutive nights. To welcome the cattlemen, city officials stretched banners across Congress Avenue, bearing legends in big red letters. (One read, "Greetings Texas Cattle-men!") At the Cattleman's Ball, the highlight of the convention, large decanters of whiskey were placed on every table and steaks were served as thick as a man's arm. The cattlemen stood and made toasts: "To Texas' cowboys, sentinels on the outposts, may their shadows never grow less!" "To the grain fields of Texas, that must feed more of our long-horns!" They drank from their decanters of whiskey, they danced with what one newspaper called "Austin's most beautiful belles"—single women who had been invited to the ball—and at the end of the night, some of them slipped away to the Variety Theatre at the foot of the Avenue to watch Miss Ida St. Clair, a scantily dressed blond beauty "whose skill in lofty kicking," one newspaperman earlier had penned, "has commanded the admiration of every cowboy from Austin to the Rio Grande." Other cattlemen visited the brothel of Guy Town's most prominent madam, Miss Blanche Dumot, who according to another newspaperman was always dressed in "silk" and "lace." In her beauti-fully modulated but entirely fake English accent, Miss Dumot let the cattlemen know that her lovely *nymphs du pave* were available for two dollars a session, which she promised would be money well spent com-pared to the dollar fee charged by the whisker-burned prostitutes at the cheaper whorehouses down the street.

In late January, there was a brief item in the *Daily Statesmen* about Lem Brooks being released from the calaboose. Apparently, the police hadn't been able to find any new witnesses who could link Brooks to Mollie Smith's murder, and the Travis County grand jury—made up of a group of Austin men who decided which felony arrests should be taken to trial and which ones should be no-billed and dismissed—had decided there was not enough evidence to indict him.

But no one in Austin—at least no one who was white—seemed particularly bothered by the news of Brooks's release. The white citi-zens were convinced that Mollie's death was nothing more than a "Negro killing" committed by "a jealous or deceived Negro lover"—a murder that had all the significance of a hangnail that had been snipped off someone's finger. Instead of trying to meet the governor to ask for improved seating arrangements on the railroad trains, wrote the Austin-based reporter for the *Galveston Daily News*, Austin's black pastor Reverend Grant "would serve his race better by addressing his efforts to the suppression of their murderous instincts."

As the weeks passed, there were more parties, including an "onion sociable" held at the home of a young Austin socialite. (The socialite and five of her female friends went into a bedroom, where one of the women took a bite of an onion, after which they all walked out into the parlor and were kissed by a young man who tried to guess who had onion breath.) At Turner Hall, the Austin Press Club hosted its annual "Grand Literary and Musical Concert," featuring young ladies from the city's more prominent families who gave recitations and sang such popular songs as "Thou Art So Near and Yet So Far."

And Miss Louise Armaindo of New York City, billed as "the lady velocipede champion of the world," came to Austin to race the city's best trotting horses at the fairgrounds. Her thighs as muscled as tree trunks, Miss Armaindo sped down the track before an enthusiastic crowd of spectators, covering a quarter mile on her velocipede in forty-six seconds, beating the closest horse by a full length. Later that evening, she put on a weight-lifting exhibition, holding heavy Indian clubs above her head and waving them back and forth in the air.

Meanwhile, over at the temporary state capitol building, the legislators gathered for their biannual session. They walked to the podium to make one grandiloquent proposal after another to improve their beloved state. One politician, his beard as luxuriant as mink, called for more money to be spent on public education, another to spend more money on railroad tracks, and yet another wanted to deepen the harbor in the coastal city of Galveston so that bigger ships could come in from Europe, thus expanding international trade.

There was even a radical proposal made by a couple of state senators—one of whom was Temple Houston, the liberal-minded son of Sam Houston—asking that half the clerks employed in the state government's main offices be women. According to newspaper reports, "scores of handsomely dressed and intelligent ladies" came to the capitol building to show their support for the bill. They applauded "vigorously" when Houston rose to speak. Although the proposal had no chance of passing, the women were thrilled. Women's rights were coming, of all places, to Texas! Maybe, the women said, the politicians will someday give us the right to vote!

Then, on the twelfth of February, a wedding was held at the State Lunatic Asylum between Miss Ella Denton, the lovely and delicate nineteen-year-old daughter of Dr. Ashley Denton, the asylum's superintendent, and Dr. James P. Given, the asylum's thirty-two-year-old first assistant superintendent.

The Texas State Lunatic Asylum was a three-story building with a classical façade, great Corinthian columns, long clerestory windows, and a huge porch. It stood two and a half miles north of downtown, in an area of the city where there were no houses, only one lonely dirt road (called Asylum Road) that led to the asylum's cast-iron front gates. Adjoining the sides of the main building were the dormitories: one for the men and one for the women. A third dormitory for the "male colored lunatics" was located a short distance away—the "female colored lunatics" stayed in the basement of the main building—and farther on was the Cross Pits, a small building with barred cells that housed the most violent patients.

In past years, few people in Austin would go near the place. One resident recalled that he and his friends grew up riding their horses past the asylum "at a gallop so that an escaped lunatic couldn't come out of the woods and catch us." A newspaperman who had taken a tour of the institution in 1880 wrote that the cells and day rooms were "crowded to suffocation with inmates in insufficient clothes, dirty and untidy." Up and down the long corridors could be heard screeches and "caterwaulings," wrote another reporter, and the odor of unemptied bedpans and unwashed bodies was "so stifling" that it was hard to breathe.

Since his appointment in 1883 as superintendent, however, Dr. Denton had been carrying on an extensive renovation program to transform the asylum into what he described as "a refuge for those unfortunates whose voices cannot be heard." The forty-eight-year-old Denton was the portrait of the distinguished gentleman, with swept-back graying hair and a carefully cultivated beard. He had used a generous $200,000 appropriation from the legislature to buy new beds for

Superintendent Dr. Ashley Denton (above left) and his son-in-law Dr. James Given (below left) oversaw the 550 "lunatics" housed at the Texas State Lunatic Asylum (right).

the patients' rooms, paint all the walls a gleaming white, and relandscape the main asylum grounds, adding lily ponds, gazebos, benches, flower beds, ornamental shrubbery, statuary, and dirt paths—the paths always curving, which according to such scholarly periodicals as *The Journal of Insanity* were more therapeutic than paths that were straight. While Denton's staffers were required to wear gray uniforms with long sleeves and high necks, he allowed his patients to wear ordinary clothing so that they would feel more dignified. To further improve the patients' dispositions, he ordered that fresh flowers be placed in the hallways, and he allowed cats and dogs to wander the asylum grounds.

As opposed to previous superintendents, Denton gladly took in anyone who was brought to him, regardless of their affliction—and that year, the asylum was filled to the brim with more than 550 patients who embodied almost every nervous disorder known in that day. Denton believed that within the quiet confines of the asylum, all of his "unfortunates" had a better opportunity to regain at least a portion of their sanity and perhaps someday return to the real world.

So that they would not, as he put it, feel "penned up like prisoners," he had the ten-foot-high picket fence surrounding the main grounds torn down and replaced with a much smaller fence, only four feet in height. He also had the asylum's cemetery, where unclaimed dead lunatics were buried, moved from its spot next to the main building to a plot of land over a hill so that his patients would not have to see it and be overcome with morbid thoughts.

He also set up a daily schedule for the patients in which they were awakened before dawn, given a bountiful breakfast (a leading theory of the day was that much of insanity was due to a lack of proper nutrition), sent off to work (most of them labored on the asylum's 120-acre farm or its 15-acre orchard), and then encouraged at the end of the day to develop what Denton called "their gray cellular material" by reading books and newspapers in the day rooms, singing patriotic songs around a piano, playing cards, chess, or billiards, or bowling on the single ten-pin lane in the asylum basement.

Denton envisioned the wedding of his daughter Ella to his young assistant Dr. Given as the ideal opportunity to introduce his modern asylum to members of Austin society. Dressed in their most fashionable clothes, his guests rode up Asylum Road in their varnished carriages, went past the front gates emblazoned with the letters SLA (State Lunatic Asylum), stopped in front of the main building, and walked up the steps carrying tasteful wedding presents: bronzes, sterling silver, china, linen, and laces.

Some of the guests had to have felt a little jittery as they looked around the nearly fenceless asylum. A few of them, no doubt, peered in the direction of the Cross Pits building, which that day housed fifty-two criminally insane lunatics, including an infamous madman named Lombard Stephens, who had sent Governor Ireland several letters vowing that he would eat the governor's brains if he was not paid $500,000.

But standing with his wife, Margaret, in the high-ceilinged foyer, Denton let his guests know that they had nothing to fear. He liked to point out that the bell installed in front of the main building, which was to be rung whenever a patient was seen fleeing for the distant fields, had not clanged in the last several months. His patients had no desire to run away, Denton said. For them, the asylum was a rural paradise, a peaceful refuge, an Eden-like outpost far away from the unbearable rigors of civilization.

The guests were led to the asylum's chapel. An organist played Mendelssohn's *Wedding March*, and everyone stood. Miss Denton, dressed in white with a train that flowed behind her, walked down the aisle to the front of the chapel, where Dr. Given waited to take her hand.

Given was a striking young man—tall, trim, and athletic, with dark brown hair, eyes that gleamed like marbles, and a beautiful handlebar mustache, the tips perfectly oiled. An Episcopalian priest performed the traditional wedding ceremony, and then the entire entourage recessed out of the chapel and headed for a dining room, where steaming dishes of breakfast food were brought forth by waiters, some of whom were patients at the asylum.

Several friends of Dr. Given and Ella rose from their seats to toast the couple. Dr. Denton himself made a toast, asking that good fortune follow his daughter and son-in-law for the rest of their lives. At the end of the breakfast banquet, Denton led his guests to the asylum's front door to watch the newlyweds ride off in the back of a carriage to the downtown railroad depot to begin their honeymoon in St. Louis and New Orleans.

Everyone cheered and waved. The asylum's patients, standing at their dormitory windows, their faces pressed against the glass, cheered and waved along with them. For Denton, the wedding had been a success beyond his wildest dreams—"the most enjoyable event that ever occurred within the asylum," wrote one of the reporters who also attended. If someone had come out onto *that* porch and told Denton and his guests that Austin soon would be descending into chaos, they too would have laughed out loud. For a few precious hours the sane had come to the land of the insane, and not a single person there had been afraid.

CHAPTER FIVE

March arrived, and according to one reporter visiting from the town of Waco, Austin remained caught up in "a pitch of gaiety." On March 2, the forty-ninth anniversary of Texas's independence from Mexico, Mayor Robertson and other city leaders put on what was unquestionably the biggest event in the city's history: a lavish parade up Congress Avenue to celebrate the laying of the 16,000-pound granite cornerstone for the new state capitol. Weeks earlier, announcements had been placed in the state's newspapers encouraging all Texans to come to Austin to watch the cornerstone being lowered into the earth. Circulars had been sent to Texas public schools, inviting students and their teachers. More than 3,000 invitations had been mailed to prominent citizens outside of Texas, including an invitation to the president of Mexico.

Just before the parade began, at least 25,000 people were lined along the downtown streets, "and it is safe to say ten thousand of that number were visitors," wrote William P. Lambert, a local writer who would

Architects planned for the Texas state capitol, under construction in 1885, to be larger than the U.S. Capitol.

later publish a pamphlet about the celebration. The upper stories of buildings along Congress Avenue were "thronged with ladies and children dressed in holiday attire," and the buildings themselves were festooned with bunting and large Texas flags. The sun was high and bright and a breeze blew off the Colorado River. From somewhere in the distance, the fourteen-piece Manning Rifle Band started to warm up, the high notes of the trumpets hanging in the air. At the stroke of noon, a whistle blew and the crowd let out a roar.

The parade lasted for close to an hour. Governor Ireland, Mayor Robertson, and at least one hundred other government officials rode up the Avenue in open-topped buggies. Marching on foot were representatives from Austin's workmen's unions, professors and students from the new University of Texas, wrestlers and boxers who trained at the Austin Athletic Association, a contingent of Jewish citizens (Lambert called them "Austin's Israelites"), members of Austin's German immigrant community, and a small group of "colored representatives." Local businessmen rode by on "floats"—decorated horse-drawn wagons. The home builder S. W. French had doors, window sashes, glass windows, and buckets of paint on his float; Charles Lundberg the baker featured pastries and cakes on his float; and R. W. Bandy, the owner of a tack and saddle shop, had a float displaying "full cowboys' outfits" as well as his best horse-riding gear. At the back of the procession were the owners of the Iron Front Saloon, probably a little tipsy, their float covered with signs advertising their drink specials and casino games.

After the last float had passed by, the celebration moved to the capitol grounds, where a half-dozen construction derricks rose high in the air. (One observer earlier had said that the derricks made the capitol site look like "a harbor of big ships.") Suspended from the front derrick was the cornerstone. Inside the cornerstone was a zinc box containing more than two hundred trinkets and mementoes that had been donated by Austin citizens. There were photographs and drawings of such famous Texas personalities as Sam Houston, photographs of prominent Austin families, and various photographs of Austin itself. The Austin Bible Society had donated a Bible, the Texas State Dental Association had donated a set of artificial teeth, and the Texas State Grange, a farmer's organization, had donated two ears of corn. Austin's most beloved poet, the portly Mrs. Martha Hotchkiss Whitten, had submitted a poem, "Austin City," that she had written in iambic pentameter especially for the occasion. ("Austin! Fair city of our Southern Land," the poem began. "By Nature's gifts adorned on every hand!") Mayor Robertson, predictably, had placed several reports in the cornerstone detailing the excellent state of affairs in Austin along with a city directory listing the names of all of Austin's residents as well as a roster of all the children who were attending Austin's public schools.

After a speech in which Governor Ireland described the capitol as "a monument to the wisdom, taste and energy of our age . . . as durable and substantial even as Austin's everlasting hills," the cornerstone was carefully lowered into place by officers of a Masonic lodge and, in the distance, the Travis Light Artillery fired a rousing forty-nine-gun salute, the smoke from their guns floating across the capitol grounds like gray ghosts.

One week later, a young servant woman awoke in the middle of the night and swore she saw a ghost standing by her bed.

III

The young woman, a recent immigrant from Germany, lived in a one-room servants' quarters that adjoined the kitchen in the back of a large home on Hickory Street, close to downtown. She later told police that the man just stood there for a few seconds, his face hidden in darkness. Suddenly, he said, "Your money or your life." The young woman screamed. He whacked her over the head with a hard object, cutting her scalp. Hearing his servant woman's screams, the homeowner in the front part of the house headed toward her quarters, but by the time he got there, the man was gone.

Four nights later, a black cook who worked for a physician was awakened by what was later described as "a violent shaking" at the locked door to her servants' quarters. When the cook looked out the window, no one was there. Within an hour, in a nearby neighborhood, two young black women were awakened by the rattling of the locked doorknob at their servants' quarters, located behind a mansion owned by their employer, Major Joseph Stewart, a former Confederate officer who spent his time touring the state, delivering a lengthy prose poem he had written on the glories of the Old South. One of the women opened the door and stepped outside to see who was there. Suddenly, she felt herself being grabbed from behind. She cried hysterically for help, and her assailant, whom she never saw, released her and disappeared.

Too terrified to be alone, the Stewarts' servant women spent the rest of that night in his kitchen. But when they returned to their quarters the next morning, they discovered that a lamp, which was not lit at the time they raced away from the room, was mysteriously burning. They also found their clothes and bedding in a great heap in the middle of the room. Apparently, whoever had tried to get inside earlier had slipped back into the quarters while the women were in the main house just to tear their room apart.

Two nights after the incident at Major Stewart's, an intruder slipped into the servants' quarters attached to the back of the home belonging to Abe Williams, the owner of a shop that sold fine suits and silk dresses. In the darkness, the intruder committed what one of the newspapers would later describe as "a determined and brutal assault" on Williams's housekeeper, "tearing the covering off her bed, and several times striking her on the head and face" before vanishing as quickly as he came.

For a couple of days, the attacks stopped. Then, on March 19, there was a tapping on the window of the servants' quarters located just behind the residence of Col. J. H. Pope, a cotton planter who owned a large farm outside of Austin. Pope's two servant girls—Swedish immigrant teenagers named Christine and Clara—lay in their beds, too scared to move. The tapping stopped and there was the sudden sound of a pistol shot. The bullet passed through the window and lodged in a wall. Screaming, the girls raced outside and headed toward the main house. One of the girls, Clara, was grabbed from behind, but she was not able to turn around to see who it was. She kept screaming, which brought Colonel Pope and others outside with their guns. But they could not find the man. He had let Clara go and disappeared almost instantly.

The Swedish teenagers returned to their room, and they locked and barricaded the door. But within minutes, another shot was fired through a window into their quarters. The bullet hit Christine between her shoulder blade and spinal column, knocking her to the ground, but it did not hit any of her vital organs.

III

Like so many other growing cities, Austin had been experiencing an increase in thefts and property crime. "The anticipated lively times in Austin have brought an influx of thieves," one newspaper had reported back at the first of the year. In January, a thief had entered the house of a family on East Walnut Street and, according to another newspaper story, "took all the eatables." A few days later, a thief had thrown a heavy piece of wood through the bedroom window of an elderly woman named Mrs. Cope and grabbed her small purse lying on a table.

There were black chicken thieves in Austin who stole chickens from the backyards of the city's white residents, which they then sold to poorer black residents for mere pennies. Men who traveled the country on freight trains occasionally jumped off at the Austin depot and wandered the city for a day or so, looking for something to steal before they returned to the trains.

But these crimes were perplexing. Whoever was trying to break into the servants' quarters seemed far more interested in attacking the women—or just frightening them—than taking their money or their meager belongings.

The assumption—at least the assumption among Austin's white citizens—was that the servant quarter "invasions," as one reporter called them, were being carried out by black men. "Bad blacks!" the *Daily Statesman* called them. "It seems from the sameness of the deviltry and its constant repetition that there must be a regular gang of these brutes who perambulate the city at the small hours of night to do their unholy work."

In 1885, about 3,500 black citizens were living in Austin—20 percent of the population. Many lived in servants' quarters, or "alley houses," in their employers' backyards; others in one-room apartments above the stores or restaurants where they worked; and still others in small, all-black neighborhoods (which the white citizens called "nigger patches") that were on the edge of the city. One of the black neighborhoods, known as Clarksville, had been built on several acres of land that a former governor of Texas, Elisha Pease, had given to his emancipated slaves at the end of the Civil War, twenty years ago. The typical Clarksville house consisted of three rooms, one room directly behind another. Sometimes as many as ten members of a family lived in a house. The front doors were so small and the ceilings so low that everyone had to stoop to avoid bumping their heads. The roofs leaked and the thin wooden walls strained and groaned, pushing against the nails. A creek carrying sewage periodically flooded the homes.

And Clarksville was one of the nicer black neighborhoods. Austin's poorest black neighborhood, which consisted of nine shanties, was located right next to the city dump. On windy days, trash and refuse blew into the homes. The neighborhood's residents regularly scoured the dump, gathering watermelon rinds, rotting fruit, potatoes, and dog-chewed bones for their meals.

Most of Austin's black adults were still uneducated, unable to read or write. Their working life consisted of the lowest-paying jobs in two fields: common labor and domestic service. The men were employed as janitors, barbers, porters, carriage drivers, cloakroom attendants, bootblacks, waiters, and bellhops. They shoveled coal for the railroads, worked at the sawmills and the brick yards, and picked cotton on farms just outside of town. A few worked as "Negro cowboys," watching over white men's cattle.

The city's black women mostly did servant work. Their days began as early as four in the morning. They'd wash themselves with rags dipped in pails of water, eat a breakfast of molasses and cornmeal, and head to the kitchen of the main house, where they'd remove the ashes from the previous day's fire, gather more firewood, and carry the wood back into the kitchen to start a new fire. The rest of their day was filled with dozens of duties: cooking, cleaning, scrubbing, mopping, emptying chamber pots, hauling garbage and liquid waste to the refuse pile, and doing all the laundry, which was a Herculean task in itself, requiring endless cycles of soaking, rinsing, scrubbing, starching, drying clothes on lines out in the backyard, and ironing with a scalding hot flatiron that had been heated over the fire.

Finally, after serving dinner and cleaning the kitchen again, they would eat scraps of leftovers that had been set out for them by their white employers, and they'd head back to their quarters to fall asleep on thin mattresses. They got one day off each week: Sunday, or at least part of a Sunday, so that they could attend one of the black churches.

Compared to the years of slavery and post–Civil War Reconstruction, when "darkies" who were deemed "insolent" were viciously beaten—"getting Ku-Kluxed" was the term used—or even hanged in a grove of oaks on the city's east side, black life definitely had improved in Austin. In their neighborhoods, black residents had opened shops and churches. The members of Rev. Abraham Grant's African Methodist Episcopal Church had pooled their money and raised an astonishing $8,000 to build a new church building, forty by seventy feet in size, with a Gothic roof and a church bell that had been made in Baltimore. On the eastern edge of downtown, a group of black businessmen had formed a business district of sorts. One of those businessmen, a former slave named Thomas Hill, ran a grocery and an unofficial bank, loaning money to other black residents from his office in the back of the store. A block away was the *Austin Citizen*, a weekly newspaper for those black residents who could read. (No copies are known to exist today.) A restaurant also opened, as did a blacksmith shop, a dress shop for women, and the Black Elephant, an all-black saloon.

On weekends, Austin's black residents entertained themselves with horse races, baseball games, and dances at Sand Hill. A group of men formed the Austin Cadet Band, described in the *Daily Statesman* as "a colored marching band," and another group of men formed a fraternal society called the Dark Rising Sons of Liberty. Black traveling acts came to Austin to entertain the residents—among them a man who gave glass-eating demonstrations, a man named Joe Slick who played the banjo, and a black cowboy who called himself "Dick the Demon Negro" and who wrestled steers to the ground, holding on to them only with his teeth.

The most exciting news for black residents, however, was that their children were finally being educated. In 1885, three state-funded "colored schools" were open in Austin, serving up to four hundred students who were learning to read English from first-year Freedman's Readers and Webster's blue-back spellers. Students who reached their teenage years could attend the Tillotson College and Normal Institute, a building on Austin's east side that had been opened by the American Missionary Association, an all-white Christian organization based in Albany, New York, that was devoted to creating black colleges throughout the South. Tillotson not only offered classes in arithmetic and English composition, it provided practical training in such fields as carpentry, home building, farming, canning, cooking, sewing, bookkeeping, and teaching. One of the white teachers gave a course in public speaking, claiming that his goal was to eliminate his students' "old-time thick and indistinct plantation pronunciation."

Several white citizens did their best to be pleasant—"accommodating" was the word they used—to Austin's black residents. Julia Pease, the ex-governor's daughter, hosted an annual Christmas party at the Pease estate for the residents of Clarksville, giving each child a bag of candy or a dime. The German-born owner of Pressler's beer garden allowed blacks to rent out his establishment to celebrate Juneteenth, their day of freedom from Confederate rule. (Texas slaves didn't go free until June 19, 1865, the day Union troops landed in Galveston, two months after General Robert E. Lee's surrender at Appomattox.) Some of the city's white businessmen had begun to allow blacks to shop at their stores at specified times; a couple of the white-owned saloons had created black areas at the end of their bars (one saloon put a black-only craps table in its gaming room); and Charles Millett, the owner of Millett's Opera House, periodically allowed blacks to buy tickets to sit in the upper balcony for some of his shows—but never for operas, which he believed were too artistic for black tastes. In 1883, Austin's white leaders had even allowed a black man named Albert Carrington, the owner of a blacksmith shop, to be elected as one of the city's aldermen, representing the black-dominated Seventh Ward on Austin's east side.

No white leader in Austin, however, was ever heard promoting equal rights for blacks. In Austin—as well as in much of the United States, for that matter—the prevailing belief among even the most educated of white men and women was that blacks were intellectually and morally inferior. In that era, doctors and anthropologists published papers in medical journals declaring that blacks had smaller brains than whites and that the shape of their bodies was conclusive proof that they had developed from "primitive" lower organisms. Newspapers didn't hesitate to describe blacks as "coons," "Senegambians," "Ethiopians," "Africans," "sons of Ham," and "dusky denizens."

In Austin, residents regularly wrote to the *Daily Statesman* complaining about the city's blacks. They were indignant over such issues as the "raucous" noises that blacks made at their Sunday church services and the way they "loitered" on the downtown street corners. There were also dozens of complaints about Austin's younger black men. Compared to older blacks who had been raised in slavery, the whites said, the new generation of black men didn't seem to be as "deferential" or "respectful." It was a theory widely held throughout the former Confederate states. Some southern writers went so far as to declare that all black men "coming to maturity after Reconstruction" had "a more decided tendency to retrograde and act upon their natural impulses, like the original African type" because they had not been given the chance to experience "the benefits of slavery," which had functioned as "a civilizing force" for "uneducated Negroes."

As a result of such bias, young black men were constantly blamed for all sorts of crimes simply because they were young and black. A *Daily Statesman* editorial put it this way: "Idleness and drink will lead off these ignorant creatures, and there is no telling, if they are permitted to idle about a town of this size, what they will do finally. There is no doubt but they will resort to theft and then it is but a small step to murder."

Curiously, none of the servant women who had been assaulted during the month of March had been able to get a good look at her attacker. A couple of women had told police and newspaper reporters that they believed black men had come after them, but they weren't completely sure. One of the women said the man who had tried to break into her quarters was possibly "yellow." Another said her attacker had painted his face coal black like a performer in a minstrel show. And the teenage servant girl from Germany said that she thought the man who had struck her over the head a few days after the capitol cornerstone ceremony was actually *white*.

Nevertheless, Austin's white citizens simply could not imagine that white men would want to terrorize harmless servant women for no particular reason at all. Surely, they said, the German girl, overcome with fright, had to have been mistaken about the skin color of the man she had seen. The string of attacks almost certainly had to be the work of blacks—"ruffians on the rampage," one man called them—who had *retrograded*.

One man was so angry over the servant women assaults that he proposed that Austin's police department round up the city's known black criminals, take them outside the city limits, whip them to within an inch of their lives, and tell them never to return. Another man sent a letter to the *Daily Statesman* encouraging all homeowners to pull out their guns and fire away, no questions asked, whenever a late-night black intruder was seen around a servant's quarters. A *Daily Statesman* editorialist made the same recommendation, writing that "the killing of one or two of these characters cannot help but have a wholesome effect on the remainder of these night hawks. . . . The first citizen who plants a charge of buckshot where it will do the most good in the car-cass of one of these 'toughs,' should be voted a gold medal and the thanks of the community."

There were a few older white citizens who thought whippings or buckshot didn't send a strong enough message. They wanted to form "vigilance committees"—in other words, lynching parties—just like the ones that had been formed back in the slave days to help patrol the city. "And if one of the scoundrels who have been out scaring and shooting our servant girls can be caught," declared one man in his own letter to the *Daily Statesman*, "let him be strung up to a limb or a lamp post with-out mercy or delay."

III

Hoping to find out more details about what was happening, a couple of reporters headed to city hall and took the stairs up to the police depart-ment to talk with Marshal Lee, who had recovered from his bout with the dengue fever that had kept him out of the office through much of January. Tall and fence-post lean, with a long, narrow face and the elongated arms and legs of a marionette, Lee was only twenty-nine years old. He had been appointed marshal by a vote of the mayor and aldermen in December 1883, just a year and three months earlier. Prior to his appointment, he had spent six months on a tour of duty with a battalion of the Texas Rangers, followed by a three-year stint as a dep-uty to the county sheriff, in which he mostly performed minor tasks. One of his duties was to find cattlemen in rural parts of the county who were grazing cattle on lands that did not belong to them.

Austin's previous marshals had been swaggering men who were very good with guns. The city's most famous marshal, who had been elected in 1880, was Ben Thompson, an English-born gambler and deadeye pistoleer who dressed in a high silk hat, a morning coat, and silk trousers. He was the master of the spin move, able to whip around on his heels while simultaneously drawing his Colt pistol from his belt, cocking the hammer, and firing away at his adversary. In his book *Gunfighters of the Western Frontier*, Bat Masterson, the buffalo hunter, frontier lawmen, and best-selling author, wrote of Thompson, "It is doubtful that there was another man who equaled him with the pistol."

The problem, however, was that after Thompson had downed a few drinks, he liked to engage in what the newspapers described as "promiscuous shooting." One evening, he had drunkenly risen from his seat at Millett's Opera House and shot off his pistol because he believed the performance was poorly staged. In 1882, a year after he was elected marshal, he was forced to resign when he killed a politician in a San Antonio shootout. In 1884, Thompson himself was shot to death in another San Antonio gunfight.

After Thompson's demise, the city aldermen decided to find a marshal who would not pull any Thompson-like escapades, and as far as they were concerned, Lee was the perfect candidate. For one thing, he was a teetotaler—"the first city marshal in Austin history to decline the bottle," a Dallas newspaper noted. He was also a blueblood, the son of one of the city's senior statesmen, Joseph Lee, a lawyer and former judge who had lived in Austin since the 1830s. The elder Lee was described as "a great lover" of the city: he had lobbied legislators to approve building the University of Texas, and he had helped plan the creation of the new state capitol building. Surely, said the aldermen, young Grooms would have no desire to embarrass the city.

According to one reporter who met him, Lee was indeed "polite" and "efficient." In one of his first acts as marshal, he purchased new uniforms and copper badges for his officers. He also took down a shaggy buffalo head on one of the department's walls and replaced it with solemn portraits of past Austin mayors. When he appeared at city council

The University of Texas was then "overflowing" with 230 students.

meetings to discuss police matters, he gave very formal speeches. At one meeting, when he was asked to discuss a new hiring method for police officers, he read from a prepared statement that concluded with the lines, "It becomes my duty to suggest a remedy, and fear that in so doing I may be but able to dimly indicate what you, in your superior wisdom, may be able to more fully digest and mature. . . . I am not prepared to say how far such a plan of appointment may conflict with the existing city charter, and ordinances under it upon the subject, but feel satisfied that if such change can be legally made it will result in great good. . . . Hoping that these suggestions may receive your favorable consideration, I have the honor to subscribe myself, H. G. Lee, City Marshal."

Needless to say, Lee was not exactly the second coming of Wyatt Earp. But then again, Mayor Robertson and the majority of the aldermen believed that as long as they had the always reliable Sergeant Chenneville around to handle the criminal investigations, they had little to worry about. In fact, they gave Ronnie O Johnnie a raise soon after they appointed Lee to the marshal's post, paying him $1,500 a year—only $500 a year less than what Lee himself made—to make sure he didn't leave.

Marshal Grooms Lee and his officers were utterly
baffled by the killings.

Besides, the mayor and aldermen were starting to realize, Austin
no longer needed an old-fashioned, gun-slinging marshal who could
hold his own against an outlaw in a street showdown. The fact of the
matter was that almost all of the old outlaws who used to terrorize
Austin were long gone, shot dead or hanged or sent off to prison. Even
the blue-eyed "bad man" John Wesley Hardin, the most feared desperado in Texas history, whose quick-draw ability reportedly had sent
forty-four men to their graves, was in the state prison in the town of
Huntsville, running the prison Sunday school and studying to become
a lawyer.

True, there were plenty of men who still harbored outlaw
ambitions—"embryo desperadoes," one of the reporters called them.
They tried to stop trains and get to the money bags locked away in the
mail car's safes, using the latest in criminal technology, nitroglycerin
instead of gunpowder, to blow open the safes. What's more, a few
women were getting into the business. Belle Star, dubbed "the Bandit

Queen," was said to be rustling cattle and stealing horses around the Texas-Oklahoma border and posing for photographs in a plumed hat with a pistol strapped around her waist. But this new crop of outlaws rarely came to the cities like Austin. They didn't have to be told that they had a better chance surviving in the state's hinterlands, where there were no gun-toting ordinances, like the one that Austin had passed, which levied a twenty-five-dollar fine on anyone caught carrying firearms in public without a license. The city's leaders were convinced that their new marshal would do just fine.

When the reporters came to see Lee about the attempted break-ins of the servants' quarters, he had no new information whatsoever to pass on to them. He did say, however, that more police officers were needed to keep up with Austin's growth. According to law enforcement manuals that Lee had been reading, police departments should have at least one officer for every 500 inhabitants. For Austin's 17,000 inhabitants, that would equate to 34 policemen. "That I have too few officers with which to properly guard the city, every man who will give the subject the least attention, is bound to admit," Lee declared in his typically convoluted style.

On this point, Lee was exactly right. In 1883, when two humor writers, Alexander Sweet and J. Armory Knox, published what became a national bestseller about their Texas travels—*On a Mexican Mustang Through Texas, from the Gulf to the Rio Grande*—they noted that the policemen in Austin were so scarce that they were forced to "walk over more ground in a day than a professional pedestrian does," and that at night "they are so far apart that they cannot hear each other snore."

The department's twelve-man roster included Bart Delong, the day clerk; Henry Brown, the night clerk; and "Uncle" Dick Boyce, the elderly boss of the chain gang who each morning took prisoners out of the calaboose to clean the horse manure off the streets. One of Austin's officers, Fred Senter, took a leave of absence every June so he could work as a cowboy on one of the few remaining cattle drives that came out of Texas. (His nickname was "Hit the Trail Fred.") Also working part-time in the department were two black men, Lewis Morris and

Henry Madison. They were known as the city's "Negro police officers." They were allowed to interrogate and arrest other black citizens but were not allowed to interrogate or arrest whites. They could wear uniforms, but were not allowed to carry guns.

On most nights, only four officers were working the streets, and they were stationed downtown. But Mayor Robertson and the aldermen rolled their eyes over Lee's proposal to triple the size of his staff. If they did such a thing, they said, the city's budget would be swamped and taxes would have to be raised. Voters would no doubt throw them out of office during the next elections.

At a city council meeting which was convened after the March attacks, one of the aldermen, James Odell, the manager of the Singer Sewing Machine office, suggested that instead of hiring more police officers, the city offer a $500 reward to anyone who shot a black man invading a servants' quarters. Alderman Radcliff Platt, the owner of a livery, feed, and seed company, said that the reward should instead go to the first servant woman who "plugged" her assailant with "buckshot." Platt's suggestion was met with laughter. Everyone knew servant women couldn't shoot.

More ideas were thrown around. Alderman Lou Crooker, the owner of a lumber and home building company, proposed the idea of "special policemen." What if some of the city's white men were temporarily deputized and ordered to patrol the white neighborhoods, essentially acting as night watchmen, until Chenneville and his officers found the "responsible parties"? Alderman Max Maas, an employee of the U.S. Internal Revenue Service, seconded the proposal, but he suggested that no public announcement should be made about the temporary policemen. That way, he said, the bad blacks wouldn't be tipped off that a manhunt was on.

Nonsense, said Alderman George Brush, who had become wealthy selling flush toilets and new gas stoves at his hardware store. The "class of people committing these crimes," he said, "are unable to read."

At the end of the meeting, the aldermen agreed to pay about a dozen

A saloon in Austin with black employees. The immediate suspects in the murders were young black males.

men two dollars a night to work the white neighborhoods. Many of those hired were friends or acquaintances of the aldermen who needed a little extra spending money or who just wanted to get away from their wives for a few nights.

By the last week of March, the temporary policemen were walking the streets and alleys. Meanwhile, Chenneville and his officers threw a couple of black men into the calaboose. Gus Johnson, a laborer, was charged with breaking into the quarters of one servant woman, and Abe Pearson, who worked in a barber shop, was charged with breaking into the quarters of another servant woman and raping her.

Both men claimed they were innocent. Nevertheless, after the arrests, the attacks on the servant women came to a stop. There were no more assaults or shootings, no more tappings on servant women's windows. The only reported instance of anyone using a gun on an intruder involved, of all people, Chenneville's young wife, Ellen. Late one night, while Chenneville was working the streets, she heard a noise in the front yard, saw the outline of a man, pulled out a six-shooter, and started firing.

It turned out she was shooting at a neighbor who had been drinking at a saloon and was so intoxicated that he had no idea he had stumbled into the Chennevilles' yard.

Fortunately, she missed.

PART TWO

APRIL 1885 – AUGUST 1885

"Who was it? Who did this to you?"

CHAPTER SIX

Another crime-free week passed, and then another. By mid-April, some of the temporary policemen were so bored that they began slipping away from their beats to spend their two-dollar daily pay at one of the saloons or brothels. Mayor Robertson and the aldermen, however, decided to keep the special policemen working at least through April 21. That date had been deemed "Texas Day" by the organizers of the World's Industrial and Cotton Centennial Exposition in New Orleans, a kind of world's fair that had opened in December and was expected to draw as many as four million visitors from around the country and even from as far away as Europe before it closed in June.

Despite being the largest state in the union (the state of Alaska, of course, did not yet exist) Texas had never before participated in any expositions, which were taking place every few years in different cities around the country. It had bypassed the 1876 Philadelphia Centennial Exposition, celebrating the hundredth anniversary of the signing of the Declaration of Independence and attended by ten million people, and it had missed the Atlanta World's Fair and Great International

Exposition in 1881 and the Southern Exposition two years later in Louisville. But Governor Ireland himself had decreed that the New Orleans Exposition would be Texas's great coming-out party—its moment to show the rest of the nation that it was no longer a second-rate state filled with gun-toting outlaws and savage Indians. It also would be his first opportunity to introduce himself to voters from other states in case he decided someday to run for president, as some of his supporters were encouraging him to do.

The exposition had been built on a 249-acre former plantation located between downtown and the Mississippi River. Among the structures erected on the site were the Horticultural Building, the Machinery Building, the Factory Building, four buildings to accommodate all the horses, and two buildings to accommodate all the cattle. There was an observation tower with never-before-seen electric elevators and an outdoor exhibit of experimental electrically powered streetcars.

The centerpiece of the exposition was the massive U.S. Government & State Exhibits Hall, thirty-three acres in size—at the time, the largest roofed structure in the world—and illuminated with 5,000 electric lights. Toward the front of the hall was the historic Liberty Bell, which had been brought from Philadelphia by train in the care of armed guards. Nearby, surrounded by velvet ropes, was one of Davy Crockett's rifles, lying on a table.

Ireland's staff had rented nearly half an acre on the main floor of the U.S. Government & State Exhibits Hall for the "Texas Department." No other state had come close to securing that much space. Spelled out in bales of cotton at the entrance to the department were the words "Lone Star," and spelled out in sacks of grain was "Welcome to Texas." Printed in big block letters on a giant billboard, easily ten feet high and ten feet across, was the slogan: "Texas! A Most Healthful State. A Cotton State. A Grain State. A Sugar State. A Tobacco State. A Garden State. A Fruit State. A Livestock State. A Timber State. An Iron and Coal State. A Marble and Granite State. A Manufacturing State. A Mercantile State. A Superbly Sceneried State."

And just to make sure visitors got the message, there was a marble globe in the center of the exhibition that showed Texas to be bigger in size than the United States and all the countries of Europe combined. (The phrase "Everything is bigger in Texas," which would become the state's most popular motto, probably was first uttered in New Orleans in April 1885.)

Wide-eyed visitors wandered through the Texas Department and stared at displays of everything Texan: bark from 150 Texas trees, tufts of 860 different Texas grasses, specimens of 220 types of rocks and minerals, and 207 kinds of Texas cactus. In large cabinets were 10,000 different Texas insects and 350 species of Texas spiders pinned to cushions. In one corner, mounted on wooden stands, were several hundred stuffed Texas birds and wild Texas animals. In another corner were poems on poster boards written by Texas poets, including, naturally, a poem by Austin's portly Mrs. Martha Hotchkiss Whitten. In another corner were paintings of Texas landscapes, pottery made from Texas clay, and Texas-made curtains, quilts, and furniture, including a chair built out of Texas cattle horns.

The Texas Department became the surprise hit of the entire exposition. A correspondent from the *Fort Worth Gazette* wrote that "people from Europe and the South American Republics seem much more interested in the display Texas is making, and many intelligent people from the North who know Texas only through the medium of the yellow-back novel and who expected to see her represented by mustang ponies, bowie-knives and six-shooters, stand amazed at the display." A *New Orleans Picayune* reporter noted that after seeing the exhibits of the Texas Department, even women and children "were expressing the most vehement desire to purchase a [railroad] ticket to go over to the country [of Texas]."

For the April 21 Texas Day ceremony, Ireland was scheduled to make the keynote speech. At least 10,000 people, twice the expected number, purchased tickets for the ceremony. Seated on the front platform, which was the size of a horse corral, were at least 800 Texas dignitaries, ranging from politicians to University of Texas professors to a handful of Houston socialites.

Ireland spoke about Texas's unprecedented new prosperity, calling the state "an empire of itself, with an insignificant debt and bonds valued so highly that they command a forty percent premium." He moved on to the subject of crime in Texas. "True, you occasionally hear of a six-shooter and a Bowie knife," he told his audience, "but after living in the state for thirty-five years, and never in that time having found it necessary to carry either a six-shooter or Bowie knife except during the war, I can say that in Texas no man need go armed to protect himself."

Ireland was getting excited—a reporter there noticed spittle whitening the corners of his mouth. The governor raised his hands and proclaimed, "There seems to be a circle of inspiration about the very name of Texas! Its mere utterance visionizes the brain! It causes troops of thought to come tripping on the tongue, and the lips refuse to be dumb. So on behalf of Texas, we extend an invitation to the world to settle within our limits, where we promise everyone a hearty welcome, education for your children, health and prosperity!"

The applause was deafening. A little girl came to the stage to present flowers to Ireland, and he leaned down to give her a tiny kiss on the lips. A young woman, completely entranced with the tall Texas governor, walked up to present him with another bouquet. According to a newspaper report, the crowd began "to cheer vociferously," hoping he would kiss her, too.

Ireland hesitated, glancing over at his wife, who was seated on the platform. Mrs. Ireland was a very proper woman. Because she believed that dancing was sinful, she had refused to go to either of her husband's inaugural balls. She gave her husband a pinch-faced stare. Observed the *Daily Statesman*, "If ever John Ireland was thoroughly nonplussed, this was the time." Ireland turned to the young lady and puckered his lips. But at the very last moment, he made a deep bow—and the crowd groaned. Yet they gave him one more ovation. They had loved his speech. His future on the national stage seemed certain.

Afterward, invited guests adjourned to the Texas Department, where champagne punch was served and ladies were presented with bouquets of artificial flowers that had been made in Texas. The party lasted into the night, but when everyone left the building, it still looked as if it was the middle of the day. Throughout the exposition's grounds were 125-foot-high towers that held giant, newly invented electric "arc lamps," each of which emitted "36,000 candlepower." They created so much light that the exposition's visitors literally could see blades of grass on the lawn.

The Austin visitors were impressed, but for many of them, the lamps appeared to be more like a pointless curiosity than a helpful invention. Why, they asked, would anyone want to go to such expense to light up a city throughout the night? What possible purpose would it serve?

III

By the time everyone got back to Austin, the spring temperatures were perfectly splendid and the downtown sidewalks crowded with shoppers. On tables in front of Gammell's Book Shoppe, the manager was displaying the science-fiction novels of Jules Verne along with the perennial bestseller *Ben Hur: A Tale of the Christ* (written by Lew Wallace, the former territorial governor of New Mexico). On wooden stands in front of his Congress Avenue office, one of the city's dentists, Dr. C. B. Stoddard, displayed his collection of biblical scenes, which he had purchased in Europe, and in front of his shop, Dr. Albert Hawkes, an optician, offered passersby the opportunity to try on the latest optical invention: "Patent Extension Spring Eye-Glasses," spectacles with dark green lenses that were guaranteed to block the glaring rays of the sun.

Several citizens stood in line at the Capital Gaslight Company to buy incandescent lamps that they planned to install in their homes, while others lined up at the Southwestern Telegraph and Telephone Company to order telephones. (Among those who had ordered a phone was the pastor at the First Baptist Church, who planned to use his to "broadcast" his sermons on Sunday mornings to all of the party-line subscribers.) A couple of salesmen were on the Avenue hawking "patent medicines": pills and ointments that cured everything from acne to baldness to farting. Down at Radam's Horticultural Emporium, at the southern edge of downtown, florist William Radam was not only selling freshly cut flowers, he was offering his customers samples of a pinkish elixir that he was calling Radam's Microbe Killer. Although the elixir was actually nothing more than 99 percent water along with a few dashes of red wine and some hydrochloric and sulfuric acid, Radam claimed that he had tried out his concoction on a group of Negro men as well as on himself and that within six months, "all those minute but evil creatures of the body" had disappeared. Radam, who smelled like cabbage, solemnly told his customers that his product could very well become "the greatest discovery of the age."

Over at city hall, Mayor Robertson and some of the city's leading businessmen were working on a 220-page catalogue which was titled *The Industries of Austin, Texas. Commercial Manufacturing Advantages & Historical, Descriptive and Biographical Facts, Figures & Illustrations. Industry and Improvement and Enterprise!* Robertson planned to send copies to libraries and bookstores around the South and Southwest in hopes of encouraging even more businesses to relocate to Austin. In gloriously flowery language, the catalogue's text gushed on and on about Austin's "new wealth"—enough to keep five jewelry stores in business, the catalogue proclaimed—as well as its "elegant homes," its "upright churches" (eighteen in all), and its numerous "institutions of learning," ranging from the University of Texas, which that spring was "overflowing" with 230 students studying English literature, European history, ancient languages, law, physics, and "moral and mental philosophy," to the Stuart Seminary for young ladies desiring a classical education, to the Capitol Business College for those wishing to master the typewriter. All in all, the catalogue's text concluded, Austin was "the American Oxford of the Southwest . . . the seat of rare intelligence, culture and wealth . . . with unrivaled advantages for establishing greater distinction in the near future."

Finally, on April 27, Mayor Robertson and the aldermen disbanded the temporary police program. All remained calm—for exactly two days. On the night of April 29, a man entered a small cabin in the backyard of a home on West Walnut Street, grabbed a German servant woman in her bed, covered her mouth with his hands to stifle her screams, threw her to the floor, and disappeared.

Later that same evening, a man entered the servants' quarters of a home on Mulberry Street. The cook who lived there was gone but a female friend was sleeping in a bed. The man grabbed her throat with one hand, held a razor with his other hand, and threatened to kill her if she screamed. At that moment, the cook and another black woman came into the backyard, and seeing the open servants' quarters door, called to their friend inside. The man raced out the door and ran away. Once again, it was dark and difficult to see, but one of the women said she could have sworn the man was wearing a woman's dress.

The next night, someone hurled a large stone at a servant woman's cabin in the backyard of a home on Rio Grande Street. A neighbor heard the woman's cries, ran outside, and shot at a man he saw running away. He missed, and the man kept running. An hour later, J. M. Brackenridge, the president of the City National Bank, was awakened by a noise in his backyard. Looking out a window, peering into the darkness, he saw his cook, an elderly black woman, struggling with a man. Brackenridge shouted at the man, who fled. But a few hours later, either the man or someone else returned and "rocked the house" (the phrase that police used to describe someone throwing rocks at a home).

Over the next couple of days, Chenneville and his officers arrested three more black men—Andrew Jackson, Newt Harper, and Henry Wallace—who were described in the newspapers as "hard-looking Negroes." They also arrested Jack Ross, a black man who worked as a janitor at the Variety Theatre (where the blond Miss Ida St. Clair danced for the cowboys), and an elderly black man who was known around Austin as "Old John."

Old John had spent some time over the past year at the State Lunatic Asylum after he was heard telling people he was worth $260 million in gold, which he secretly had buried beside the Colorado River. He had been released by Dr. Denton, who decided that he was completely harmless. But now, reported the *Daily Statesman*, the police "believed on good grounds" that Old John was the man seen in a dress during that attack of the servant woman at her quarters on Mulberry Street. "It is also thought that he had a hand in the outrageous attacks made a few weeks ago [in March]," added the newspaper.

In truth, Chenneville and his officers had no idea at all whether

Old John, or any of the other men they had arrested, had committed any of the attacks. Hoping to get someone to break, they chained the black men to iron rings cemented to the floor of the calaboose and subjected them to brutal interrogations—"examinations," one of the newspapers reporters euphemistically called them. Yet none of them confessed to anything. The suspects insisted that they had never broken into anyone's servants' quarters and that they had no desire to harm servant women.

Nevertheless, with the latest round of arrests, the attacks once again came to a stop. During the first week of May, there were light rains, which were followed by spectacularly beautiful sunsets. As dusk descended, church bells tolled, and bats flew out from their hiding places and turned long, dark circles in the sky, the sound of their beating wings like a deck of shuffling cards. Henry Stamps, the lamplighter, walked the downtown streets, lighting the gas lamps. One by one, they sprang to life, a row of flickering isolated globes. Saloon owners propped open their front doors, out of which poured the sound of laughter and rinky-tink piano music. Because women weren't allowed into saloons in 1885, a couple of the saloon owners had their waiters carry out gin fizzes to their male customers' wives and girlfriends who were sitting by the curb in their carriages.

On the afternoon of May 6, there was another rain, followed by another stunning sunset. Over on the city's east side, some of the black residents went to a black Baptist church to witness the wedding of Miss Lucie A. Lomax, the daughter of a shopkeeper, to Mr. H. G. Grant, a young schoolteacher. A thirty-one-year-old servant named Eliza Shelley did not attend the wedding. She was working at the home of her employer, Dr. Lucian Johnson, a medical doctor and former state legislator who had been described as "a well-known citizen of the city."

That evening, Eliza fixed dinner for the Johnson family. Afterward she cleaned the kitchen, polished the stove and silverware, and then retired to her little cabin in the Johnsons' backyard, forty or fifty steps from the main house—a cabin so small that she had to stoop to avoid bumping her head as she came through the door. Inside the cabin, she fed her three young boys, the oldest of whom was seven, with scraps of food she had collected from the Johnsons' dinner table, and soon she and the children climbed into their bed.

Eliza and the two smallest boys were at the head of the bed; the seven-year-old was at the end. Eliza's husband, William, was not there; in early 1884, he had been sent to the state penitentiary for five years for stealing a horse.

The next morning at six, just at the break of day, Dr. Johnson rose and left for the market to buy groceries for the family. While he was gone, his wife heard Eliza's children screaming—"crying and hallooing at a fearful rate," she would later say. She sent her young niece, who was barely a teenager, out to the cabin. Within a couple of minutes, Mrs. Johnson heard her niece screaming, too. The girl ran back to the main house and collapsed into Mrs. Johnson's arms, so terrified she couldn't speak a word.

Dr. Johnson returned from the market, spoke to his wife, walked out to the cabin, and opened the door. In a corner of the room were Eliza's three boys, huddled together. On the floor next to the bed, wrapped in a quilted bedspread, was Eliza. Parts of her brain were oozing out of a gaping wound in her right temple.

CHAPTER SEVEN

When Sergeant Chenneville arrived at the Johnsons', he walked into the cabin and noticed that both of Eliza's trunks had been broken open and her garments scattered over the floor. He ordered that Eliza's body be taken out to the backyard, where there was more sunlight. Police officers removed the bedspread from Eliza's body, only to find that underneath was a white counterpane (quilt) that had also been wrapped around her. When the counterpane was removed, everyone finally got a look at the extent of Eliza's wounds.

Besides an ax wound to her skull, there was a small hole between her eyes that looked as if it had been made by a screwdriver or some sort of thin iron rod, and there were several knife wounds up and down her body. Some of them were easily four inches deep: the blade had been plunged all the way into her body and pulled directly out, severing blood vessels, muscle tissue, and cartilage.

Everyone in the yard stood still, trying to keep their stomachs from heaving. The reporters soon arrived, their Faber notebooks in their hands. They watched as Chenneville's bloodhounds circled Eliza's body like vultures. The dogs sniffed what were described as "large, broad, barefoot tracks" that had been found leading to and from Eliza's cabin. They ran out to the back alley. But once again, Chenneville was out of luck. To quote a San Antonio newspaper reporter who was there, "Mr. Chenneville's bloodhounds refused to take a scent."

Chenneville went over to speak to Eliza's seven-year-old son. The boy said that he had been shaken awake in the middle of the night by a man who was wearing a white rag over his face with two holes cut out for the eyes. The boy couldn't tell whether the man was black or white, but he thought he was white. He said the man asked him where his mother kept her money, and he replied that he didn't know if his mother had any money. The boy said the man ordered him to put his head under a pillow and not look out again, or else he would kill him. The man then told him that he would be on his way to St. Louis the next morning on the first train.

Eliza's son said he went back to sleep—(his two little brothers never awakened)—and he had no idea what the man had done to his mother until the first light of the morning sun seeped through the cracks of the cabin and he saw her on the floor.

The boy's story, of course, sounded completely preposterous. A man in a mask had come into the cabin, slammed an ax into Eliza's skull, pulled her off the bed, jammed some type of rod between her eyes, stabbed at her with a knife, wrapped her in a counterpane that he must have found in one of the trunks, wrapped her again in a quilted bedspread—and then woke up the seven-year-old boy to ask where any money was? And, to top it all off, he said he was going to St. Louis on a train?

Was the boy in some sort of shock when he told the story? Maybe. But when Chenneville was finished with his interview, a correspondent from the *San Antonio Express* took the boy aside, asking him several times to go through what had happened, and the boy repeated the same story "without varying it at all."

Dr. Johnson, clearly distraught, came outside to the backyard and told reporters that Eliza was "an excellent woman." He described her as hardworking, reliable, and honest—so exemplary, he said, that he, his wife, and children had tended to treat her like a lesser member of the family.

Johnson also said it made no sense that someone would want to murder Eliza for her money, claiming that she had "only a few paltry cents" to her name. Surely, he suggested, a thief would have tried to get into his home instead of his servant's cabin. A coin collector, Johnson was well-known around Austin for a very valuable coin he owned that had been made during the reign of Marcus Aurelius, emperor of Rome in the year AD 161.

Someone asked Johnson if Eliza had had any enemies. Johnson replied that he had no knowledge of anyone disliking her and that he knew of no men with whom she was romantically involved. He said she seemed very devoted to her husband and was patiently waiting for him to serve out his prison sentence. She did not deserve to die in such a manner, regardless of her race, Johnson said. Then he turned around and went back inside his house.

Because of the footprints found by the cabin, Chenneville and other police officers went looking for a barefoot black man. Within a couple of hours, a shoeless black teenager, nineteen-year-old Andrew Williams, who lived near the Johnson residence, was brought in for questioning. He was described as a "half-witted colored boy" who previously had been jailed for "stealing buttons."

Williams, however, didn't incriminate himself during his police interrogation, and his footprints didn't match the measurements of the footprints found in the yard. A justice of the peace convened the inquest, the jurors ruled that Eliza's death was a murder that had come "at the hands of a person or persons unknown," and the black undertaker arrived at the Johnsons' to pick up Eliza's body and carry her to the hospital for her autopsy and then on to Colored Ground, where she was buried only yards from Mollie Smith's grave.

Afterward, Mr. Nitschke, the cemetery's elderly sexton, opened his beautifully bound ledger to add Eliza's name to those who had been buried at the cemetery. But once again, he was reluctant to go into the details of what had happened to her. He simply wrote that her death was due to a "wound on the throat."

III

The sexton's sense of propriety didn't exactly carry over to the newspapers. "Inhabitants of the Capital City Are Again Shocked by a Blood-Curdling Murder," trumpeted the next day's *Fort Worth Gazette*. "A Mother Butchered in the Presence of Her Children," cried the *San Antonio Daily Express*. The *Daily Statesman*'s headline, ghoulishly alliterative, was thirty-three words long: "The Foul Fiends Keep Up Their Wicked Work—Another Woman Cruelly Murdered at Dead of Night by Some Unknown Assassin, Bent on Plunder. Another Deed of Deviltry in the Crimson Catalogue of Crime."

The *Daily Statesman*'s story noted that "clear-headed, conservative men" were huddling on Congress Avenue's street corners to discuss the attacks on the city's servant women. Some of the men theorized that there must be some sort of black gang—"a band of colored fiends," one man said—that was behind the assaults and the killings. According to one rumor circulating up and down the Avenue, the gang worked for a black labor union that had been trying to recruit the city's servant women to join and demand higher wages—fifteen dollars a month—from their white employers. The gang supposedly had been hired to attack those women who wouldn't sign up.

William Sydney Porter, the young drugstore clerk who wanted to become a writer, actually came up with a nickname for the gang. After Eliza's murder, he wrote a friend who recently had moved to Colorado that life in Austin had been "fearfully dull . . . except for the frequent raids of the Servant Girl Annihilators, who make things lively during the dead hours of the night."

In Austin's black neighborhoods, however, no one was talking about a gang. Many of the black residents were literally saying that a "demon" or an "evil one" with an "evil eye" had come to Austin. Some of the city's elderly blacks who still practiced hoodoo, a slave-era folk magic, gave servant women special powders to scatter around the doorways of their quarters that supposedly would keep them safe from the "evil one." They made "nostrums," specially brewed tonics that were supposed to bring long life, for the servant women to drink, and they

The young Austin writer William Sydney Porter
nicknamed the killers the "Servant Girl
Annihilators."

created "mojo bags," little leather pouches filled with herbs, roots, seeds,
minerals, animal parts, silver dimes, shiny rocks, and shoestrings that
were supposed to bring good luck, for the servant women to carry. It
was likely that at least one of the hoodoo practitioners performed one
of the more honored hoodoo rituals: boiling a black cat in a pot of
scalding water, pulling out its bones, and then giving the bones to a
servant woman to protect her from evil.

Yet even then, the servant women didn't feel remotely safe. At
night, they stacked furniture against the doors of their quarters. One
black man who lived with his wife in the quarters behind the home of
a white family said he never expected to leave the quarters ever again
at night "for fear his wife would be killed."

As for Sergeant Chenneville, he met with his "pals" and the department's two "Negro" officers to find out what they had learned. They
told him they had no information at all. On his big bay horse, Chenne-

ville rode through the black neighborhoods, staring intently at every black man he saw, and he dropped into the Black Elephant saloon, which was always a convenient place to find a suspect when an arrest was needed.

On May 10, five days after Shelley's murder, Chenneville got a break—or so he thought. A black resident named Andrew Rogers came to the police department and said that he believed he knew who had murdered Eliza.

Rogers stated that one of his neighbors, a young black man named Ike Plummer, had carried on a brief romantic relationship with Eliza earlier that year while her husband was in prison. Rogers said that a few weeks prior to Eliza's murder, he had seen Eliza arguing with Plummer, who was angry with her because she wouldn't loan him money. Rogers added that he had happened to pass by Dr. Johnson's home the day of Eliza's murder and seen Plummer and Eliza arguing again. According to Rogers, Plummer said, "I want some money," and Eliza replied, "I have none for you. What little I have is for my children, and I don't want you around me." Then, said Rogers, Plummer walked off, yelling at Eliza, "I'll see you again!" Rogers claimed that he noticed either a hammer or a hatchet protruding from Plummer's pocket.

And that wasn't all, continued Rogers. Later that night—sometime after one in the morning—he had been awakened by a sound outside his window and had seen Plummer entering his own shanty.

After hearing Rogers's tale, Chenneville immediately had one of the department's black officers, Lewis Morris, go to Plummer's shanty and arrest him on a charge of "suspicion of murder." (Chenneville would later say he worried that Plummer would run, or maybe even pull out a knife, if he saw the sergeant coming after him.) Reporters who got a look at Plummer in the calaboose described him as "a tall, ungainly, ill-kempt Negro" with "a half imbecile grin" and "a countenance suggestive more of idiocy than brutality, and about thirty years of age." Although Plummer did have a minor criminal record—he had been arrested a couple of times for vagrancy—he had never before been charged with committing a violent crime. A man who had hired Plummer to do some work on his cotton farm told the *Daily Statesman* that "there was nothing of a vicious disposition about him."

It turned out that there was no physical evidence linking Plummer to the killing: no blood was found on his clothes, and his footprints didn't match the footprints around the front door of the cabin. Moreover, the police could not find anyone who could corroborate Rogers's story.

At least a couple of couple of reporters were suspicious about what Rogers had said. Would Plummer really have gone after Eliza with a hatchet, a knife, and some sort of ice pick all because of a dispute over a very small amount of money? And if he did, wouldn't Eliza's son have recognized Plummer—or at least recognized his voice—even if he was wearing a mask? Wasn't it more likely that Rogers had made up the story for his own reasons—perhaps he was in some sort of feud with Plummer and saw a chance at putting him behind bars?

"It is scarcely probable that the slight circumstantial evidence pointing to his [Plummer's] guilt will ever warrant a conviction," noted the Austin-based reporter for the *San Antonio Express*, who also predicted that it would only be a matter of time before "the regular nocturnal Negro carving of the Capital City" would again be taking place.

The reporter's prediction came true only two weeks later. On the evening of May 22, a shoemaker named Robert Weyermann, who lived with his family northeast of downtown, just across the street from a popular German-owned beer hall called the Scholz Garten, heard a low, painful moan coming from the backyard. The moan turned into a scream: a terrible, piercing scream.

Weyermann and other family members ran outside and found Irene Cross, their thirty-three-year-old black cook, lying on the ground. Her right arm was nearly severed in two. A long horizontal gash extended halfway around her head, from her right eye past her right ear. It looked as if someone had tried to scalp her.

Irene tried to speak, but blood was running out of the gash in her head and into her mouth. More blood was spurting from her half-severed arm. Weyermann had her carried to a spare bedroom in his home—something that was at the time considered an amazing act of generosity by a white man, to let a black servant bleed to death in one of his beds. A cloth was wrapped tightly around her arm and another cloth around her head.

"Who was it?" someone asked. "Who did this to you?"

Irene tried again to say something to those around her. But there was a look of confusion on her face and no words came out of her mouth.

CHAPTER EIGHT

After sunrise, a steady parade of visitors came to the Weyermanns' home hoping to get a look at Irene through the bedroom window. She was, amazingly, still alive. A *Daily Statesman* reporter was allowed to come inside and talk to her. "Familiar as he was with repulsive sights, the reporter could not help being horrified by the ghastly object that met his view," he wrote, referring to himself in the third person. The reporter added that when he bent down toward the bed and asked Irene if she could identify her attacker, she was only able to emit a faint groan.

Meanwhile, Chenneville's bloodhounds were brought to the Weyermanns' yard—and for the third murder in a row, they failed to find a scent. Some of the men who were there, leaning against the fence, just shook their heads. Had the dogs again been overwhelmed by all the blood? Was there too much blood for the bloodhounds? Or had Chenneville simply been sold some bad dogs?

As was the case with Eliza Shelley's killing, all that the police had to go on was the story of another child. Irene's twelve-year-old nephew, who lived with her, had been sleeping in one of the cabin's two rooms. The boy said that he had opened his eyes and glimpsed the shadowy figure of a man coming through the outer door leading into his room. The man, who was holding a knife, had quietly told the boy that he was not there to hurt him, and ordered the boy not to scream or yell. The man then walked into Irene's room, which contained two single beds: one for her (her husband had left her years earlier) and one for her seventeen-year-old son, who was not there (he worked nights as a porter at one of the city's saloons). According to the nephew, the man spent just a couple of minutes in his aunt's room, and then ran out her door leading into the backyard.

Later, when the newspaper reporters interviewed the nephew, he said that he believed his aunt's attacker had been "a big, chunky Negro" wearing a brown wide-brimmed cloth hat, a ragged coat, a blue shirt, and black pants rolled up over his bare feet and ankles. For at least some of the reporters, the boy's statement was baffling. It was hard for them to imagine how, in the pitch-black darkness of that cabin, he had been able to get such a good look at the man, considering that he was there for only a few seconds. Had the boy, in his excitement, gotten carried away and made up parts of his story to please Chenneville and the other police officers? Had he, perhaps, been prompted about what to say?

Irene hung on for another day, finally dying in the early morning hours of May 25, mumbling words to herself that no one could understand. A court of inquest ruled that she had been killed by "a party or parties unknown," and the black undertaker arrived to carry her away to Colored Ground. After her burial, Mr. Nitschke, the cemetery sexton, once again opened his ledger to note Irene's passing. He was still having trouble coming to terms with what was happening. This time, under the listing for cause of death, he wrote, "Wounds."

III

Austin's clear-headed, conservative businessmen gathered for another day on Congress Avenue. Several of them continued to insist that a murderous "Negro gang" was at work. At least one man speculated that the gang lived like "a band of outlaws" in one of the caves or cliffs along the Colorado River just outside of Austin, and that they swooped into the city at night to do their killings, which was the reason Sergeant Chenneville had not been able to find them.

A couple of men on the Avenue believed that the gang was made up of "escaped convicts" who had vowed eternal "enmity" against servant women in Austin because the gang's leader had received some sort of venereal disease, or maybe even tuberculosis, from a servant woman. Others believed that the gang was a "secret, oath-bound association" made up of religiously fanatical black men who disapproved of black women having "sexual relations" with men who weren't their husbands. The goal of this association was to "stamp out Negro prostitution" and "compel the members of the Negro race to live in the bonds of matrimony."

And then there were a few men who had come up with an even more astonishing theory. They had concluded that some sort of mystical "killing mania" was sweeping over Austin's black neighborhoods. The way they saw it, the murder of Mollie Smith had inflamed the blood-thirsty instincts of other young black men, leading them to commit similar murders of those black women they didn't like.

For his part, Marshal Lee did his best to reassure the public that nothing was amiss, saying that Chenneville and his officers were pursuing several good leads. But on June 2, two weeks after Irene Cross's murder, someone stuck his pistol through the slightly raised window of the servants' quarters adjoining the home of Henri Tallichet, the professor of modern languages at the University of Texas, pulled the trigger, and shot a .42-caliber bullet into the arm of the Tallichets' young black servant woman. Hearing the shot, Professor Tallichet seized his own pistol and hurried toward the kitchen. Just as he opened the door of the servants' quarters, a bullet whizzed past his head. The intruder fled before Tallichet got a chance to get a look at him.

That same night, someone visited the residence of Major Stewart— the same Major Stewart whose two servant women had been attacked back in March—and threw a large rock through the window of the servants' quarters. Sleeping in the quarters with the servant women was a black man—the women had asked him to stay there at night to protect them—who grabbed his pistol, ran after the rock thrower, and fired away. But the invader quickly disappeared down an alley, and no one had any idea what he looked like.

Chenneville and his officers did the only thing they knew to do— they chased down more black men and arrested them for various infractions—vagrancy, disturbing the peace, public intoxication— hoping that one of them, during his uncomfortable stay in the cala- boose, would confess that he knew something about the murders.

There was one man in particular whom Chenneville wanted to arrest and interrogate: a twenty-two-year-old chicken thief named Oliver Townsend. Although he was only five feet, seven inches tall and 150 pounds, Townsend was a larger-than-life figure in the black neighborhoods. According to stories told about him, he was able to slip into a white man's chicken coop "as noiselessly as a cat," grab some sleeping chickens, snap their necks, and disappear into the darkness, running away as quickly "as a deer" before the other chickens awakened and began their frantic screeching. During the previous Christmas season, an Austin homeowner had paid a couple of night watchmen to keep watch on his residence, where he had a coop full of fattened turkeys and chickens for his holiday dinners. The next morning, six of the fowl were found missing, and the assumption was that only Townsend could have pulled off such a theft.

Chenneville apparently had decided that if anyone in Austin had the ability to get in and out of a servant's quarters without being seen, it was Townsend—"the great and bloodthirsty robber of the hen roost who has figured in several daring midnight hen murders," the *Daily Statesman* called him.

On June 6, two officers found Townsend at the Black Elephant. They dragged him to the calaboose, where they were "forced to listen to some ugly cuss words that the prisoner used in giving vent to his opinion regarding them. . . . In the choice slang of the day, Mr. Townsend is a tough, and though he may be proof against bullets, is liable to have a hard time with hemp."

The implication was clear: Townsend was about to get the beating of his life with a rope whip.

However, just like every other black man who had been arrested and interrogated since Mollie Smith's murder, Townsend swore that he hadn't attacked any of the servant women and that he didn't know anyone who had. Chained to an iron ring cemented to the floor, he was beaten again. And still he confessed to nothing.

Eventually, Townsend was released, and Chenneville and his officers returned to the streets to look for more black suspects. Worried that they too would be arrested and hemp whipped, black men began walking to and from their homes with their arms held out so that the officers would know they were not carrying axes or knives. Some of the men were so terrified that Chenneville's bloodhounds would chase them down that they covered their feet and legs with asafoetida, a strong-smelling putty composed of old tree roots, soured vegetables, herbs, and spices that had been used since slavery days to confound bloodhounds.

As for the servant women, several of them quit their jobs and moved away, carrying with them a couple of tin pots and a bag of clothes. Those who stayed wouldn't budge from their quarters after sundown. Or they spent nights inside their white employers' homes, lying on pallets on the kitchen floor. Some held their mojo bags to keep away the demon with the evil eye. They quietly sang spirituals and prayed, asking God to let them fall asleep at least for a few hours before they had to awaken at 4 in the morning to begin another day of work.

III

By mid-June, the attacks again came to a stop: not even a rock was thrown at a servant woman's quarters. Residents speculated that the bad blacks had been scared off by the police department's strong-arm tactics. Either that, wrote the *Daily Statesman*, or they had been frightened by all the homeowners who had been sticking rifles and pistols out their windows and "firing away" at anyone they felt was coming too close to their servants' quarters.

In truth, there was little crime at all in Austin during the month of June except for the usual saloon brawls and a couple of run-of-the mill burglaries. On June 16, William Howe, the young police officer who had conducted the initial investigation into the Mollie Smith murder, did issue a ticket to Governor Ireland for illegally parking his carriage at a street crossing down by the railroad depot, which gave the newspaper reporters a day's worth of entertainment. ("Something near a dozen assassins and would-be assassins of servant women go scot-free, but a governor is nabbed!" chuckled the *Fort Worth Gazette*.) Mayor Robertson and the aldermen were so angry at Howe for embarrassing the governor that they fired him. But they still didn't feel a need to do much more to protect Austin's citizens, such as voting to hire more police officers. They too seemed to believe that Chenneville and his officers had chased off the "midnight miscreants" who had been committing "deeds of deviltry."

By July 4—Independence Day—Austin's pitch of gaiety was back in full swing. There were boat races on the Colorado River and tug-of-war contests at a city park. Some families rode in their carriages to Barton Creek to swim and eat picnic lunches. Men pitched horseshoes. Children attempted to capture an oiled pig. In a "ladies only" section of Barton Creek, a few daring young women jumped into the water wearing bathing dresses that revealed their knees.

At sunset, between 4,000 and 6,000 citizens gathered on Pecan Street in the heart of downtown to celebrate the laying of the cornerstone for a new hotel that Col. Jessie Driskill, a rich cattleman who had lived in Austin for many years, was building. Driskill had announced he would be spending $400,000 of his fortune to construct what he called "the most sophisticated hotel west of St. Louis," four stories high, with hydraulic elevators, and flush toilets on the top floors. The blueprints called for a large saloon on the first floor along with a billiards room and a barber shop. On the second floor would be a dining room, a bridal apartment, parlors, and a ladies' dressing room. Each of the hotel's sixty rooms on the top two floors would contain a chandelier, a large couch, a red rocker, a four-poster bed, a private balcony, and an electric bell to ring for a porter. The twelve corner rooms would come with private bathrooms, an almost unheard-of feature for any hotel in the region.

To top it all off, Driskill had ordered that enormous stone busts of

In July, 6,000 citizens came downtown for the cornerstone ceremony of the Driskill Hotel, said to be the finest hotel west of St. Louis.

himself and his two sons, Tobe and Bud, be carved into the exterior of the hotel because he relished the notion of future generations of Texans looking up to see his family. To show his unending loyalty to the old Confederacy—he had made his fortune supplying beef to Confederate troops throughout the Civil War—Driskill had ordered that his own bust be facing south.

For the cornerstone ceremony, hundreds of small incandescent lights were strung over Pecan Street in front of the hotel. Both a brass band and a string band performed. Edward Shands, a popular Austin real estate agent, entertained the crowd with a Jules Verne–like speech predicting what Austin would look like on July 4, 2000, 115 years away. Shands announced that 75,000 people would be living in Austin, that 60,000 copies of the *Daily Statesman* would be delivered each day through pneumatic tubes to every building in Austin, and that the U.S. mail would be transported in "electrical airships" and dropped directly onto people's yards. He also declared that "modern aerial flights" in those electrical airships would take passengers "from Austin to San Francisco, then thence to China and Japan, then over Europe and across the Atlantic to home . . . a pleasure trip around the globe in a few days."

Most exciting, Shands concluded, was that electricity would be used "to send shock waves through people, causing them to live longer and end all diseases," and that "entire armies and navies" that dared to attack America would be "instantaneously destroyed with one electrical bolt!"

The crowd roared its approval. Fireworks were set off: Roman candles and sky lanterns and firecrackers that battered the ear. Showers of red, white, and blue fell like stars and then burst. Afterward, citizens lingered on the streets, many of them greeting one another by name, the men tipping their derbies or their Stetson hats at the ladies. A group of businessmen and politicians headed down to the Pearl House Hotel and Restaurant, just across the street from the railroad depot, for a dinner to honor Colonel Driskill. Seated at one long table, they consumed a lavish eight-course meal and drank Mumm's champagne. At the end of the night, amid curls of cigar smoke, they rose to make increasingly inebriated toasts to everything from the new hotel to the city's banking system to the entire educational system of Texas.

Mayor Robertson gave the final toast, and it was, of course, a masterpiece of booming. "To the Capital City," he declared, "with the natural beauty of its location, the salubrity of its atmospherical influences, and a proper diversification of its labor and investment of its money. . . . No city has the promise of a more healthful prosperity!"

III

Later that July, Mayor Robertson held a meeting of the Texas Semi-Centennial Organizing Committee to begin planning the fiftieth celebration of Texas's independence, which would be held in Austin in March 1886—seven months away. Although the mayor had no idea what he would do to surpass the parade and cornerstone ceremony from the previous March, he vowed that the coming celebration would "eclipse anything ever attempted in Texas."

In early August, he headed down to the railroad depot to greet J. W. Olds, a very important visitor who was coming in from San Francisco. Olds was a researcher and ghostwriter for Hubert Howe

Bancroft, one of the most popular American historians of his day. For the last several years, Bancroft had been working on a massive thirty-nine-volume project detailing the history of the western half of the continent, from Central America to Alaska, and he recently had decided to devote a volume to Texas. Bancroft had ordered Olds, who was one of his chief ghostwriters, to come to Austin to "collect material" on Texas's history, beginning with the arrival of the first white settlers in the 1520s and concluding in the 1880s, with Texas, and its capital, Austin, on the very cusp of modernity.

Robertson was determined that Olds see the best of Austin. It was arranged for him and his wife to stay in a suite of rooms in one of the city's finest boardinghouses. Dinners were thrown in his honor. Governor Ireland and William Swain, the state's barrel-chested comptroller who was already campaigning to be the next governor, met with Olds, hoping to be included in Bancroft's book. ("An excellent man," Olds later wrote about Swain.) As part of his research, Olds visited the shops and restaurants of Congress Avenue, went to talk to the professors at the new University of Texas, and even made the two-and-a-half-mile trip north of downtown to the sprawling State Lunatic Asylum, where the effusive Dr. Denton showed off the newly landscaped grounds, the freshly repainted dormitories, and the lovely, flower-laden chapel, where his daughter and his son-in-law Dr. Given had been married.

And, of course, Olds took a tour of the new state capitol, which was still under construction—by all accounts, the biggest and most expensive construction project in the country, costing at least $3.7 million ($85.3 million in today's dollars). More than five hundred workers were swarming over the twenty-two-acre capitol grounds, erecting iron girders and pillars, excavating the basement, constructing the foundation walls, and installing water pipes and ventilation shafts. Every afternoon, on a narrow-gauge railroad track that ran straight from the quarry to the site of the capitol, a locomotive called *The Lone Star* pulled flatbed cars laden with red granite, which were unloaded by cranes and cut into perfect rectangular blocks by trained stonemasons who had been brought in from England and Scotland. Olds was so overwhelmed with the capitol that he wrote that upon its completion, it would "rival in dimensions and magnificence any other edifice of its kind in the United States."

Olds was almost certainly told about the servant women attacks. In his notes, he wrote that citizens periodically had to endure the behavior of "debased Negroes" who "engaged in frays among themselves, which generally terminated in bloodshed." But he made it clear that the "frays" were of little significance. He noted that the state's criminal laws were being enforced "with undeviating justice" and that violent criminals were being taken off the streets and put in the penitentiary. All in all, concluded Olds, the state once known as "the abode of savages" was being converted "into a civilized country."

III

Throughout the month of August, several residents left the city to go on their summer vacations, some traveling back to their old family homes in the South, and others taking the train to Galveston to stay at the Tremont Hotel and swim in the Gulf of Mexico. Sergeant Chenneville himself took a few days off because there was little to do. "If something doesn't turn up soon," wrote a reporter, "Austin's police force will probably adjourn for a fishing frolic."

In the last week of the month, the temperatures soared, thermometers hitting 100 degrees Fahrenheit. A crew of men in a water wagon traversed downtown's heat-baked streets, spraying them with water to keep down the dust. On Saturday, August 29, a couple of hundred residents who were not on vacation trooped out to the fairgrounds to watch the Austins, the city's semi-professional baseball team, play the neighboring Georgetowns for the regional championship. Before the game, the Austins donned new uniforms made of gray flannel pants that came down to their knees, gray flannel jackets trimmed in white, gray flannel caps, blue stockings, and black shoes. The players were so hot that sweat poured down their bodies. Still, they won by a convincing score of 19–10 to advance to the state playoffs.

That night, there was the usual activity on the downtown streets. Couples dined at the restaurants and later dropped by the "air-cooled"

An Austin ice-cream parlor. Through much of the summer, the people of Austin thought the murders had come to an end.

ice-cream shop owned by Julien Prade. At the saloons, the usual array of men gathered to drink and play cards. On the Avenue, a salesman sold a new soap that he vowed would remove all grease spots from skin and clothing, and a self-described "street astronomer" offered sidewalk strollers the opportunity (for a small fee) to look through his telescope and view the heavens. It was a beautiful night, he said, to see the moons and the stars—which was no exaggeration. There were only a few clouds in the sky.

Then, a short time past midnight, just a couple of blocks southeast of the Avenue, a man made his way down an alley behind the home of Valentine Osborn Weed.

CHAPTER NINE

Valentine Weed was a successful young businessman who owned a downtown livery stable that leased horses, wagons, buggies, and carriages. He and his family lived in a two-story Queen Anne home, which was only a block away from Dr. Lucian Johnson's residence, where Eliza Shelley had been murdered back in early May.

On pallets in Weed's kitchen that night were his servant woman, Rebecca Ramey, and her eleven-year-old daughter, Mary. The two had been sleeping in the kitchen because they, like so many other servant women, were too afraid to sleep in their own quarters. Rebecca was about forty years of age, a large woman, weighing close to two hundred pounds. She was well known in the black community—her brother was Albert Carrington, Austin's lone black city alderman. Rebecca formerly had worked at the Austin Steam Laundry and had been married to a man who was a bellhop at the popular Avenue Hotel. But when he disappeared from Austin a couple of years earlier—rumored to have run off with another woman—Rebecca had come to work for the Weeds so she could always have her daughter, Mary, at her side.

Mary spent the mornings at the all-black Central Grammar School. In the afternoons, she helped her mother. She did everything—iron clothes, make beds, chop wood, bring in water, start fires, clean, and cook. Because of her education, she had a bright future: someday she would be able to enroll at the Tillotson College and Normal Institute to study and become a teacher.

The man in the alley opened the back gate to the Weed home. He probably stood there for several seconds, completely still, to avoid spooking Tom Thumb, Weed's miniature Shetland pony that lived in the backyard.

The yard was dry, the fallen leaves from the surrounding live oak trees even drier. As the man started walking toward the house, however, he didn't make a sound. Nor did the floorboards creak when he slipped onto the back porch—or at least they weren't loud enough to wake Rebecca or Mary, or any member of the Weed family. Like a highly skilled burglar, he slowly and silently opened the kitchen door.

In his hand was a club, about a foot long, containing several ounces of lead packed in sand that was all wrapped in buckskin. A leather strap was at the bottom end of the club, which the man had wrapped around his wrist. He stepped into the kitchen and loomed over Rebecca and Mary.

When Rebecca realized someone was there, she tried to get her eyes to focus so that she could see just who it was. But the man was a dark silhouette against the blackness. Rebecca didn't have a chance to draw a breath, let alone scream, before he slammed the club against the side of her head. It hit her so hard it was like a fist going through a light plaster wall. But because of the sand surrounding the lead, the sound was muffled—a dull *thunk*. Rebecca fell back to the floor, knocked completely unconscious. The man dropped the club and grabbed little Mary.

III

At some point in the early morning hours, Rebecca regained consciousness and began to groan. V. O. Weed awakened, lit a small lantern, and walked toward the kitchen, his wife in her nightgown following him.

He opened the door. Her eyelids fluttering, Rebecca was on her hands and knees, her head lowered to her chest. She must have crawled into that position without thinking, like a wounded animal that had retreated to a corner. Blood was flowing from two cuts in her left temple. Part of her forehead looked caved in and the line of her jaw was crooked. The pain was so great she could barely speak. "I'm sick," she murmured to Weed. When he asked about her daughter Mary's whereabouts, she just shook her head.

Weed noticed the club on the kitchen floor—left there almost as a taunt. He grabbed his shotgun, stepped outside, and yelled toward the home of his next-door neighbor, Stephen Jacqua, the co-owner of a flour, feed, and hay supply store. Jacqua met Weed at the fence, where Weed told him that someone had attacked Rebecca and dragged away her daughter. He asked Jacqua to come with him to look in the back-yard shed, where tools were stored. "I carried the light and Mr. Weed pushed the door of the outhouse open with the barrel of his gun," Jacqua would later say. "We saw the girl lying on the floor, as I supposed, dead."

Mary, however, was not dead—not yet. Her eyes were partly open, dazed, peering up at the two men with no expression at all. Blood was trickling out of her ears and blood bubbles coming out of her nose. The men stepped out into the yard and looked around, as if expecting to be attacked. But there was only silence.

Weed told Jacqua to remain in the yard and not to allow anyone to come in. He was smart enough to realize that the crime scene needed to be preserved until the police arrived. He had his wife run to the home of Dr. Johnson and ask him to come tend to Rebecca and Mary. Then Weed himself either ran or rode a horse to the home of Sergeant Chenneville, who lived only a couple of blocks away, to ask him to come with his dogs.

Dr. Johnson arrived, examined little Mary in the shed, and realized there was nothing he could do. Whenever she took a breath, more blood poured out of her ears and spread below her body. Another doctor, Richard Swearingen, also came into the shed and stared at Mary. Chenneville then showed up. The men conjectured that an intruder, after attacking Rebecca, had grabbed Mary, clamped one hand over her mouth so she could not make a sound, and carried her to the shed, where he had jammed some sort of long iron rod into the cavity of one of Mary's ears, piercing one side of the brain. Then he had pulled out the rod and jammed it again into her other ear, piercing the other side of the brain—essentially lobotomizing her—before he ran out to the back alley and vanished.

Dr. Johnson cradled Mary's head in his hand. Just as dawn arrived, she made a tiny *ooh* sound as the life drained out of her.

III

Next to the gate leading from the Weeds' backyard into the back alley, a police officer found some footprints in the sandy soil. Chenneville's bloodhounds sniffed the prints and hit a scent. They ran down the alley and came to a stop two blocks away at a stable, where a young black man named Tom Allen was found sleeping in a hayloft.

Allen, whose nickname was River Bottom Tom, worked on the water cart that sprayed the downtown streets to keep down the dust. Chenneville's dogs lunged at him, sinking their teeth into his legs and arms and hands. He was arrested on a charge of "suspicion of murder" and taken to the calaboose.

By then, a crowd was starting to gather around the Weed home. Some people were wearing their Sunday-best clothes and holding Bibles, on their way to church. They watched as Mary's body was carried out of the shed and loaded onto the black undertaker's wagon so that she could be taken to the dead room of the City County Hospital for her autopsy. They kept watching as Rebecca was placed either beside her daughter or in a separate wagon so she could be taken to the hospital's "Negro Ward," a small windowless room containing a few beds that was located just down the hall from the dead room.

When the newspaper reporters gathered around Weed, he told them that Rebecca and Mary "were good workers and of quiet habits." He added that Rebecca "had no men going to see her, and I think her a good and virtuous woman." She led an "orderly life," he said. He mentioned that he gladly would give money for a reward fund for the capture of Mary's killer.

At 11 a.m., a full seven hours after Weed had found Rebecca and Mary, Marshal Lee arrived at the Weed home. Because it was a Sunday, his day off, he had slept late in the back bedroom of his father's house, where he lived, and by all indications, Chenneville and his officers had been just fine with their marshal staying there. No one from the department had called Lee and no one had come to knock on his father's front door to awaken him.

Lee talked for a few minutes to Weed. He inspected the backyard shed. Then he headed to the police department and sat behind his desk. He must have felt utterly ridiculous that he had been left out of another murder investigation.

But the investigation was going nowhere. Although one police officer told a reporter that River Bottom Tom's feet perfectly matched the footprints that had been found next to the Weeds' backyard gate, even to a "peculiarly shaped toe" on one foot, the fact was that it wasn't all that surprising that his footprints might have been in the alley, because he lived close by. What also pointed to his innocence was that the police had not found a drop of blood on him or on any of the hay in the stable where he slept.

Nor could Chenneville find anyone who had a story to tell about River Bottom Tom holding some sort of grudge against Rebecca and Mary. Chenneville did his best to get River Bottom Tom to confess, subjecting him to another one of his "examinations." Like all the other black suspects who had been brought in, however, River Bottom Tom kept saying he had nothing to do with the attacks on Rebecca and Mary and that he knew nothing about any of the other attacks.

Determined to make another arrest before the day was over, Chenneville and his officers went looking for another black man named Aleck Mack, who over the years had been described in newspaper articles as "a petty thief of a particularly quarrelsome nature," "a very impudent Negro," and "a notoriously bad darkey." Among Austin's white citizens, Mack was especially notorious because he had once defiantly taken a drink from a whites-only water bucket at a construction site on a hot summer afternoon.

Although Mack hadn't been seen around Austin for several months, he had returned earlier that summer. When officers tracked him down in a black neighborhood in east Austin, his feet and legs were covered with asafoetida, which for Chenneville was proof that Mack was up to no good.

During his own examination, however, Mack, like River Bottom Tom, professed complete ignorance about the attacks on the Ramey women. He said he barely knew Rebecca or her daughter. He told a reporter for the *Daily Statesman* who came to visit him in the calaboose that the only reason he had used the asafoetida was because he was hoping to throw Chenneville's dogs off his scent so that they would not drag him to the ground and chew him up.

III

On Monday, Mary's body was placed in a small coffin and taken by the Negro undertaker to Colored Ground. Waiting by the cemetery's front gate, as always, was Mr. Nitschke, the sexton. He pointed mourners in the direction of the grave he had picked out for Mary, underneath a pretty live oak tree, and then he returned to his office to fill out Mary's death record. When Nitschke got to the column asking for Mary's cause of death, he wrote, "Murdered." At this point, he finally realized, it was pointless to pretend that nothing was happening.

It was indeed pointless. By now, all the newspapers in Texas were running stories about the murders, and many of them were lambasting Austin officials for not finding the "bad blacks." Even the editorialists for the *Daily Statesman* were losing their patience. "We pay for protection, but why is there none—absolutely none?" one of them wrote. "The citizens are overcome with terror, not now at the bold daring desperado in the open street, but at sneaking midnight prowlers, seeking an opportunity to outrage the unprotected and to shed the blood of the innocent."

On Congress Avenue, there were more calls for more full-time police officers—as many as twenty—to be hired to work at night. Some

An Austin newspaper reporter. The reporters likened the
killings to an Edgar Allan Poe short story.

men continued to demand that vigilance committees be formed. "If such
a step is taken," one man told a San Antonio reporter, "it will not only
certainly put a stop to these nightly outrages, but it will be the means
of ridding this city of a horde of loafing, shiftless, vagrant Negroes who
have infested it for years."

Several citizens said the time had come for Mayor Robertson and
the aldermen to impeach the polite and efficient Marshal Lee. One citizen put it this way: "The present marshal is a good, honest, well-meaning
man, but he is deficient in the ability which should characterize a man
occupying the important position that he does. And if the chief of
a police force is inefficient, the force is so, too, no matter how capable
the men comprising it may be. . . . A change is imperatively demanded.
The reputation of the city marred and blackened by a fearfully bloody
record, demands it."

Austin's black leaders were so anxious that they made an extraordinary decision to gather at the county courthouse to ask that the city's black residents be given better police protection. Among those there were Reverend Grant; Alderman Carrington; Dr. Quinton B. Neal, the city's sole black physician; William Wilson, the principal of one of the all-black public schools; and Jeremiah J. Hamilton, the publisher of the *Austin Citizen,* the weekly black newspaper. Two black porters who worked for the state government and were therefore on speaking terms with many white government officials—Lewis Mitchell from the department of the secretary of state and Henry Hollingsworth from the General Land Office—also came.

One of the men stepped forward to read a formal statement: "Whereas, the city of Austin has been wronged, outraged and thrown into the intensest excitement; and whereas, not one of the fiendish scoundrels has been caught and punished; therefore, be it resolved, that we, the colored citizens of Austin, pledge ourselves to use every lawful means to aid the civil authorities in arresting and punishing

For most of the year, white Austinites still believed that only black women were being targeted.

these villains to the fullest extent of the law." The statement concluded with a request that "the mayor, city council and governor" offer "a suitable reward for the arrest and punishment of the parties who committed the murder upon Mrs. Ramey's daughter last Sunday morning."

The black leaders tried to meet with Governor Ireland and hand him their statement, but they were told he had the dengue. Ireland, of course, wasn't about to jeopardize his political future by getting involved with the Austin killings. Nor did Mayor Robertson meet with the committee. He didn't want his constituents to think that he was, God forbid, getting advice from black men.

But Robertson did not have to be told that his own political future would be in grave jeopardy if he could not bring the killings to an end. The city elections were scheduled for early December, and Joseph Nalle, a wealthy lumberman who had lost to Robertson in the last mayoral race, had already let it be known that he planned to run for the office again. Nalle was telling voters that if he was mayor, they would not have had to worry about their servant women being attacked. He said Austin would not be overrun with Negro criminals, because he would make sure a real marshal was in charge of the police force, not some rich man's son who knew nothing at all about law enforcement.

And so, determined to save his reputation and win the election, Robertson came up with a plan. He wrote a letter to the owners of the Noble Commercial Detective Agency in downtown Houston, asking if they would send him their best private detective, a man named Capt. Mike Hennessey.

PART THREE

SEPTEMBER 1885– CHRISTMAS DAY 1885

"A woman has been chopped to pieces! It's Mrs. Hancock! On Water Street!"

CHAPTER TEN

In 1885, every city in Texas had a private detective agency. Austin's was the Capital Detective Association, a three-man operation that had opened in 1884. The tasks that the detectives performed were almost always routine. They were hired by merchants to watch over their establishments at night, or recover stolen merchandise, or track down an employee who had run off with a store's strongbox—crimes that the local police didn't have the time or manpower to solve. Periodically, a bank asked them to look for a swindler who had cashed a forged check and left town.

In Houston, however, the owners of the Noble Commercial Detective Agency—C. M. Noble, a former Houston sheriff, and John F. Morris, a former marshal of the Houston Police Department—were promoting themselves as the Texas version of the legendary Chicago-based Pinkerton National Detective Agency, which had opened in 1850. Every American knew the Pinkerton motto: "The Eye That Never Sleeps." Many of them bought books, published by the agency itself, that dramatically recounted the tales of its "private eyes" chasing bank

C. M. NOBLE, Principal. | J. F. MORRISS, Supt.
Ex-Sheriff.   Ex-Chief of Police.

NOBLE'S

Commercial Detective Agency

OF TEXAS.

Fox Building, Cor. Main and Preston,

HOUSTON, TEXAS.

We are prepared to furnish Detectives of unquestioned ability to perform all Railroad, Bank, Insurance and all branches of Detective Work. We are in daily communication with the Pinkerton Agency, East and West. All communications for the State of Texas should be addressed to

NOBLE DETECTIVE AGENCY,
oc10-85tf   Houston, Texas.

When the murders resumed, Mayor Robertson hired a famed Houston private detective agency to come to Austin.

robbers, railroad bandits, swindlers, kidnappers, political assassins, and such cold-blooded outlaws as Jesse James and the Dalton Gang. In the books—which had such titles as *The Molly Maguires and the Detectives* and *The Railroad Forger and the Detectives*—the Pinkerton men were always able to "penetrate beneath the thick veil of night," "lay bare the fearful mysteries of the metropolis," and "see things that others cannot see." No criminal, no matter how smart, was able to get away from the Pinkertons.

Noble and Morris unabashedly claimed their team of six detectives were of "Pinkerton quality." The owners had gone so far as to take out ads in the state's newspapers that made them look as if they were the Pinkertons' affiliate in Texas. "We are prepared to furnish Detectives of unquestioned ability to perform all Railroad, Bank, Insurance and all branches of Detective Work," the ad read. "We are in daily communications with the Pinkerton Agency, East and West."

Actually, Noble and Morris were not in touch with the Pinkertons at all. But their marketing campaign was definitely getting them business. In the last year, they had opened branch offices in San Antonio and Dallas. To drum up even more work, they gave interviews to the newspapers trumpeting their detectives' latest arrests. Most of the publicity was focused on the thirty-nine-year-old Hennessey, a former New Orleans police captain. According to one laudatory story in the *Houston Daily Post*, Hennessey had both a national and a "foreign reputation" as "one of the most skillful detectives in the profession." Among the cases he had solved, the *Daily Post* noted, were "the celebrated Diamond Robbery, the Meade Murder, the case of the celebrated Italian bandit Espiloso, and that of Johnson the Fire Bug."

Built like a boxer, with broad shoulders and a tapered waist, Hennessey was considered to be an expert tracker, able to slip into a city and hunt down either a criminal or a witness to a crime whom no one else could find. Recalling how he had once caught a man who had gone into hiding in New Orleans after being accused of murder, Hennessey proudly said in an interview, "By day and night, I was upon his track. When he moved a shadow was after him. When he slept, his very breathing was watched and reported."

Hennessey intrigued Robertson. At that point, the mayor did not have to be told that Marshal Lee was utterly helpless when it came to hunting down the killers. Nor did Sergeant Chenneville seem to have any idea what to do. The fact was that the sergeant, for all his reliability, had all the intellectual depth of the tacks that held up the wanted posters on the walls of the police department. Robertson called the aldermen to city hall and told them that Captain Hennessey was just the man they needed.

Impressed, the aldermen agreed to pay for Hennessey's services—he cost ten dollars a day, plus expenses—and on September 9 he arrived in Austin with his assistants George Hannah and Ike Himmel. Using assumed names, the detectives checked into rooms at the Carrollton House, a hotel only a couple of blocks off Congress Avenue. They also brought along their own bloodhound, which they put in the hotel's small backyard.

The three men headed over to the police department, where they were brought up to date on the details of the various murder investigations. They then went to work. Hats pulled down over their eyes, they walked past the homes where the murders had occurred. They visited with some of the servant women who had survived attacks, trying to get them to reveal new information about whomever they had seen in their rooms. In the evenings, dressed in seedy clothes, wigs, and false whiskers, the detectives slipped into the saloons in the poorer First Ward and eavesdropped on conversations. At the end of each night, they went back to their rooms at the Carrollton House and scribbled notes on sheets of paper about what they had learned.

Their anonymity didn't last very long. Austin was soon buzzing with the news that the Noble detectives had come to town. Reporters began hanging out in the lobby of the Carrollton House, hoping to land interviews. Women came to the hotel just to swoon in the great Hennessey's presence. Kids went out to the Carrollton's backyard to pet the bloodhound.

Hennessey clearly loved all the attention. A few days after his arrival, he told newspaper reporters that he and his two assistants were already "drawing a net pretty closely around a number of suspicious characters," and that "developments may be looked for at any time."

Indeed, said Hennessey, there was nothing to fear. He, Hannah, and Himmel would find these killers. All they needed, he said, was a little time.

III

The Noble detectives prowled around Austin for a few more days. At least one reporter—the Austin-based correspondent for the *San Antonio Light*—began to get the sense that they had no better idea how to catch the killers than Chenneville did. "The detective force that has been trying to run down the murderers of the girl, Mary Ramey, reported some days since they had a clue to the fiends," the *Light*'s man wrote sarcastically on September 22. "They left the trail to go and inform the newspaper reporters of the fact, and thereby lost it [the trail], which they have not been able to find since, even with the aid of their bloodhound."

Hennessey replied that he and his assistants were definitely making progress. Good detective work required large amounts of patience, he liked to say. Sources had to be carefully cultivated and physical evidence collected. The key was to accumulate all the facts—and then pounce upon the killers.

On the last weekend of September, Hennessey decided to take a short break and return to Houston to catch up on personal matters.

And it was on that very weekend that all hell broke loose.

III

It began on Saturday night, September 27. Two black servant women who lived in the quarters behind a home on Rio Grande Street, close to downtown, heard a noise. One of the women saw a man at the door. "I'll kill you if you open your mouth," the man whispered. The woman screamed anyway, and the man fled. When Chenneville and other officers arrived, she couldn't offer any description of the man at all except to say that she believed he was white.

The next evening—Sunday, September 28—a cook residing in the servants' quarters of Dr. Wade A. Morris, who lived just a couple of blocks west of the site of the new state capitol, began screaming because she had heard a noise at her window. Once again, the woman had no physical description of whoever it was making the noise.

An hour or so later, W. B. Dunham, the publisher of the *Texas Court Reporter*, a journal that covered Texas legal matters, was awakened by some sort of muffled cry coming from his servants' quarters in the backyard of his north Austin home on Guadalupe Street, just past the University of Texas. Dunham's cook, a pretty young black woman named Gracie Vance, lived in the quarters with her boyfriend, Orange Washington, who worked at Butler's Brick Yard. Also staying in the quarters were two young black servant women, Patsy Gibson and Lucinda Boddy, who worked for other Austin families. They were there because they were too afraid to sleep alone in their employers' quarters.

Figuring that Orange and Gracie were arguing, Dunham went to his back door, shouted at the couple to quiet down, returned to bed, and drifted back to sleep. But several minutes later, he heard another noise. This one sounded like a groan. He grabbed his pistol and walked into the yard just in time to see Lucinda Boddy, one of Gracie's visitors, staggering out of the shanty. Her head was bloodied and she seemed completely disoriented.

"Mr. Dunham, we are all dead!" she screamed.

Dunham ordered her to lie on the back steps of his house. Right about that time, his next-door neighbor, Harry Duff, the co-owner of the Iron Front Saloon, came into the yard holding a lantern. He told Dunham that he too had been awakened by a noise and that he had called the police department.

The two men stepped into the shanty. Duff held up his lantern. Patsy Gibson was barely alive, lying on her side, blood flowing from her head. Orange was dead, lying facedown on the floor between the bed and the wall in a pool of his own blood. A bloodied ax was on the bedspread beside him. Gracie was nowhere to be found.

Chenneville and another police officer, James Connor, galloped up to the Dunham residence on their horse and dismounted. Holding lanterns, they followed a bloody trail leading out of the servants' quarters. They climbed over the backyard fence, which was about four feet high, and kept following the trail of blood into another backyard that abutted the Dunhams'. That yard, belonging to the Hotchkiss family, was at least fifty yards in length, and was used as a small horse pasture. As Chenneville and Connor came closer to the Hotchkiss stable, one of them stumbled over something soft. Under the yellow light of their lanterns, the men stared at what they now realized was the corpse of Gracie. She had been beaten so viciously in the face that it was mostly a mass of bone and skin and blood. Her head was somewhat off center, as if knocked from its moorings. Her hair and her nightgown were smeared with blood. Beside her was a brick covered with blood and bits of her face. The only thing that wasn't bloodied on her body was a beautiful silver open-face watch, attached to a delicate silver chain that was wrapped around her wrist.

Suddenly, from an upstairs window, the elderly matriarch, Mrs. Hanna Hotchkiss, shouted, "There he goes toward Nigger Town!" She had seen someone—or she thought she had seen someone—running toward a black neighborhood that was west of the Hotchkiss home.

Chenneville and Connor fired shots into the darkness—at least eight shots in all, hoping that one of the bullets would hit whoever was supposedly running from them. The two police officers ran back to the Dunham home and mounted their horses. The horses reared, wheeled, and bolted away, raising a cloud of dust in the darkness. Chenneville and Connor held their guns out before them, ready to shoot again. But they couldn't see anyone. Whoever was there had vanished like a phantom.

More police officers rode up to the Dunhams', including the Travis County sheriff, Malcolm Hornsby, and a couple of his deputies. Marshal Lee also showed up. (He had made it clear to his officers that he wasn't going to be left out of any more murder investigations.) Some of the officers began searching the nearby houses and servant quarters, looking for a lead. Except for Mrs. Hotchkiss, however, none of the residents had seen or heard anything. The officers rode into the black neighborhood in hopes of finding men who were awake and on the streets at that hour. But the streets were empty and all the homes were shuttered.

Dr. C. O. Weller, a physician who lived in the neighborhood, arrived at the Dunhams' and did quick examinations of Lucinda and Patsy, discovering that each woman had been hit one time in the head with a blunt object, probably with the back of the ax that had been found in the quarters. Weller studied Orange's wounds. He had been hit at least twice in the head. Then Gracie was carried in from the Hotchkiss backyard and placed on the bed. Dr. Weller noted that besides having the same head wound as the others, she had been hit at least twelve times in the face with the brick. One blow had caught her on the bridge of her nose, shattering the bone, and other blows had smashed against her temples, her jaws, her cheeks, and her eyes. Her face, one reporter would later write, was "like jelly."

Inside the shanty, Chenneville and his police officers snipped off the ends of cigars and smoked to keep the smell of the blood out of their noses. Trying to reconstruct what had happened, they figured that someone had slipped into the shanty and quickly whacked Gracie, Orange, Lucinda, and Patsy on their heads. Perhaps because Orange continued to struggle, the assailant had hit him again, killing him. The killer had carried Gracie out of the shanty, lifted her over the Dunhams' back fence, and taken her into the Hotchkiss yard, where he brutally beat her to death with the brick. The entire attack, they figured, had taken place in complete darkness within a space of five, no more than ten minutes.

III

By sunrise, the news of the attacks was whipping through the city. Soon, the crowds at the Dunham home were so large it was like a carnival. According to the *Daily Statesman*, mule-driven streetcars were doing "a thriving business" as they hauled sightseers from downtown to the scene of the murder. College boys walked over from the University of Texas hoping to get a look at Orange Washington and the bludgeoned servant women, and a group of Mexican-born citizens also showed up, one of them shouting *"Viva los vigilantes!"* The *Daily Statesman* reporter wrote that when he got to the Dunhams' home he had trouble getting to the window to "obtain a glimpse at the prostrate forms within."

Eventually, a path was cleared and Gracie and Orange were carried away to the City-County Hospital's dead room. Lucinda and Patsy were taken to the hospital's Negro Ward to join Rebecca Ramey. At some point that morning, the police learned that a black man named Dock Woods had tried to win Gracie's affection earlier in the year and had gotten upset when she turned him down in favor of Orange.

Woods resided in a shanty on a cotton farm about eight miles south of Austin. A posse of officers, along with Marshal Lee, rode to the farm and found him picking cotton in one of the fields. He seemed flabbergasted. He said that he had not left the farm the previous night. But the officers noticed some blood on the bottom of his shirt. Woods was arrested for "suspicion of murder" and hauled back to Austin.

As word spread of his arrest, a group of saloon men, fortified on

Several of Austin's 3,500 black residents moved out of the city, terrified of the killer they called "the evil one."

whiskey and Budweiser, began making plans to march to the calaboose, take Woods away, and string him from a lamp pole on the Avenue. A *Fort Worth Gazette* reporter raced to the telegraph office and dictated a dispatch that began: "There is definitely a deep-seated intention to lynch Woods, provided he can be got at." Incredibly, added the reporter, "a large body of Negroes" were also gathering in east Austin to form their own lynching party to take their revenge on Woods, if it turned out he was guilty. "The indignation of the Negroes themselves is terrible," the reporter noted.

But within hours, the case against Woods was falling apart. A doctor who examined him discovered that he had an open wound on his genitalia, the result of an untreated venereal disease, which was the cause of the blood on his shirt. Moreover, the owner of the cotton farm told police that he not only had seen Woods at the farm the evening of the murders at 10 p.m. but also had seen him the next morning at four o'clock, when all the workers had been awakened to start work in the fields.

As the men at the police department were pondering the latest information about Woods, a man named John R. Robinson, the owner of a dry goods store, arrived at the police department with his Swedish teenage servant girl. He said that since Mary Ramey's murder, the girl had been sleeping in a bedroom in the main house, only going back to her quarters behind the house during daylight hours to change clothes.

That very morning, Robinson continued, when his servant girl had walked into her quarters, she had discovered that someone had been there. Her dresses had been pulled from the closet and thrown to the floor, her trunks filled with clothes had been upended, and her sheets and blankets had been torn off the bed. The girl had gone through her belongings and realized only one item was missing: a silver open-face watch, attached to a delicate silver chain, which she had received from her father when she still lived in Sweden.

One of the officers retrieved the silver watch that had been found on Gracie's wrist and showed it to the girl. She gasped, turned over the watch, and pointed to her name inscribed on the back. When asked if she knew how her watch had ended up on the wrist of a murdered black servant woman, she shook her head. She said she didn't even know who Gracie was.

There was a long silence. The men at the police department just stared at one another, trying to put everything together. Why would someone break into the quarters of Robinson's servant girl, steal her watch, and make his way to the Dunhams' home (with perhaps a stop at Dr. Morris's home along the way in order to frighten the cook) to brutally assault Gracie Vance and her three friends? Why would he then drag Gracie away to bash her face in until she was dead, and afterward take the time to wrap the Swedish girl's watch around Gracie's wrist before disappearing into the night?

Was someone out there toying with the police—letting them know that there was nothing they could do to stop him?

No one seemed sure what to think—or what to do. And then the door to the police department was flung open. Captain Hennessey had returned to Austin.

CHAPTER ELEVEN

Hennessey was filled in on the details of the attack at the Dunhams', and soon he was on the streets with his assistants Hannah and Himmel, interviewing sources they had been cultivating. Two days later, he asked the newspaper reporters to meet him on the front steps of the temporary state capitol. There he announced that the Noble Commercial Detective Agency had made a break in the case.

The reporters looked at him expectantly. Hennessey said that he and his assistants had come across a black teenager by the name of Jonathon Trigg who had agreed to reveal some very important information.

According to Hennessey, Trigg claimed to have been at the Black Elephant on August 29, the night of the murder of Mary Ramey. There he found himself standing near Oliver Townsend, Austin's fleet-footed chicken thief. Townsend was telling one of the saloon's patrons that he was preparing to murder little Mary. Trigg decided to follow Townsend as he walked from the Black Elephant to V. O. Weed's residence, but he left before seeing what Townsend actually did.

There was more, Hennessey told the reporters. Trigg claimed that he ran across Townsend again on the night of September 28—the night of the attacks on Gracie, Orange, Lucinda, and Patsy. This time, Trigg saw Townsend in the heart of downtown, on the corner of Congress Avenue and Pecan Street, the busiest intersection in the city, talking with another black man Trigg didn't know. As Trigg got closer, he heard the man say to Townsend, "You will be caught up with." And Townsend replied, "I have been killing them all and I have not been caught up with yet." Townsend added that he was going to murder Gracie Vance that very night, and he started walking north up the Avenue. Trigg followed him to the Dunham home, where Townsend met yet another black man Trigg didn't know. Moments later, the two men walked toward the Dunhams' servants' quarters and stepped inside. A woman cried out, "Please don't kill me." Fearing for his own life, Trigg ran away.

Standing before the reporters, Hennessey held up a typed statement that he said Trigg had signed detailing his allegations. "I am certain Oliver Townsend is the man I followed to the house where the murder [of Gracie Vance] was done," the statement quoted Trigg as saying. "The reason I followed Oliver Townsend was because I heard him say he was going to kill Gracie Vance, and I wanted to see if he would do what he said he would. The reason I did not tell [the police] that I saw Oliver Townsend go to Mr. Weed's, on the night Mary Ramey was killed, was because I did not know for certain that he killed her. I thought I would wait and see, so when I heard the other threats made by him and followed him and learned what he did, I told what I knew."

Hennessey wasn't finished. He announced that he had gone to the City-County Hospital to talk with Lucinda Boddy and Patsy Gibson, and that Lucinda had reiterated that she had seen Dock Woods, Gracie's former suitor, standing at the window of Gracie's servant quarters just before the attacks began. Clearly, said Hennessey, Woods and Townsend were the guilty parties.

So what about the watch on Gracie's wrist? Hennessey and his assistants had an explanation for that as well. They said that Woods must have slipped away from the cotton farm in the afternoon—the farm's owner must have been mistaken about seeing Woods—ridden into town on a stolen horse, and taken the watch from the Robinsons' servants' quarters, hoping to give it to Gracie at the Sunday night church service held at Reverend Grant's church, thinking the gift might win her away from Orange Washington. When she had refused to accept the watch, Woods had contacted Townsend, who had agreed to help him exact his revenge.

The reporters stared at the detectives in disbelief. Did he really expect them to believe that this teenager just happened to be close enough to Townsend on two occasions to hear him talk about murdering servant women? And that this same teenager had followed Townsend to the scenes of two murders without ever being seen?

It wasn't long before the reporters learned that Trigg worked as a waiter at the Carrollton House, the very hotel where the Noble men were staying. Obviously, many residents surmised, Hennessey and his assistants had gotten to know Trigg and persuaded him—perhaps even bribed him—to make up a story fingering Townsend and Woods.

To make matters worse for Hennessey, a *Daily Statesman* reporter made his own visit to the hospital's Negro Ward to interview Lucinda Boddy to see if she would verify that she had seen Woods. What he discovered was that both Lucinda and Patsy Gibson were in such extreme pain from the blows to their heads that they were unable to carry on any conversation whatsoever. Lucinda's "brain matter," the reporter later wrote, was "oozing from the wounds in her skull every few moments." He stated that Dr. Burt, the hospital's staff physician, was preparing to subject her to trepanning, a medical operation in which a hole would be drilled into her skull in hopes of relieving pressure on the brain. "There appears to be a chance for the loss of her mind," the reporter added.

Trying to save face, Hennessey said that perhaps Lucinda Boddy, in her delirium, had misidentified Dock Woods during their conversation. He also acknowledged that Trigg could very well have exaggerated parts of his story. But the detective insisted that he was certain of one thing: Oliver Townsend was the leader of what he called "a gang of scoundrels" that was murdering the city's servant women. What's more, he said, he was already accumulating more information on other members of Townsend's gang and soon would be making another arrest.

On Saturday night, October 3—one week after the attack at the Dunhams'—Hennessey let Marshall Lee know he was ready to make that arrest. He told Lee he had new evidence linking Aleck Mack, "the impudent Negro" who already had been questioned and released by police, to the gang of scoundrels.

Perhaps to keep watch on Hennessey and his assistants, or perhaps because he was so determined to be involved in the murder investigation, Lee said he would be coming along to help make the arrest. (Significantly, Sergeant Chenneville did not. He obviously had lost all trust in Hennessey.) Hennessey and his two assistants and Lee and two of his officers headed over to the Black Elephant, where Mack was drinking. Hennessey asked Lee to go inside the saloon and tell Mack that he wanted him to answer a few questions.

Because Mack didn't fear Lee, he didn't try to run. He followed the marshal out the front door and down the street, where he was suddenly grabbed by the detectives and the officers. When Mack tried to fight back, they kicked and pounded him with their fists. A white resident named Press Hopkins, who was standing on his front porch, watching the encounter, would later say that Mack's screams woke up everyone in the neighborhood.

Mack was dragged to the calaboose, thrown into a cell, and chained to the iron ring cemented to the floor. For the next couple of days, Hennessey used all his interrogation skills to get him to confess. But Mack continued to say—just as he had earlier told Chenneville—that he was completely innocent. He went straight to the newspaper reporters when he was released and accused Marshal Lee and the Noble detectives of wrapping a rope around his neck as if to hang him—what was known in those days as "nigger neck stretching."

In his typical formal style, Lee released a statement calling Mack's allegation "a malicious falsehood, concocted in the most damnable spirit. . . . If Mack has any bruises or scars on his person, they are the result of his own desperate efforts to resist arrest and incarceration. I never struck him, nor saw any one else strike him. Only one pair of nippers were used on him. He was not maltreated in any way, and only such force used [as] was absolutely necessary to conquer him."

As for Hennessey, he too said that he and his assistants had not physically abused Mack. By now, however, it was becoming clear to just about everyone in Austin that the Noble men were abject failures. And things only got worse. Hennessey's assistant Himmel spent an evening at one of the saloons, ostensibly in hopes of picking up gossip about potential suspects. Instead, he drank too much, got into an argument with another patron, and pulled out his pistol and shot a bullet into the ceiling—a violation of a city ordinance.

III

In mid-October, Robertson and the aldermen voted to cancel their contract with the Noble Agency. One of the alderman, Joseph Platt, snapped that the only thing the private detectives had done during their month-long stint in Austin was "stand on the capitol steps" and "with a great flourish of trumpets announce the arrest of a nigger." An indignant Hennessey and his men packed up and left for Houston with their bloodhound. The mayor and the aldermen then passed a broadly written ordinance offering a reward of $250 to anyone who provided evidence leading to "the arrest and conviction of any party for murder, rape, arson, burglary or assault with intent to murder in the nighttime in Austin."

Determined to get the reward money, some Austin citizens arrived at the police department to pass on names of even more black men they believed were responsible for the attacks. A few people got so caught up in the guessing game that they spent their evenings leafing through the city directory, studying the names of all the city's black men, wondering which one could be a killer. (In the directory, there was a little *c* at the end of black residents' names to denote that they were "colored.")

Based on the citizens' tips, the police did make some more arrests, one of whom was a black man named James Thompson, who supposedly was overheard making a drunken confession at a black saloon that he had murdered one of the servant women. A fourteen-year-old black boy was also arrested after he had been seen carrying a knife. But after brief interrogations, they were released.

Acting on another tip, a couple of officers spent a few days following a man known only as Maurice, an immigrant from Malaysia, in southeast Asia. Maurice, who looked to be in his early thirties, worked as a cook at the Pearl House (the restaurant where Colonel Driskill had held his July Fourth dinner celebrating his new hotel) and he lived in a cheap boardinghouse not far from the Weeds' home, where Mary Ramey had been murdered.

It was said of Maurice that he would get "beastly drunk" after work and wander the city late at night. What's more, "fresh blood" supposedly had been discovered in a pool of water not far from Maurice's boardinghouse on the day after little Mary's killing.

During the period that Maurice was being watched, however, he did not engage in any suspicious behavior. He went to work each night at the Pearl House, did his cooking without complaint, and returned straight to his room at the boardinghouse.

As October came to an end, the newspapers were writing that the Austin police remained clueless about what to do. "It is beginning to be believed that the detection of the Austin servant girl murderers is as far off as ever," noted the *Galveston Daily News*. More newspapers, including the *Fort Worth Gazette*, went after Austin's leaders for not being able to stop the murders. "If a radical change is not made in the government of the city so that crimes may be prevented and glaring vices suppressed, it will be far better for Texas to close her university and cast the keys into the sea," wrote a *Gazette* editorialist. "A city incapable of governing itself is not a place for building up a university of a first class."

In Austin itself, worried homeowners stood in line at J. C. Petmecky's to buy guns and ammunition. Those who couldn't afford Petmecky's prices went to Heidbrink and Co. Pawnbrokers, which sold secondhand guns. A few elderly residents pulled out rifles so old that one police officer said they could have been used in the Texas Revolution back in the 1830s. "It may be safely stated that Austin is the best armed city in the United States," wrote the *Daily Statesman*. "It is probable that each home in town contains at least fourteen rounds of ammunition."

Some men took their servant women out into the backyard, gave them pistols, and taught them to shoot bottles off fence posts. Yet even with all the guns and bullets, more servant women were leaving Austin—so many, in fact, that the *Dallas Daily Herald* wrote, "The servant girl will soon become one of the rarest and costliest of capital luxuries."

One black woman in Austin who was too old to move was an eighty-year-old former slave known fondly around town as Aunt Tempy. She was so terrified of being killed that she not only kept the doors and windows of her shanty bolted and barred, she left a lamp burning next to her bed throughout the night. In early November, a few hours before sunrise, the lamp fell onto the bed. Within seconds, Aunt Tempy's sheets and blankets were on fire. Within minutes, the shanty was in flames. Outside in the yard, people could hear Aunt Tempy's screams.

A man finally got inside the shanty and dragged her out into the yard. Aunt Tempy gripped the man with charred fingernails, screamed again, and died.

III

Finally, on the evening of November 10, one week after Aunt Tempy's death, Mayor Robertson decided to give a formal speech about the murders. The occasion was his annual State of the City address, which he had titled "The Report of the Mayor on the Work of the Present City Administration." Robertson had spent days on the speech: he knew it had to be good. Joseph Nalle, the lumberman who was running against him in the upcoming city elections, was breathing down his neck, gaining support among voters. He was even having large banners that read "Joseph Nalle for Mayor!" attached to the sides of downtown buildings.

Predictably, Robertson began with good news. He told the

standing-room-only crowd that the finances of the city were in "excellent order." Debts had been paid, he said, and the cash balance in the treasury was $31,048.30. There was plenty of money available to build new bridges over the creeks, regrade the streets, and perhaps add a new wing to the hospital.

Robertson paused, looked down at his written speech, and read:

> During the last year, a number of the most dastardly crimes known to the law have been committed in this city. These crimes have been of the most revolting character, attended with evidences of the grossest brutality, and perpetrated at the dead hours of night, in nearly every instance upon unprotected colored females.
>
> Much has been said and written about these crimes, and the city government has been subjected to severe criticism, sometimes unfriendly and sometimes bordering on the malicious. I undertake to say that the city authorities, ably aided by the state and county officers, have faithfully and earnestly labored to detect the perpetrators of these crimes and to bring them to punishment, but they have failed at success. I employed detectives who came with the highest endorsements as honest and skillful men. They, too, have failed to detect the guilty parties. Great vigilance and energy has been displayed by private citizens, who have devoted much time and labor to bring to light the real criminals. They have accomplished nothing.

There was a silence in the chambers. Robertson kept reading:

> The crimes still remain a mystery. They are abnormal and unnatural, as compared with ordinary crimes among men. No one, not even the expert, skilled in the detection of crime, can find a plausible motive. The mutilated bodies of the victims

are always found in parts of the city where crime is not expected or anticipated, and beyond the fact of the murders we have never been able to penetrate.

Robertson did his best to reassure his audience that the killings soon would come to an end. "I have faith to believe that the authors of these crimes will yet be discovered," he declared. "No human is strong enough to hold such a secret. Some guilty conscience will unburden itself sooner or later."

He then tried to raise everyone's spirits, booming, "This city has a great future. Its magnificent location, its picturesque surroundings, its invigorating and healthful climate, and its refined and cultured people, invite the stranger to make his home among us. I hope that before many years we may see a great population dwelling upon these hills!"

But the men who had come to hear his speech were hardly reassured. They walked out of city hall, gathered on the Avenue, and started talking. Had Robertson really said that the only way the murders would come to a stop was when one of the killers *confessed*? Did he genuinely believe that there was nothing more that anyone could do?

III

Everyone agreed that Robertson was right about one thing: the murders were "abnormal and unnatural." At this point, four servant women and one servant woman's daughter—Mollie Smith, Eliza Shelley, Irene Cross, Mary Ramey, and Gracie Vance—had been slaughtered with axes, knives, iron rods, and a brick. It wasn't clear whether any of the victims had been raped, but the fact that many of them were half naked and organs exposed suggested some twisted sexuality was involved. What was peculiar was that two of the women apparently had been "decorated" after their deaths, with blankets wrapped tightly around Eliza's mutilated body and a silver watch wrapped around Gracie's wrist.

What was even more peculiar was that all of the victims had been left in full view for everyone to see, as if they were works of art. None of them had been carried away to confound the police—hidden, for instance, in a thick grove of woods or thrown into the Colorado River.

There was one other bewildering detail: a potential witness had been left alive at the scene of each murder. Whoever had slaughtered Mollie Smith back in the early hours of New Year's Eve had allowed her boyfriend, Walter Spencer, to live. Whoever had killed Eliza Shelley in early May hadn't touched her three boys, who were in the bed with her, and whoever killed Irene Cross didn't harm her young nephew. On that August night when little Mary Ramey had been brutally attacked, her mother, Rebecca, had been struck with a club that had only rendered her unconscious. And during the September rampage at the Dunhams', Gracie's friends Lucinda Boddy and Patsy Gibson also had been knocked unconscious before Gracie herself was dragged away and beaten to death. True, Gracie's boyfriend, Orange Washington, had been killed by two blows to his head, but the doctors and police believed that that had happened by accident.

For the first time, some of the men on the Avenue were beginning to talk openly about the possibility that the murders, for all their gruesomeness, were not the work of "ordinary" Negro criminals. In their own way, the men said, these murders were very well planned— "carefully directed" and "intelligently consummated."

The Austin-based reporter for the *San Antonio Daily Express* actually suggested that one man was behind all the murders. He even came up with his own moniker for this man. He called him the "Midnight Assassin"— a killer, he wrote, who "strides at will over Austin's sacred soil."

The correspondent went on to explain: "The fact that this series of crimes is composed of some of the boldest, most startling flagrations in criminal annals, that they have extended over a period of many months, and that the perpetrator has, so far, not only accomplished his ends but successfully escaped and blinded the police, would seem to indicate that he is a criminal of no mean ability . . . but one of the most remarkable ghouls known to the death history of any section of the country."

Today, of course, no explanation would be required: everyone would know that a depraved but brilliant serial killer was at work. The Austin Police Department would be putting together a task force. "Profilers" from the Federal Bureau of Investigation would be flying in from their offices in Quantico, Virginia, to study similarities of the physical evidence at the various murder scenes in hopes of creating a psychological profile of the killer. A large Crimestopper reward would be offered in hopes of encouraging citizens to reveal what they knew.

In late nineteenth century America, however, the term "serial killer" did not yet exist. It wasn't that people were unfamiliar with the concept of one person committing multiple murders. Periodically, there would be headlines about "maniacs," gripped by psychotic rages, who had gone on killing sprees. One of the most infamous of these maniacs was a twelve-year-old boy in Boston named Jesse Pomeroy, dubbed the "boy fiend," who in the early 1870s was imprisoned for life after he stabbed at least two other children to death. And, of course, the old outlaws were, in their own way, serial killers who didn't hesitate to shoot or stab anyone who got in their way.

But the maniacs clearly looked and acted insane, and they were almost immediately identified by police because they rarely attempted to cover their tracks. As for the outlaws, they seemed to act out of clear self-interest, killing other men for a financial reward, or dispatching rival outlaws who posed a threat. What's more, most outlaws rarely operated under the cloak of anonymity. The blue-eyed Texas bad man John Wesley Hardin actually wrote an autobiography in which he proudly took credit for his killings, saying the men he had shot deserved to die.

What no one in that era had ever heard about was an anonymous killer who set out to mutilate women, one after another, in almost ritualistic fashion in order to satisfy some private libidinous craving or a pathological hatred. Even writers of fiction had not yet invented such a character. Edgar Allan Poe's short story "The Murders in the Rue Morgue," which had been published in 1841, begins with a mother and daughter who have been ripped apart in a bedroom in Paris. The killer in Poe's story, however, turned out to be an escaped orangutan, not a human being.

As a result, for the vast majority of Austin's residents, this concept of a Midnight Assassin was extraordinarily difficult to grasp. For them, it was almost impossible to believe that someone could act perfectly normal during the day, with nothing in his looks or manner to attract attention, let alone raise alarm, and then at night walk out of his house to perform acts of sadism that surpassed anyone's comprehension. Surely, they said, such a crazed, bloodthirsty killer could not have gone unnoticed for so long in their small city.

The members of the Travis County grand jury certainly weren't buying into a Midnight Assassin. In fact, a mere two weeks after Mayor Robertson's speech, the grand jurors released the list of its most recent indictments. Toward the bottom of the page was the name "Walter Spencer"—the boyfriend of Mollie Smith, who had been murdered in the early hours of New Year's Eve 1884, exactly eleven months earlier. The grand jurors had determined that when Spencer burst into the home of Mollie's employer, W. K. Hall, frantically crying that Mollie was nowhere to be found, he was only pretending to be innocent. They claimed that enough evidence existed that proved Spencer was Mollie's killer and they wanted him put on trial, charged with first-degree murder.

CHAPTER TWELVE

The man who had presented the case against **Walter Spencer** to the grand jury was the county's thirty-one-year-old district attorney, James Robertson. It just so happened that he was the younger brother, by thirteen years, of Mayor Robertson. In the mid-1870s, James had followed his older brother to Austin from the family home in east Tennessee, studied law at his brother's firm, taken the bar exam, and moved to the small town of Round Rock, just north of Austin, where he married, started a family, and began his own law practice. In 1884 he had returned to Austin to run for district attorney.

Although James didn't have his brother's oratorical skills, he was regarded as a very bright lawyer, and with the support of his brother and other members of the city's establishment, he handily won the election. (It didn't hurt his campaign when the incumbent district attorney, James Sheeks, had decided to withdraw from the race after he was arrested for drunkenly driving his carriage too fast along Congress Avenue and making crude remarks at women.)

So far in his short tenure, which had begun in January 1885, the

Mayor Robertson's brother James, the
district attorney, was pressured to
prosecute an innocent black man.

younger Robertson had prosecuted a handful of felony cases and had
won convictions for a couple of routine killings. As for the servant
women murders, however, he had never pushed for indictments of any
of the black men who had been arrested, concluding that there had
been too little evidence to take their cases to court.

Obviously, the young district attorney's opinion had changed. There
is no documentation—no paper trail whatsoever—indicating exactly
what led to Spencer's indictment. But *something* had to have happened.
Had new evidence been discovered that proved Spencer's guilt? Or was
it possible that Mayor Robertson, who realized his political future
was on the line, approached his younger brother and begged for help?
The city elections, after all, were just a couple of weeks away. Or was it
even possible that District Attorney Robertson himself had decided,
on his own, to help out his older brother by securing an indictment
against one of the murder suspects?

Whatever took place, the grand jury's announcement must have
pleased Mayor Robertson. During his strolls up and down Congress
Avenue, he was able to say to all his detractors that justice in the

servant women murders was being served. On Election Day, December 8, he was out early, shaking hands with voters. Joseph Nalle was also on the streets, asking for votes. "The friends of both candidates were everywhere, watching and working as if everything depended on their individual efforts," noted a *Daily Statesman* reporter. "Hacks, loaded down with voters, hurriedly deposited their loads at the polling places and whirled off after others."

That day, there were allegations that Nalle had brought in more than a hundred men from out of town, paying them to cast "illegal votes." If so, he could have used fifty-three more men. Robertson was narrowly reelected by a vote of 1,390 to 1,338. In an interesting side note, Albert Carrington, the lone black city alderman, representing the Seventh Ward, lost his election to Dennis Corwin, a white surveyor who had been a captain in the Confederate army. A large number of Austin's white residents had organized an "Anti-Colored Movement" to prevent Carrington's reelection. For them, the servant women murders had only proven that the black race could not be trusted with any civic responsibility. They were also no doubt infuriated by newspaper reports claiming that members of the Carrington family believed the servant women were being killed by a white man.

Later in the evening, after all the votes had been counted and recounted, Robertson's supporters came to his home and shouted his name. The mayor and his socialite wife, Sophronia, a descendant of Stephen F. Austin's, stood on their porch and waved—and then, of course, Robertson gave one of his speeches about Austin's golden new era. The future, he said, never looked better.

III

One week later, the trial of Walter Spencer began. District Attorney Robertson told the jury that Spencer most likely had caught Mollie with another man and decided to get even. During the fight that had ensued between the couple, either Mollie had hit him with the back of an ax before he grabbed it away and began attacking her, or he had hit himself on the head with the ax after having murdered Mollie, which was his attempt to make himself look like a victim instead of a killer.

But it quickly became clear that there was no new evidence whatsoever pointing to Spencer's guilt. Robertson didn't even have a witness who could tell any tales about Mollie and Spencer having any sort of disagreement. All Robertson was able to tell the jury was that because Lem Brooks (Mollie's ex-boyfriend, who was initially arrested) had such a good alibi, the only possible person in Austin who would have had any reason to kill Mollie was Spencer.

After a single day of testimony, the district attorney rested his case. Spencer's court-appointed lawyer called a couple of witnesses who spoke about Spencer's peaceful relationship with Mollie. The jury learned that since Mollie's murder, Spencer had been staying with his mother in east Austin. Although he still suffered headaches from his wounds, he had returned to his job at the brick factory. He also had joined an all-black baseball team that played against other black teams. He was living a very quiet life, avoiding any trouble with the police.

Regardless of the lopsided testimony, there was still a good chance that Spencer would be convicted. He was, after all, a poor young black man facing an almost entirely white jury. (There was one black man on the panel.) A quick conviction would be the easy thing to do. Such a move would, for the first time in months, give Austin's citizens some sort of reassurance that Austin's bad blacks were finally being taken off the streets.

But the jurors, one of whom was J. B. Blocker, a successful cattleman who had hired black men to work as cowhands on his trail drives, were suspicious of young Robertson's case from the start. They quickly voted to acquit Spencer—and he walked out of the courthouse a free man.

Obviously humiliated, the district attorney made no public comment about the verdict. As for Mayor Robertson, he too said nothing. But to show the citizens that he was still taking action to keep them safe, he called the aldermen to city hall and proposed that a search immediately begin to find a new marshal to replace Grooms Lee when his term ended on December 22.

By all accounts, it had been a very long autumn for Marshal Lee. Residents were still talking about how he had overslept on the morning of Mary Ramey's murder, and how his attempt to gain respectability by teaming up with the Noble detectives to arrest Aleck Mack had turned out to be a fiasco.

Lee had done his best to defend himself. He had issued a report noting that his officers had collected a record $9,025.90 in fines for misdemeanors committed in the last fifteen months. But Robertson and the aldermen were ready for him to go. He spent his last days on the job sitting in his office, concentrating on paperwork. According to the *Daily Statesman,* he "succeeded in obtaining a fine picture of [former mayor] J. T. Cleveland, thus completing his pictorial collection of Austin's chief magistrates at the City Hall." He told his friends that, when his term as marshal came to an end, he planned to get out of law enforcement altogether and become a surveyor—a quiet occupation that he had once tried and which seemed to be more fitting to his personality.

Twelve men submitted their names to replace Lee, including a deputy U.S. marshal, a former county sheriff who was now running a feed store, an attorney, and the proprietor of the Proper Star Saloon on Congress Avenue. Chenneville added his name to the list of candidates, though he probably knew Mayor Robertson and the aldermen were content with him remaining as sergeant.

He was right. The candidate who most impressed the city officials was James Lucy, a captain with the Texas Rangers, the famed state police organization. Since the end of the Civil War, the Rangers had been "ranging" through the hinterlands of Texas, fighting the last of the Indians and arresting (or shooting) gunslingers, bandits, cattle rustlers, and horse thieves. Although Lucy was not the most physically imposing of Rangers—he was described in one article as "no taller than Napoleon"—he was fearless, and, yes, he was very good with guns. In 1878, he and some fellow Rangers had gotten into a famous shootout with the infamous Texas train robber Sam Bass and his gang in the town of Round Rock, north of Austin. (Bass was killed.)

The other quality about Lucy that impressed Robertson and the aldermen was his intelligence. He had graduated from the University of Missouri, and when he came to Texas in 1873 to join the Rangers, he had been assigned a series of complicated land fraud cases that resulted in at least a dozen convictions. If there was anyone who could stop the murders, said Robertson and the aldermen, it was Lucy.

III

With the announcement of Lucy's appointment, Austin's citizens did feel a definite sense of relief. Now, they told one another, life can go back to normal.

Which was exactly what happened. There was a dedication ceremony at St. David's Episcopal Church for its new stained-glass window that depicted the Virgin Mary holding the infant Jesus. Over at Austin High School, a group of students played a "football game" against a group of students from the Texas German and English Academy. (It was perhaps the first high school football game ever played in Texas.)

As the Christmas season approached, shop owners decorated their windows with ornaments, red and green crepe paper, and heaps of pine boughs. One merchant placed a string of incandescent lightbulbs

Texas Ranger James Lucy was brought in as the new marshal to restore law and order.

around his front window, which featured a stuffed Santa Claus and tiny elves surrounded by fake snow, and another filled his window with a plethora of presents for children: dolls, hobbyhorses, baseballs and base- ball bats, bows and arrows, tambourines, accordions, tea sets, and red- topped cowboy boots. At Stacy and Baker's newsstand and tobacco shop, one of Austin's portlier citizens dressed up as Santa Claus and sat on a large chair by the front door, where he asked the children who came to see him if they had been good that year.

Newspaper reporters wrote that the downtown streets were "liter- ally thronged with all sorts of people" and the stores "jammed with purchasers." L. Schoolherr & Brothers, one of the city's better dress shops, held a Christmas sale on shawls, robes, silk gowns, and silk handkerchiefs. Hirschfield's Dry Goods advertised "Christmas prices" on its sewing machines. And Austin's most well-known photogra- pher, Mr. Samuel B. Hill, offered discounts on his "portraits." Many men brought their entire families to his studio. Standing before a painted backdrop—a pastoral landscape, a ruined castle, the hills of Italy—they held themselves still for several moments, looking as dig- nified as possible, while the negatives were exposed. Women arrived at the studio to have individual portraits made, which they planned to give to their husbands as Christmas presents. The women stared directly at the camera with their backs straight, their mouths slightly pouted, and their noses turned delicately upward. Because Hill used incandescent lamps to light the studio, their eyes shone, and their skin seemed as pale as milk.

On the evening of December 22, after the 9 p.m. roll call at the police department, Lee turned over his badge to Lucy. According to the *Daily Statesman*, Lee gave a farewell address, "indulging in a few appropriate remarks, referring to his past pleasant relations with the force, and trusting his successor's administration would be fruitful of much good." Sergeant Chenneville and the other officers then stood at attention as Lucy spoke to them about his determination to keep Austin free of crime.

That night, Lucy helped patrol the streets. He was on the streets the next day, December 23, and again on December 24, Christmas Eve, greeting residents who came downtown to do the last of their Christmas shopping. Throughout that day, people lined up at Bill Johnston's market to buy meats for their Christmas Eve dinners, the counters loaded with steaks, hams, turkeys, venison, and some of the last buffalo meat left in Texas. Others went to Prade's ice-cream parlor, where clerks were selling Christmas fruit baskets, ornamented cakes, and French candy for twenty cents a pound. Men drove their wagons to Radam's Horticultural Emporium to buy Yule trees to carry back to their homes for their children to decorate. (Some of them, no doubt, also bought bottles of the florist's Radam's Microbe Killer.) A man pulled up in his wagon at H. H. Hazzard's music shop to purchase a piano as a Christmas gift for his family. At his livery stable just off Congress Avenue, Osborn Weed, who had been the employer of Rebecca and Mary Ramey, offered the city's children Christmas rides on Tom Thumb, his gentle Shetland pony. Attempting to show goodwill to all, Charles Lundberg the baker provided a Christmas meal to all the prisoners in the county jail.

As the sun began to set, Henry Stamps performed his usual role lighting the gas lamps. The owners of the restaurants and saloons turned on their incandescent lights. Dr. J. J. Tobin, one of the city's pharmacists, invited fifty of his friends to his home to watch fireworks. Children from the state's Asylum for the Blind held a concert, performing a popular new song about Santa Claus coming to town, and over at the state's Asylum for the Deaf and Dumb, another group of children stood around a Christmas tree decorated with candy and popcorn, making what one reporter said were "mute testimonials of affection."

There was even a Christmas party at the State Lunatic Asylum, north of the city. Dr. Denton had arranged for selected patients to gather in the main day room, eat popcorn, sing Christmas carols, and stay up one hour past their usual nine o'clock bedtime curfew, and he had one of his employees dress up as Santa Claus and pass out candy.

An hour passed, and then another. The shop and restaurant owners turned off their lights, locked their doors, and headed for their homes. Throughout the city, families ate their Christmas Eve dinners and decorated their Christmas trees, covering the branches with ornaments, strings of popcorn, candy-filled paper cornucopias, candles, and Japanese lanterns.

Eventually, parents put out the fires in the fireplaces, telling their excited children that they didn't want Santa to burn himself on his way down the chimney. A thin breeze swept through the city, carrying with it the aroma of evergreen and cinnamon and wood smoke. Soon, the moon rose. The stars appeared. According to what a reporter for the *Daily Statesman* would later write, the moon and the stars "were at their most effulgent and shot their mellow light over all the earth and in nearly every crevice of our houses and garden fences."

At midnight, the clock above city hall began to chime. Marshal Lucy, Sergeant Chenneville, and several of the officers remained on the downtown streets, keeping watch. A couple of officers checked the saloons to see if any suspicious characters were drinking at the back tables; a couple of other officers walked the alleys behind the Congress Avenue buildings, looking for tramps; and a couple more wandered through Guy Town to make sure the men at the brothels were behaving themselves.

Suddenly, there was sound of hoofbeats. A horse was seen coming straight up Congress Avenue from south of downtown, and it was coming fast, whipping through the cones of light thrown out by the gas lamps. On the back of the horse was a man named Alexander Wilkie, who worked as a night watchman for one of the saloons.

"A woman has been chopped to pieces!" Wilkie yelled. "It's Mrs. Hancock! On Water Street!"

CHAPTER THIRTEEN

Susan Hancock was the forty-three-year-old wife of Moses Hancock, a prosperous carpenter, and the mother of two daughters. People who knew Mrs. Hancock would later describe her as "one of the most refined ladies in Austin," a "handsome woman" who "bore an unblemished character" and was a "tender mother" and "devoted wife." She was also white.

The police officers leaped on their horses and raced to the Hancocks' home, which was at the southern end of downtown, just a block off the Colorado River. Those who didn't have horses simply began running. They ran so hard that their stomachs heaved and their breath tore at their throats. Marshal Lucy and a *Daily Statesman* reporter, who happened to be standing together outside of Martin's Shoes and Boots on Congress Avenue, piled into a hack. It barreled down the Avenue, rocking back and forth like an old stagecoach.

Lucy found Moses Hancock in the parlor of his one-story home. He was dressed in his long underwear, which was stained with blood. On the floor of the parlor, lying on a quilt, was his wife. There were two deep wounds in her head—the result of ax blows. One blow had cut into the cheekbone. The other, which was between her left eye and left ear, had perforated her skull and sunk into her brain. Her right ear also had been punctured by some sort of rod.

Mrs. Hancock was breathing erratically. According to the *Daily Statesman* reporter who had taken the hack to the house with Lucy, "cupfuls of blood" were pouring from her mouth. From a back bedroom could be heard the desperate cries of the Hancocks' daughters, one fifteen years old, the other eleven. Dr. Burt, the physician from the City-County Hospital, arrived, as did another physician, Dr. R. S. Graves. They worked feverishly to save Mrs. Hancock's life, pressing bandages over her wounds to stop the bleeding, giving her a shot of morphine and pouring a little brandy into her mouth to see if she would swallow it. She couldn't. Nothing but the whites of her eyes could be seen beneath her half-closed lids. In the gaslight, the blood over her skin had an almost glossy sheen.

Although it was just his third day on the job, Lucy made it clear that he alone would be in charge of this murder investigation. He interviewed the fifty-five-year-old Hancock, who was leaning against a

On Christmas Eve, Susan Hancock became the first white woman to be murdered. Her husband, Moses, told police he had found her in their backyard.

wall of the parlor. In what would later be described as a "distracted, disconnected narration," Hancock told Lucy that his wife had spent the late afternoon shopping downtown. After she returned home, the two Hancock daughters had gone to a Christmas party, escorted by a neighbor. He and Susan had sat by the fireplace, reading and sharing a piece of cake. They had gone to bed between ten and eleven o'clock, sleeping, as they always did, in adjoining rooms. A gas lamp had been left burning by the front door.

According to Hancock, the two daughters returned home from their party a little after 11 p.m. and went straight to bed. Just before midnight, Hancock was awakened by a noise. He walked into his wife's room and saw that her sheets and bedspread were piled in a heap on the floor. Her trunks were open and her clothes pulled out. The window of her room, facing the backyard, was also open and blood was on the windowsill.

Hancock said he walked out to the yard, where he found his wife lying in a pool of blood. As he bent over her, he heard a noise coming from behind the back fence. He turned and saw a shadowy figure, wearing dark clothes. The man—Hancock could not tell if he was white or black—jumped over the fence and ran off down the alley. Hancock started yelling, grabbed a rock, and threw it in the direction of the man. His next-door neighbor, a brick mason named Harvey Persinger, came into the yard and helped Hancock lift Mrs. Hancock from the ground and carry her into the parlor. Then Persinger ran for help. He found Wilkie, the night watchman, who rode up Congress Avenue, crying out the news of the Hancock attack.

Mayor Robertson, alerted by telephone, arrived at the Hancocks' home, as did District Attorney Robertson. Within minutes, the front and back yards were filled with men from the surrounding neighborhood and the nearby saloons. Some of the men struck matches to their oil lamps, dialed the flames to the highest possible height, and held the lamps above them, trying to cast as much light as possible into the shadows. Dr. Burt's teenage son Eugene, who was there, spotted a bloodied ax three feet from the window of Mrs. Hancock's bedroom. He picked it up and waved it around. When Hancock was shown the ax, he said it belonged to him and that he kept it on top of the woodpile by the back fence.

A police officer arrived with Sergeant Chenneville's bloodhounds. They sniffed the ax, the woodpile, and the spot where Mrs. Hancock had been found. But because so many men had already tromped through the yard, the dogs could not find any tracks to follow. They were led out to the alley, where they began running westward, alongside the Colorado River. A group of officers chased after the dogs. They slid their six-shooters out of their holsters in case they saw someone to shoot. But they came across no one. Minutes later, the dogs lost whatever trail they were following.

The men at the Hancocks' kept waving their lamps over the back-yard, hoping to find some piece of evidence.

Then, in the distance, there was the sound of more hoofbeats.

III

Henry Brown, the night clerk at the police department, was on his horse, coming at a full gallop straight for the Hancock residence. When he saw Marshal Lucy, he began yelling that a woman had been found on Hickory Street, on the northwest side of downtown, just two blocks from city hall.

Lucy and the other men in the yard stared at him.

"It's Eula Phillips!" Brown shouted. "Her head's been chopped in two!"

The men kept staring at him. Eula was the seventeen-year-old wife of Jimmy Phillips, who was the twenty-four-year-old son of James Phillips, a very successful Austin architect and home builder. Slim as a fawn, barely one hundred pounds in weight, Eula was regarded as one of Austin's most beautiful young women, with eyes the color of syrup, a delicately cut chin, a Mona Lisa–like smile, and auburn hair that she swept back from her temples and bunched in curls on the nape of her neck. Whenever she walked the sidewalks of Congress Avenue, she was stylishly dressed, wearing broad hats heaped with feathers and tight crinoline dresses, underneath which were wiggling bustles and corsets that pushed up her bosom.

"It's Eula!" the man cried again. "She's in the Phillipses' backyard!"

Men began jumping on horses or piling into hacks and racing back up Congress Avenue. They made a screeching left turn at city hall, and headed for the Phillips home. Whips could be heard cracking against the horses' flanks. Chenneville's dogs also sprinted up the Avenue, baying all the way.

The Phillips home was one of the city's finer two-story residences, built by Phillips himself. Lucy and the other men were led to the backyard and taken to the outhouse. Next to it was Eula, her nightgown pulled up to her neck and her hair rolled in brown curling paper. She was on her back, the blood around her "warm and scarcely coagulated," a reporter would later write. She had been struck directly above the nose by the blade of an ax: a perfect vertical blow, splitting her forehead wide open. There was another horizontal ax cut across the side of her head. Because her nightgown was tightly twisted around her neck, the police speculated the killer had used it like a rope to drag Eula across the yard.

And there was something new about this murder scene: three small pieces of firewood had been placed, almost ceremoniously, on Eula's body—two across the breast and one across her stomach. Her arms had been outstretched. It was as if she had been posed to look like a figure in some twisted Crucifixion scene.

Lucy went inside the house and was directed to the room—in a back wing of the house, at the end of a long hallway—where Eula, Jimmy, and their ten-month-old baby boy, Tommy, stayed. Jimmy was still in bed. There was a large gash above his ear. The Phillipses' family doctor, Dr. Joseph Cummings, who lived in the neighborhood, was already there, pressing a pillow against the wound. A bloody ax was at the foot of the bed.

Jimmy seemed to be in a stupor, unable to communicate at all. His mother, Sophie, told Lucy that at sometime after midnight— maybe around 12:15 a.m., she said, or maybe later—she heard Tommy crying. She walked into Jimmy and Eula's room and almost fainted when she saw Jimmy curled under bloody sheets and the baby sitting up, holding an apple, unharmed even though his nightclothes were crimson with blood.

Eula Phillips was murdered one hour after Susan Hancock. Her husband, Jimmy, was found in their room, wounded from a blow to the head.

Sophie said she ran back to the master bedroom to alert her husband. Using Jimmy's nickname, she shouted, "Bud is knocked in the head and Eula is gone!" The elder Phillips went outside and with the help of other men in the neighborhood eventually found Eula. One of the neighbors then ran over to City Hall and took the stairs up to the police department to alert the night clerk about the killing.

After Lucy finished speaking to Mrs. Phillips, he was shown a bloody bare footprint on the wooden floor in the hallway outside Jimmy and Eula's room, right next to a door leading to the backyard. He ordered that the planks containing the footprint be cut from the floor and taken to the police department. He also ordered that the ax in the bedroom—which the elder Mr. Phillips had identified as his, saying he had last seen it on top of his woodpile behind the house—be brought to the police department and placed next to the ax found at the Hancocks'.

Meanwhile, in the backyard, someone spotted drops of blood on the top rail of the back fence. Chenneville's dogs were led into the alley and headed off into the darkness, the sound of their baying echoing against the other houses. But soon they again came to a baffled stop. It was as if the scent—if there had been a scent—simply had vanished.

A blanket was placed over Eula's body and she was carried back into the house. Jimmy, who seemed to be regaining consciousness, murmured to Dr. Cummings, who was beside him, "Where's Eula?"

But the doctor told him nothing. He later said he didn't want to say anything that might cause Jimmy to go into shock and die.

III

Within minutes, the news was spreading over the telephone party lines. There had been a double murder. Mrs. Hancock and Eula Phillips had been axed to death in their backyards. Someone was now targeting white women.

Grabbing their rifles and tearing open boxes of shells, some men shouted at their wives and children to get out of their beds and gather in one room. They stood in front of their families, the nickel grips of their rifles cold in their hands, waiting to see if whoever was out there was going to come after them.

Other men decided it was far safer to get their families out of their homes. They loaded them onto carriages or wagons and raced toward downtown. It wasn't long before several hundred people were packed on Congress Avenue, standing under the gas lamps. A reporter who worked as a freelancer for the Western Associated Press ran to the Western Union office, grabbed a clean sheet of white paper, and drafted a telegram to send to his St. Louis office. "The entire population is in the streets, excitedly conversing," he wrote.

Right behind him came the Austin-based reporter for the *Fort Worth Gazette*. His telegram began, "People tonight are in a state bordering on frenzy. Groups of excited men parade Congress Avenue and ask each other, with white lips, 'When will this damnable work end? Whose wife is safe as long as these bloodthirsty hell hounds can commit such crimes in the heart of the city?'"

At three in the morning, still more residents were pouring into downtown—shouting, panting, stumbling in the wagon ruts. Horses became spooked and tried to bolt. A carriage racing down one of the streets went up on two wheels as it turned a corner. Policemen blew their whistles and shouted at the crowd to "Stay calm!" Yet downtown remained in a lather of fury and terror. Men stood guard on street corners, holding lanterns or makeshift torches and carrying weapons of all kinds—rifles, hatchets, pipes, and sheath knives. "Had a man with a speck of blood on his clothes appeared, he would have been rent in pieces," a *Houston Daily Post* reporter would later write. To increase the amount of light, merchants came to their dark stores to turn on their incandescent lamps. Several women, tears streaming down their faces, huddled in carriages under the "outdoor lamp" that Charles Millett, the owner of Millett's Opera House, had placed by his front doors so that potential customers walking by at night could read his marquee about upcoming shows.

Finally, the sun rose. Throughout the city, church bells rang to signify the arrival of Christmas Day. But for all practical purposes, Christmas had been canceled in Austin—presents left wrapped under the Christmas trees and Christmas dinners uncooked. The priest at St. David's Episcopal (the church with the new stained-glass windows) opened his doors for a 7:30 a.m. Christmas Communion service. But only a handful of his parishioners came to take the sacraments. There was no music at the service because none of the choir members arrived to sing.

By late morning, the newsboys for the *Daily Statesman* were on the

The *Austin Daily Statesman*'s headline for the Christmas
Eve murders

Avenue, hawking the Christmas Day edition, which had been reprinted
overnight. "Blood! Blood! Blood!" screamed the new front-page headline, the ink scarcely dry on the paper. "The Demons Have Transferred
Their Thirst for Blood to White People!"

People read the story, over and over, in disbelief. Even those who
had already been told details of the killings gasped when they got to
the part of the story describing the firewood laid across young Eula
Phillips's body—"evidently used for the most hellish and damnable of
purposes," noted the reporter.

Holding their newspapers, some citizens walked down the Avenue
to the Hancocks' home and then back up to the Phillipses' just to look
at the yards where the women had been found. How was it possible,
they asked, that neither woman had cried out when struck by an ax?

And how could no one have heard the attacks taking place? Both the Hancocks and Phillipses lived in the midst of busy neighborhoods. At the time of the attacks, there were still some Christmas Eve revelers out and about on the streets. And there wasn't a single eyewitness to either of the killings?

At the police department, Lucy ordered Sergeant Chenneville and his officers to round up the usual black suspects—including Oliver Townsend, Dock Woods, and Aleck Mack—and bring them to the calaboose. In a twisted version of the Cinderella story, each man was told to remove his shoes, place his bare feet in a bowl of ink, and step down on a sheet of white paper to see if his bare footprint matched the bloodied footprint that had been cut from the floor outside Eula's room.

There were no precise matches. And none of the men cracked during their interrogations, which no doubt were fierce. They insisted they had spent Christmas Eve at their homes, or at the Black Elephant, and that they had had nothing to do with the attacks.

Later that morning, close to noon, Mayor Robertson convened a public meeting at the temporary state capitol. More than seven hundred men packed into the Texas House of Representatives' chamber. They jostled against one another, all of them talking at once, their voices thick with anger—"an infuriated multitude, white with heat," wrote the *Houston Daily Post*.

Robertson banged his gavel on the podium, begging for order. "I have called you to assemble and adopt some measures that, if possible, will bring these men to justice," he declared. "It is a matter involving the protection of life and property, as well as the name and fame of our capital city. Something must be done, and I ask you to consider and determine what expedient should be adopted."

Nathan Shelley, a former Confederate general, rose and demanded that "a cordon of sentinels" (armed men) be placed around the city's limits that very afternoon. He said he would have these sentinels start moving forward, step by step, questioning every man in their path and asking about his whereabouts in the last hours of Christmas Eve. If a man's answers were "inadequate," Shelley said, the sentinels would be allowed to take "appropriate measures."

Frank Maddox, a general land agent, called for the city to hire a hundred secret agents, known only to the marshal, who would hunt down "the assassins." He also wanted a city ordinance to be passed that would require all of the lower-class saloons, where he said "the murderers" were no doubt gathering to drink and plot their crimes, be closed by 10 p.m. each evening. Ira Evans, the president of the New York and Texas Land Company, said that it wasn't only the saloons that needed to be closed. He wanted city authorities to "shutter" all of Austin's "gambling dens," "bawdy houses," and "other means of dissipation which lead to greater crimes."

A number of men called on Mayor Robertson and the aldermen to agree to a temporary suspension of normal criminal statutes and allow for "lynch law," which would grant anyone the power to make a citizen's arrest of a murder suspect, do whatever he wanted to do to that suspect, and not suffer any legal consequences for his actions.

But Alexander Terrell, a longtime Austin lawyer, begged everyone in the hall to let Marshal Lucy handle the investigation. "A vigilance committee means blood, and is likely to victimize the innocent," he said. "When it rules, reason is dethroned and ceases to act. It would be fruitless of results and bring about calamities you would deplore."

Terrell pointed to those supporting a vigilance committee. "You men can't find the killers, marching around the city," he roared.

The men roared back that they damn well could. One of them yelled that the killers, when apprehended, should be taken to the expansive grounds of the new capitol building so that their hangings could be witnessed by all of Austin's citizens.

It was finally agreed by a voice vote that a "Citizen's Committee of Safety" be formed, made up of four men from each of the city's ten wards. The committee's task would be to raise money for a reward fund and assist in the police department's murder investigations—or, if need be, conduct its own investigation.

The meeting was adjourned, and Mayor Robertson and the city aldermen headed to city hall for another meeting. They passed an ordinance authorizing Marshal Lucy to hire twenty additional police officers, giving him thirty-four officers in all—exactly the number Grooms

Lee had asked for many months earlier. They passed another ordinance requiring all saloons, "or any place where intoxicating liquors are sold or kept for sale," to close at midnight and not reopen until 5 a.m. Finally, they then passed an ordinance authorizing Robertson "to employ the most skillful detective talent available for a period of ninety days or so long as in his judgment the present emergency may demand."

Robertson let it be known that this time he would not be hiring amateurs. He strode straight to the Western Union office and addressed a telegram to the Pinkerton Agency in Chicago, asking for its best detectives to come to Austin as soon as possible.

Meanwhile, that very afternoon, George Thompson, the "dog man" for the state prison in the town of Huntsville, got off a train at the depot with half a dozen bloodhounds. (Lucy apparently had contacted Thompson earlier that day, asking for his help.) The bloodhounds were reputed to be the finest trackers in the state—certainly better than Chenneville's slobbery dogs. It was said they could stay on an escaped prisoner's trail even if that man took off his shoes and ran through water or jumped on a horse and rode away. According to one newspaper account, the lead bloodhound, who was named Bob, was known for "his wicked but intelligent eye. . . . There is only one thing he really enjoys better than beef steak and eggs and that is to get on the trail of some fellow free from obstacles, and run him over hill and dale."

Bob and the other dogs were taken to the Hancocks' and Phillipses' backyards. But they found no scents to follow: by then, sixteen hours had passed since the killings and both of the yards had been trampled, over and over, by other men's boots. While at the Phillipses', Bob, the lead bloodhound, did do something that seemed rather peculiar. He suddenly turned to the house—"barking ferociously," wrote the *Daily Statesman* reporter who was there—and headed straight for Eula and Jimmy's bedroom. "Although there were several persons in the room," wrote the reporter, "he passed by them all, and approaching the bed, reared up on it and smelt Jimmy."

From there, Bob bounded toward the parlor, where Eula's body had been laid out, just a few feet from the family's Christmas tree. Bob began barking again, and Thompson, baffled by the dog's behavior, dragged him away because he was "frightening other ladies" who were in the room.

III

By now it was five o' clock. The sun was beginning to set. At the police department, Lucy began hiring his new officers, pinning badges on their street clothes and sending them out on the streets to work with Chenneville and the other officers. He ordered all of his men to "halt" strangers they saw, demand their name and addresses, and have them explain why they were out and about. If any stranger could not give "a good accounting of himself," he was to be taken to the calaboose, given a more "extensive interrogation," and kept there "until morning, at least."

Besides the Austin police officers, deputies from the sheriff's department and the U.S. Marshal's Office showed up to help patrol the neighborhoods. Members of the Citizen's Committee of Safety came out of their houses to walk around their wards. Even the publicly humiliated Grooms Lee showed up at the police department to man the telephone while everyone else was looking for the killers.

Despite the overwhelming police presence, however, few residents slept. Inside many of the homes, husbands pushed furniture against doors and nailed wooden planks or blankets across windows. Fully dressed, they walked their floors, cradling rifles, stopping every few moments to listen with straining ears for the sound of an invader. Those who owned telephones periodically picked them up to hear if any new attacks were being reported on the party line.

But there were no attacks and no attempted break-ins. There were no sightings of a "stranger." Periodically, a police officer would bring his horse to a complete stop because he thought he had heard the snap of a stick. He would sit there for seconds, staring at the shadows. But no one emerged. The only sound came from the officer's own horse blowing steam into the air, twitching his tail, and occasionally letting loose dollops of shit.

Twenty-four hours had passed since the Christmas Eve attacks, and still no one had a clue as to what was happening.

PART FOUR

DECEMBER 26, 1885– JANUARY 1886

"The whole city is arming.
If this thing is not stopped soon,
several corpses will be swinging
from the tree limbs."

CHAPTER FOURTEEN

By the morning of December 26, the story had gone national: newspapers from coast to coast had printed the Western Associated Press dispatch on the ax attacks on Mrs. Hancock and Eula Phillips. "A Ghastly Tale of Terror from Austin!" was the headline in the *San Francisco Examiner*. "City Cursed with a Secret Band of Woman Slayers," declared the *Missouri Republican* out of St. Louis. Even the editors of the *New York Times* had deemed the story significant enough for their subscribers, its headline reading: "Two Women Dragged from Their Beds, Maltreated and Murdered."

In Texas itself, all of the state's newspapers had devoted large swaths of their front pages to the Christmas Eve attacks, splashing such melodramatic headlines above the fold as "Another Chapter of Crime from the State Capital That Makes the Blood Run Cold" and "Hell Broke Loose. Dark and Damnable Deeds Done in the Blackness of Night by Fiends." Knowing this was their chance to sell an enormous number of newspapers—it was, after all, one thing for black servant women to be attacked, but something else entirely when the victims were proper white ladies—the reporters let loose with lip-smackingly lurid prose. They played up Mrs. Hancock's and Eula's social standing, calling them "the wives of respectable citizens" and "the ornaments of highly respected homes." They described the way the two women had been found in their backyards—"weltering in blood," "bleeding and mangled," and their limbs contorted "as if in a dance of death."

The reporter from the *Fort Worth Gazette* gave the young Eula an almost angelic portrait. He wrote that she was "so beautiful, so frail, her face turned upward in the dim moonlight with the expression of agony that death itself could not erase."

To everyone's amazement, Mrs. Hancock was still alive that morning, lying in her own bed, unconscious but at least breathing. Eula's body remained in the parlor of the Phillips home. At the request of the family, she had not been moved to the dreary dead room at the City-County Hospital. Dr. Cummings, the family doctor, conducted the autopsy. Noticing that Eula's "private parts" were "distended," he wondered if she had engaged in intercourse just before her murder—or perhaps she had been "outraged." But he could not come up with an answer.

A justice of the peace and six inquest jurors arrived from the courthouse to listen to testimony from Cummings, police officers, and various members of the Phillips household, all of whom said that they could not think of anyone who would want Eula dead. Jimmy didn't testify at the inquest due to his head wound. It was reported he was still too dazed "to give any intelligent account of the affair." When the hearing concluded, the jurors ruled that Eula's death had resulted from "wounds inflicted with an axe in the hands of parties unknown." Monroe Miller, the city's most prominent white undertaker, came into the house to prepare Eula's body for burial. Assisted by one of the Phillipses' black servant women—her name was Sallie Mack, and she just happened to be the mother of Aleck Mack, the "impudent Negro" who nearly had been lynched—Miller took off Eula's bloodied night dress, washed the blood from her body with towels, and dressed her in a lovely white gown. He used cotton balls and putty to cover up her head wounds, he brushed her hair, and he applied some makeup to her face.

Miller then put Eula into his finest casket and had it carried out to his varnished hearse, which was drawn by a gleaming black horse. He climbed up to the driver's box, flicked the reins, and headed toward the First Presbyterian Church. Behind the hearse came a cortege of Eula's relatives and friends—the men wearing mourning suits and black bow ties, the women wearing hats with black veils and hooped dresses with "mourning fringe."

Austin's citizens lined the streets as the procession passed by. Women wept. Men snatched their hats from their heads. Out of respect for the young Eula, the drivers of the mule-driven streetcars stopped in their tracks.

When the funeral service was over, Eula's body was taken to Old Ground, the highest point of the forty-acre city cemetery, a fenced-in area that was reserved for Austin's wealthiest families. Handfuls of dirt were thrown onto her casket as it was lowered by ropes into the ground, and the pastor said a prayer.

The mourners just stood there, still in shock, staring at the casket. In the distance, they could hear the faint sound of baying bloodhounds. George Thompson from the state prison was still in Austin with his dogs, and they were on the move again, crisscrossing the back streets, trying to find a scent to follow.

Of course, they found nothing.

III

For the rest of the day, hundreds of citizens remained on the Avenue. According to one reporter's count, at least three hundred people alone were gathered at the intersection of the Avenue and Pecan Street. More men stood in line at J. C. Petmecky's to buy more guns and ammunition. Some women did, too. (Besides the usual Colt pistols and Winchester "center fire" rifles, Petmecky sold "boob guns," small derringers that Austin's women could put inside their corsets or attach to garters high on their legs.) Sensing a business opportunity, a salesman arrived on the Avenue to hawk "electric burglar alarm systems," which consisted of "electric bells" that were to be placed on the doors of homes and servants' quarters and which were guaranteed to ring whenever the doors were opened. Another salesman offered Atwell's Patent Window Bolts.

"They are beyond all question the best invention for security against burglars and murderers ever offered for sale," he proclaimed in an advertisement that he later took out in the *Daily Statesman*. "In view of the recent outrages committed in this city, these locks are just the thing to secure people against the midnight invaders."

For a second straight night, all of Austin's police officers rode their horses or walked along the streets of downtown and through the white neighborhoods, looking for any stranger acting in a suspicious manner. Yet residents still did not feel safe. So few of them left their homes that restaurants closed early. The city's drinking men did show up at their favorite saloons, coming in early because of the new closing time, but they kept their conversations to a low murmur. It was as if they were waiting for the sound of running boots and the voices of police calling out that another murder had been committed.

As midnight approached, more women were overcome with fear. ("A sound in the darkness makes them unconscious," wrote one reporter.) At least a couple of women were convinced they saw a man standing by their bedroom windows, well-muscled in the moonlight. Just before sunrise, a meat delivery man accidentally slammed his wagon into a wall as he backed it up to the kitchen window of the downtown Southern Hotel. Two black female cooks, sleeping in an adjoining room to the kitchen, woke up and began screaming, "Murder! Murder!" One of the hotel guests opened his window, pulled out his six-shooter, and began firing away.

The guest missed both the delivery man and his horse before officers raced to the scene.

III

The next morning, December 27, the crowds returned to Congress Avenue. At some point that day, a rumor got started that an arrest had been made in the town of Belton, ninety miles north. A police officer there had detained two men just as they were stepping off the train that had come straight from the Austin depot. The officer had seen drops of blood on their coats and vests, the sleeves of their shirts, and their shoes.

Suspicious, he had handcuffed the men and taken them to the Belton police department to talk to the marshal.

It turned out the two suspects were poor, uneducated white brothers in their early twenties named J. T. and J. P. Norwood. They worked on a farm in Hays County, south of Austin. They had told Belton's marshal that they had gone to the town of San Marcos that morning to board a train, started arguing, and had gotten into a fistfight, which accounted for the blood on their clothes. They hadn't even been in Austin on Christmas Eve, they said.

The marshal didn't believe a word they were saying. Apparently, he suspected that the Norwoods had been infected by the same "killing mania" that had been infecting Austin's black men. He had called Marshal Lucy, told him he believed he had apprehended the Christmas Eve killers, and said he was sending them back to Austin on the next train, escorted by a couple of his officers.

On the Avenue, as word spread about the Norwoods, some men said they wanted to get a look at them. They walked to the depot to greet the train. But the brothers were not on board. Lucy and the sheriff of Travis County, Malcolm Hornsby, worried that the brothers might be dragged away and beaten or even lynched, had stopped the train north of the city, removed the brothers and taken them to the county jail, which was far more heavily fortified than the calaboose.

Their tempers rising, the men marched back up the Avenue to the jail. More men joined them. They "looked like a mob," wrote one reporter, "their faces scowling and ugly." At least one man yelled, "Bring us the Norwoods!"

Hornsby and the deputies came outside and said the brothers had been "thoroughly investigated" and were "believed to be innocent." They already been sent back to their farm, Hornsby said. There was no reason for the Norwoods to be harmed.

Reluctantly, the mob dispersed and headed for their homes, and for a third straight night, fear gripped the city like a vise. An entire black neighborhood on the east side of the city was awakened by a series of piercing shrieks coming from an elderly woman who thought she had heard her doorknob being rattled.

At the Hancock home on Water Street, Mrs. Hancock finally breathed her last, dying in her bed, surrounded by her husband, her daughters, and her doctors, who had been giving her morphine injections to ease the pain. According to a *Daily Statesman* reporter who was there, she had been given so much morphine that even after the pronouncement of her death, "the quivering nerves of the murdered woman did not quite cease their functions."

The inquest was held the next morning just after breakfast, with the jurors ruling that Mrs. Hancock's death was the result of "the effects from a fracture of the skull and from a sharp pointed instrument being driven into her right ear, inflicted by the hand or hands or a person or persons unknown." Monroe Miller arrived to place Mrs. Hancock's body in a casket, and after a funeral was held for her at a Methodist church, the casket was carried to the city cemetery, where she was buried on a hill between Eula's grave and the graves of the black servant women.

III

Since the Christmas Eve attacks, Marshal Lucy had been hanging on to the slim hope that Mrs. Hancock would be able to regain consciousness—at least for a few minutes—and reveal the name of her attacker. But now, with her death, his investigation was back to square one, and Austin's citizens could sense it. More of them lined up at Petmecky's and Heidbrink's to buy guns and ammunition. "The whole city is arming," wrote a *Houston Daily Post* reporter who was on the Avenue that day. "If this thing is not stopped soon, several corpses will be swinging from the tree limbs."

Just about everyone had ideas about how to stop the killings. Someone proposed that all Austin women be given guard dogs. Someone else proposed that twelve police officers on horseback scour the countryside "for at least six miles from Austin" to look for suspects. Meeting with members of the Citizen's Committee of Safety, Governor Ireland piped up with his own proposal—and it was a strange one. Whenever the next attack occurred, he said, someone who lived nearby

should run to the closest fire alarm and set it off. As soon as Austin's men heard the alarm, they should rush out of their homes with their guns, head in the direction of the alarm, and stop all those "passing by" who were not known as "good citizens." The men would then escort the "suspects" they had apprehended to the police department for further questioning, the governor said.

As for Mayor Robertson, he begged everyone to stay patient. There was already a near army of police officers at work on the streets, he said, keeping the killers at bay. What's more, he had some more good news to pass on. The Pinkertons—the greatest detectives in all of America— were on their way to Austin! They should be here at any time. The "mystery of the murders" soon would be solved!

Robertson asked the citizens to go on with their lives—to return to their jobs, shop at the stores, and dine at the restaurants. He encouraged them to attend a long-scheduled show which was taking place that very afternoon at Millett's Opera House, featuring the famed New York operatic diva Emma Abbott and members of her Grand English Opera Company.

Months earlier, when Charles Millett had learned that Abbott, one of the country's most popular sopranos, was planning a tour of the West, he had arranged for her and her company to come to Austin to do back-to-back operas: a matinee performance of Gilbert and Sullivan's *The Mikado*, followed by Ambrose Thomas's *Mignon*. Millett had even promised to spend $1,500 on new props for the performances and provide a local chorus.

Needless to say, after making such an investment, Millett was not about to cancel the show. And to make sure the diva didn't try to back out of her trip, Millett had arranged for an off-duty police officer to act as her bodyguard, meeting her at the train depot in San Antonio and accompanying her to Austin.

Abbott had no complaints about her bodyguard. But she had to have felt a sense of dread when she arrived in Austin and saw the newspaper boys holding copies of the *Daily Statesman* over their heads and shouting out headlines about the Christmas Eve killings. She and the members of her company were taken in carriages up Congress

Avenue, past the milling crowds, and were dropped off at Millett's, where they changed into their Japanese costumes for *The Mikado*. The city's art patrons arrived and were led to their seats. The curtain rose, and *The Mikado* began.

According to the newspaper reviewers, Abbott was "in exceedingly good voice, and musically, her performance was a treat." But they didn't mention the reaction of the audience to the opera, as they usually did. Perhaps *The Mikado*'s theme—about a young Japanese man who risked having his head cut off so that he could be with the woman he loved—didn't seem particularly enticing to the art patrons that day. Nor did the reviewers mention the audience's reaction when Abbott and her singers returned to the stage that evening to perform *Mignon*. It's possible that there wasn't much of a reaction at all. Many of the ticketholders no doubt had left, determined to be back in their barricaded homes well before midnight. They weren't even tempted to stay around to hear Abbott perform her encores—what Millett in his advertisements had described as her "famous renderings" of "Home Sweet Home" and "The Last Rose of Summer."

It's likely that Abbott herself was worried about the approach of midnight. When her encores were over, she and her fellow singers rode in carriages back to their hotel, escorted by the bodyguard. Like everyone else in Austin, they locked their doors and huddled under their blankets, praying that they stayed alive until sunrise.

III

The next morning, December 29, Abbott and the English Opera Company boarded a train and disappeared from Austin. The ever hopeful Charles Millett promptly put a sign on his marquee promoting his next event: the English Shakespearean actor Frederick Warde, who was touring the country with his acting troupe, would be arriving for the New Year's weekend to perform *Julius Caesar*.

Only a few of Austin's citizens, however, bought tickets. They obviously had no interest in theatrical tragedy. As one reporter put it that day, "The bloody and cruel murders are the only subject of conversation."

Indeed, for the fifth straight day, crowds gathered on the Avenue.

A group of businessmen passed around a petition demanding that Mayor Robertson and the aldermen close down all "bawdy houses, disorderly drinking saloons and gambling halls"—"those murdering grounds of virtue and innocence," one man called them. And from a group of progressive citizens came a rather startling idea: they wanted the entire city to be illuminated at night by powerful electric lamps—maybe even high-powered incandescent "arc lamps" like the ones that had lit up the grounds of the 1885 New Orleans Exposition, cutting through all shadows and shining on every back alley.

"The recent crimes, which have so lately horrified all lovers of peace and personal safety, would, no doubt, have been averted had there been sufficient light to prevent the fiend [from] finding easy hiding places," one man wrote to the *Daily Statesman*.

The whole notion seemed quirky and absurd: the city would spend thousands upon thousands of dollars to erect electric lamps? Electric light could save Austin from murder?

But before the conversation went any further, another train pulled into the depot. Out of a passenger car stepped two or three men, dressed in suits, carrying suitcases. Quickly, word began to spread along the Avenue. The Pinkertons had arrived! The greatest detectives in all of America!

The men were whisked away to city hall to meet a very pleased Mayor Robertson, who handed them a contract guaranteeing them at least $3,000 in payment for ninety days of work.

And here's what probably happened next: after the contract was signed, the mayor pulled out his best cigars from his humidor. He asked the detectives about their famous bosses, the brothers William and Robert Pinkerton.

The detectives shook their heads. We don't work for William and Robert Pinkerton, they said.

Robertson just stared at them.

No, the detectives continued. We work for Matt Pinkerton.

There must have been a very long silence.

Who, the mayor finally asked, is Matt Pinkerton?

CHAPTER FIFTEEN

When Robertson had sent his Christmas Day telegram to the "Pinkerton Agency," he naturally had assumed it would be delivered to the offices of the famed Pinkerton National Detective Agency. But Robertson had not written out the entire name of the agency on the telegraph. As a result, the delivery boy mistakenly had taken it to the Pinkerton & Co. United States Detective Agency, another Chicago detective outfit that Robertson didn't even know existed.

Pinkerton & Co. was owned and operated by thirty-two-year-old Matt Pinkerton, a balding, thickset man with manicured fingernails and a beautifully trimmed imperial beard in the hollow of his chin. He was not related in any way to William and Robert Pinkerton. He briefly worked for their agency as a night watchman—an entry-level position—but had been fired in 1882 for incompetence. Undeterred, he had started his own agency, advertising himself in his promotional literature as one of the Pinkerton National Detective Agency's best men—"the author of several brilliant captures." According to his lit-

Matt Pinkerton, owner of the "other Pinkerton agency," which Mayor Robertson mistakenly hired.

erature, he possessed "such a remarkable tact for detective work" that "the most difficult operations of that agency" were often placed in his hands.

Livid, the Pinkerton brothers had sent a circular to the Chicago newspapers describing Matt Pinkerton as a con man who was simply capitalizing on his last name. But the young Pinkerton somehow stayed in business, getting hired by people who had never read the circular. He was a master of public relations, portraying himself as an expert in criminal behavior. He gave speeches to civic groups and ladies' clubs about what he described as the "homicidal impulse." In a book that he wrote—which he grandly titled *Murder in All Ages: Being a History of Homicide from the Earliest Times, with the Most Celebrated Murder Cases Faithfully Reported, Arranged Under Controlling Motives and Utilized to Support the Theory of Homicidal Impulse*—he declared, "The first real clue to the perpetration of a mysterious homicide is furnished by the discovery of a tangible motive. It is this matter that instantly engages the attention of the trained detective, into whose hands a murder case is placed."

Despite his eloquence as a writer, neither Matt Pinkerton nor any of his detectives had in fact ever investigated a murder case. They were hired mostly to look into claims of divorce and small-time financial fraud. One company had employed the agency to find an ex-employee who had fled to Virginia after embezzling several hundred dollars. The owner of a Michigan wood mill had asked the agency to provide private security officers for the mill during a labor strike.

But now, Matt Pinkerton suddenly found himself being asked to investigate what at the time was the most highly publicized murder case in America.

There is no record indicating exactly who Pinkerton sent to Austin. His detectives could very well have been graduates of his "correspondence school." For a fee, a would-be detective was mailed a "certificate of membership," a "Pinkerton badge," a "letter of credential" from Matt Pinkerton himself, and a booklet that taught the detective how to stalk and interrogate suspects.

Nor is there any record indicating what Mayor Robertson did when he realized he had hired the wrong Pinkertons. The mayor had to have realized that if the news got out that he had just wasted the city's money on the wrong detectives—in the same way he had wasted its money on the Noble Agency back in September—his political career definitely would be over.

Robertson decided to say nothing about his blunder. Apparently the Pinkerton men also agreed to tell no one about their real backgrounds. The mayor introduced the detectives to Marshal Lucy and Sergeant Chenneville, who gave them an update on the Christmas Eve attacks. The detectives studied the bloodied axes found at the Hancock and Phillips homes and they examined the bloodied footprints cut out of the floor by Eula's room. They asked several questions that had been laid out in Pinkerton's correspondence school materials about the "homicidal impulse."

The fake Pinkertons then headed off to begin their own investigations, and it became clear that they were not going to be making an arrest any time soon. They walked through the Hancock and Phillips backyards, interviewing the same witnesses the police had interviewed. They trooped up and down the Avenue, hoping to pick up some new gossip. At the city's finest restaurants, they ate dinners expensed to Mayor Robertson.

A frustrated Alexander P. Wooldridge, the president of the City National Bank who had been named chairman of the Citizen's Committee of Safety, quickly realized the Pinkertons had no more idea how to solve these murders than anyone else did. He called a meeting and proposed that the committee offer a huge reward—one of the largest in Texas history—for information leading to the arrests of the killers. He believed that if the reward was high enough, there was no way the killers could remain in hiding for very long.

By the end of the meeting, the members of the committee agreed to offer $1,000 to the person who provided information leading to "the arrest and conviction of the party or parties who murdered Mrs. Eula Phillips"; $1,000 to the person who provided information leading to "the arrest and conviction of the party or parties who murdered Mrs. Susan Hancock"; and $1,000 to the person who provided information leading to "the arrest and conviction of the party or parties" who had murdered one of the five black servant women.

The committee printed up a circular—which was headlined "REWARD! $3,000!"—and had copies pasted to the walls of downtown buildings and printed in the *Daily Statesman*. "Every good citizen ought to be zealous in aid of the committee," the circular declared.

Not wanting to look stingy, Governor Ireland announced that he too would offer a reward: $300 for any information leading to the arrest and conviction of the man who murdered Mrs. Hancock and another $300 for the arrest and conviction of the man who murdered Eula Phillips. (Significantly, he didn't offer any reward for solving the murders of the black women.)

When added together, the reward money was indeed a hefty sum. With that kind of cash, a man could buy a nice home or farm and have enough left over to purchase a new set of clothes and a couple of tickets for a show at Millett's.

Just as Wooldridge had hoped, the police did receive numerous new tips. Although almost all the potential suspects were black, one man excitedly called the police department and said that he had seen a white man washing bloody clothes in a creek next to a lime kiln a couple of miles outside of Austin. Lucy quickly ordered a posse of his officers to race for the kiln, and they got there just in time to nab a poor white "wood hauler" named J. D. Echols. It turned out the clothes he had been washing had been colored reddish-brown—from pecan stains, not blood.

Another anonymous tipster was convinced that a Mexican, in fact, was the Christmas Eve killer. He recommended that the police investigate Anastazio Martinez, a middle-aged immigrant who lived in a shack next to the city dump and spent his days picking up rags, pieces of tin, scraps of old iron, and anything else that interested him. The tipster said he had seen Martinez on Christmas Day carrying a bundle of women's apparel. Perhaps, the tipster speculated, Martinez had broken into the Hancock and Phillips homes to kill the women and steal their clothes.

Two officers rode to Martinez's shack, where they did indeed discover some female apparel and white silk ladies' handkerchiefs. They also found an old six-shooter, seven butcher knives, a small ice pick, and a long iron spike, "such as might have been driven into the ears of Mary Ramey and Mrs. Hancock," the *Daily Statesman* reported. The officers quickly brought Martinez back to the police department, along with two "flour barrels full" of Martinez's items.

During his interrogation, he seemed disoriented; his mind rambled when he spoke. He launched into a bizarre story in Spanish about being "told and ordered by the Almighty to go out at night and draw blood." Well, at least that's what the police officers, who didn't speak much Spanish, believed he was saying.

But it turned out that none of the clothes in Martinez's bundle belonged either to Mrs. Hancock or to Eula. And there was something else: he didn't own a horse. It was hard to imagine that he would have had the strength and endurance to break into a house, murder a woman, carry her body out to the backyard, then run uptown to do the same thing all over again.

III

Because Martinez seemed so befuddled, he was taken by police to the State Lunatic Asylum, where Dr. Denton gladly took him in. As for the other tips that came into the police department, they too led nowhere. Not sure what else to do, Marshal Lucy announced that he was going to have his officers round up all of the city's "tramps" and "vagrants," take them to the city limits sign—or better yet force them into the empty boxcars of freight trains that were headed out of Austin—and tell them they were never to return. Essentially, in the words of one reporter, Lucy was going to attempt a "cleaning out" of Austin, getting rid of anyone who was a potential killer.

Lucy's dragnet, however, didn't seem to make anyone in Austin feel much safer. That New Year's Eve, one week after the Christmas Eve killings, there were a few parties—but only a few, as most residents stayed home. Unlike the previous year's festivities, there was no masquerade ball at the Brunswick Hotel, no roller skating at Turner Hall, no fireworks, and no exuberant champagne toasts to Austin's future.

The next day—New Year's Day 1886—Colonel Driskill, the cattle baron, did host a "calling party" at his mansion north of the university, and Dr. Johnson, whose servant woman Eliza Shelley had been murdered in front of her children back in May, hosted another at his home. And over at the governor's mansion, Governor Ireland threw his annual "open house." One reporter who was there estimated that at least three hundred "well-dressed ladies and gentlemen" arrived throughout the afternoon to shake the governor's hand, and another reporter noted that Charles Millett, no doubt hoping to boost ticket sales at his opera house, had brought along Frederick Warde, the Shakespearean actor who was performing in *Julius Caesar*.

Nevertheless, at all of the parties and at the open house, there was

An Austin saloon. By New Year's Day 1886, dozens of men, white and black, had been accused of being the killer.

little celebration. The great men of Austin huddled together, murmuring to one another about the murders as they downed cordials. Later that evening, there was another gathering to commemorate the opening of the newly built Firemen's Hall, the downtown fire station where volunteer firemen would house their fire wagons, hoses, and ladders. Mayor Robertson welcomed the crowd—about 150 in all—with a speech that completely ignored the murders. "We are here to join our social greetings on the advent of a new year, and to gather hope and inspiration from the future—hope and confidence in the continued prosperity of our common country and of our great state, of this beautiful city and we of ourselves as individuals," he proclaimed. "May the city grow and prosper, and may success, health and happiness bless the people of Austin! Let the disagreements of the old year die and be forgotten and let each one of us on this bright day declare that there shall be no bickering in 1886!"

Afterward a small band began to play waltz music, and couples walked out onto the floor of the new hall to dance. But despite the mayor's relentless positivism, the party ended early: everyone wanted to be home well before midnight. In the early morning hours, the wind rose, rattling windows and doors. Another cold front was coming in from the north, but many people woke thinking they were being attacked. Men grabbed their guns. Women put clothes over their nightgowns in case they had to flee.

Few people fell back asleep until the sun rose.

III

Since Christmas Eve, there had been more talk about the possibility that the killings had been done by one man—a "Midnight Assassin," as other reporters were now calling him, borrowing the term first used by the *San Antonio Daily Express*. Some citizens speculated that this Midnight Assassin was a deranged "maniac," perhaps a patient at the State Lunatic Asylum who had been slipping away at night—which wouldn't have been very hard to do, considering that Dr. Denton, as part of his grand plan to create a utopian outpost of civilization, had removed the high fence surrounding the asylum—making his way into Austin, murdering a random woman, washing himself off in a creek, and then returning to the asylum undetected.

Other citizens took note of the fact that all of the murders had taken place either right before, immediately after, or during a full moon. In those years, there was still a widespread belief that too much exposure to moonlight could cause someone to act in very peculiar ways. (The word "lunatic" itself comes from *luna*, meaning "moon," and *tic*, meaning "struck": moonstruck.) These citizens believed that on certain evenings, when the moon was full, some man—one who wasn't necessarily a patient at the asylum—was being transformed into a werewolf-like beast. A reporter for the *Fort Worth Gazette* actually suggested that Austin was being terrorized by a real-life version of Frankenstein's monster, the hideous, yellow-eyed creature created by Mary Shelley in her 1823 novel. (The reporter, who obviously had not read the novel, spelled the monster's name as "Frank Einstein.")

And then there was a theory proposed by one of the out-of-town reporters who came to Austin that week: a correspondent, his name unknown, who worked for the *New York World*, which was owned by the newspaper baron Joseph Pulitzer. In 1883, Pulitzer had bought the *World* from the New York railroad magnate Jay Gould, and in a mere two years had boosted its circulation to more than 150,000—a tenfold increase—largely by running sensational crime stories that he knew would grab the public's attention. Needless to say, Pulitzer and his editors didn't have to be told that the story of a Texas city under siege was perfect fodder for their readers.

The *World* correspondent filed three stories from Austin, one of which was an astonishing 7,000 words in length and ran under the headline "Those Extraordinary and Similar Assassinations of Women at Austin. Facts as Marvelous as the Most Extravagant Fiction." In his stories, the correspondent carefully detailed all the killings. He noted that not one woman had cried out prior to being attacked—"Death came always swiftly, silently and certainly," he wrote—and that at every murder scene all of the bloodhounds had been "confounded" and "baffled." Although police officers and private detectives had "sifted to the bottom of every fact connected with the appalling deeds," he continued, "the clues, seemingly fresh at the start, rapidly have drifted away into a mist of uncertainty and finally disappeared altogether. . . . Numerous arrests have been made from time to time but not one has been productive."

What most intrigued the *World*'s man was that the motive for the murders remained a complete mystery. Almost always in history, he wrote, violent murders of women "have love, passion, ambition or the supernatural for a background, as a somewhat relieving motive. But here in the city of Austin in the Nineteenth Century, these crimes seem to have nothing to palliate their naked brutality and gaping wounds. As yet, the ablest detectives can advance no satisfactory theory to account for their commission."

The reporter made it clear that he did not believe an "organized gang of vile Negroes" did the killings. Nor did he buy into the theories that the killers were hardened criminals with prison records or saloon drunks with violent streaks. He pointed out that "all the worst characters in town" had been "kept under watch" by the police since the murder of little Mary Ramey back in late August. If such men were guilty of the murders, he wrote, "they would have betrayed themselves long ago."

No, the *World* reporter suggested to his readers, the only logical conclusion was that a "cunning maniac" of "great strength, fleetness of foot, and a superior intellect" was doing the "foul deeds." The maniac was able "to plot these crimes, carry them out in every particular without a mistake" and then "disappear into thin air almost immediately." He most likely had "a secret hiding place" where he went after each murder so that he could clean off his victim's blood and change clothes before returning, chameleon-like, to the streets, looking like just one more man in the crowd—a man hiding in plain sight.

The correspondent had his own name for the killer: he called him the "Intangible Nemesis." What was especially interesting about the Intangible Nemesis, he explained, was that he was not emotionally out of control. He did not slay indiscriminately, attacking any woman he saw. "He does not thirst with the blood with insatiable desire," the reporter wrote. "This man is frugal. He kills only when necessary."

Indeed, the reporter concluded in his final article, what this killer was doing was not just a different form of murder. It was a different form of thinking. "I do not believe any man figures in the world's history with such a terrible and horrifying distinction from the rest of humanity," the reporter declared. "He may well give to history a new story of crime—the first instance of a man who killed in order to gratify his passion."

III

The *World* articles were telegraphed to Texas. The *Dallas Morning News*, which was sold on Austin's newsstands, reprinted the 7,000-word article in its entirety. Although the *Daily Statesman* did not publish any of the *World*'s dispatches, it began printing more statements and letters from citizens who were starting to believe that a very devious and very smart killer was on the loose.

One resident recommended that the police stop focusing on the "tramps" and instead "have an eye to the upper crust which may be found, after all, the author of these terrible crimes." Another man wrote that he had read about a doctor in London who had been murdering numerous people. It's almost certain the letter writer was referring to the novella *The Strange Case of Dr. Jekyll and Mr. Hyde* by Robert Louis Stevenson, which had just been published in England to great acclaim. The story involved a good man named Dr. Edward Jekyll who at night became the murderous Edward Hyde, unable to control his darkest desires. Maybe, the letter writer surmised, the police in Austin should be looking for a "practicing physician" who probably had used some of his medical instruments to rip apart his victims.

Such talk set off even more paranoia and panic. Some Austin husbands decided that their best hope for keeping their wives alive was to leave the capital city altogether. One man said he would be moving his family to Monterrey, Mexico, "where there is some protection of life and property." Another said he would be taking his family to a farm in East Texas. And more black residents were talking about moving—to Houston, to Galveston, or as far away as to Kansas, which had a reputation as a safe haven for black Americans.

At the same time, newspapers around the state began advising their readers to cancel any upcoming trips they were planning to take to Austin. A couple of editors recommended that parents who had daughters attending the University of Texas (of the 230 students at the school, 58 were women) send letters to the university's president letting him know that their daughters would be staying home until the murders came to a stop.

Maybe the lowest blow of all came from the *Laredo Times*, a newspaper from the dusty, sunbaked town of Laredo on the Texas-Mexico border. Its editors literally launched a promotional campaign hoping to persuade Austin's residents to move to their city. The editors described Laredo, which had seen its share of desperadoes over the years, as the ideal spot for those in Austin needing "a safe and quiet breathing spell" from murder.

Indeed, those first days of 1886, Austin's reputation was sinking into ruin. The *San Antonio Times* began calling Austin "the dark and bloody ground" (a phrase used twenty-five years before to describe Civil War battlefields) and the *Dallas Daily Herald* was calling it "the Criminal City." Under the headline "Worse Than Babel," the *Fort Worth Gazette* continued its attacks, writing that the city, "which once had been held up to the world as the Athens of the South, a shining example of virtue," was now "a by-word for lawlessness of the most repulsive type."

There were more calls by other newspapers exhorting Austin's citizens to bring in new leaders. The editor of the *Temple Times*, in central Texas, told his readers that Austin's voters should impeach all of its officials, "from the mayor on down." The editor snarled, "The city is a wealthy community and there is no lack of money. But nothing worthy of its name has been done to ferret out the hellhounds who with periodical regularity have butchered citizens without hindrance. . . . Austin's citizens should let the mayor know that if this thing is not stopped he will be swung by the neck!"

Although Mayor Robertson was not necessarily worried about his own hanging, he had to be feeling desperate. Every attempt he had made to stop the murders had backfired on him. If something didn't change soon, he would go down in history as the mayor who presided over Austin's downfall.

III

But something did change. An Austin man named Thomas Bailes showed up at city hall and said he had some "significant" information he wanted to pass on regarding Eula Phillips.

Bailes said that in the weeks before Christmas Eve, Eula had been leading a secret life.

CHAPTER SIXTEEN

Eula Phillips had always been the subject of curiosity in Austin. She was a descendant of one of the state's original pioneer families—her grandfather had helped finance the Texas Army during the war for independence—and her father, Thomas Burditt, had been a decorated Confederate soldier who after the war became a prosperous farmer, living outside of Austin. Eula's mother was Alice Missouri Eanes, a member of a well-known Austin family. In 1880, for reasons never publicly stated, Burditt and Alice had divorced. Alice then had moved to Austin with Eula and Eula's older sister, Alma, who was quiet, reserved, and rather homely. Eula, however, turned out to be a striking teenager—"a young woman of comely appearance," a *Daily Statesman* reporter would later write. With her lustrous curly hair, her winged eyebrows and glistening brown eyes, men could not help but look twice at her. Sometimes she carried a brightly colored parasol, which she twirled above her head.

No one in Austin was more smitten with Eula than Jimmy Phillips, whose father had been building many of Austin's finest homes and buildings for the last thirty years. The newspapers described Jimmy as "a fine-looking young man," "rather portly," with "blue eyes and light hair." He sported a barber-trimmed handlebar mustache and often dressed like a dandy, wearing red socks with his dark suits. But he had little ambition. He worked sporadically as a carpenter for his father's company, and he seemed content living in a back wing of his parents' grand home. Mostly, Jimmy liked playing the fiddle with a local band and drinking at the saloons.

Jimmy took Eula on buggy rides, and it wasn't long before she became pregnant. A marriage was hastily arranged and she moved with Jimmy into the back wing of the Phillips home.

Almost overnight, Eula was living a life of privilege. She went to ladies' teas, to church socials, to the city's finest restaurants, and to the theater at Millett's Opera House. She had her photo taken by the well-known photographer Samuel B. Hill under his incandescent lights at his Congress Avenue studio. In the spring of 1884, she gave birth to a son whom she and Jimmy named Tom, after Eula's father. Friends arrived at the Phillips home with gifts. Eula held little Tom in her arms. She smiled softly and chatted with everyone. What no one could have imagined was that the young socialite was already becoming desperately unhappy.

The problem was Jimmy. Behind his well-oiled mustache was a high-color drinker's face. Rumors circulated through Austin's upper class that when Jimmy came home from the saloons after a night of drinking, he often was surly and physically abusive. One friend of the Phillipses' would later recall watching Jimmy hurl a coffee cup at Eula. Eula's sister, Alma, said she had seen Jimmy throw a glass of milk at Eula. It narrowly missed her head and smashed into a pie safe in the kitchen. And there was one occasion when Jimmy staggered in from a saloon and started shouting at Eula and his own sister, Adelia. Terrified, they ran to another room and locked the door. Determined to get at them, he kicked in a panel to the door. The two young women opened a window and ran out of the house toward the police department, crying for an officer to rescue them.

To their credit, Jimmy's parents did their best to keep him out of the saloons. In January 1885, they sent Jimmy, Eula, and their infant son to live with a family friend on a farm near the town of Georgetown, north of Austin. When they returned early that fall, Jimmy promised he would stay sober. But soon he was back in the saloons, downing whiskey.

It was not clear to others why Jimmy had turned on his own wife. Perhaps he was angry that he had to give up his wayward life as a bachelor, get married, and become a father—responsibilities he clearly was not ready for. Or perhaps he sensed that his teenage wife was resentful that she had gotten pregnant and had been forced to marry him.

Whatever was going on, Jimmy was never arrested or even questioned by police over his behavior. In those years, men were not hauled off to the calaboose for throwing dishes at their wives or backhanding them across the face. The simple truth was that all women, including those from Eula's social strata, were expected to endure almost any degree of domestic unhappiness, even if it included violence.

Eula did seem to play by the rules, refusing to complain—at least not too loudly. As her sister Alma said, Eula always acted "lady-like." But then Thomas Bailes arrived at city hall with a very different story to tell. Eula, he said, was not ladylike at all.

Bailes was a former assistant U.S. marshal in Austin who in 1884 had gone to work as the "assistant chief" of the Capital Detective Association, the small private detective agency in Austin that mostly collected unpaid bills for local merchants. He was clearly a man with ambition: the previous December, he had submitted his name for the position of city marshal to replace Grooms Lee. But he hadn't received a single vote from the mayor and aldermen, who by then were enamored with Lucy.

During his closed-door meeting with city leaders—the Robertson brothers, Marshal Lucy, and leading members of the Citizen's Committee of Safety were most likely in attendance—Bailes said that he had learned that in the last months of 1885 Eula had been taking a hack to the foot of Congress Avenue, close to the Colorado River, in an area of downtown that was rather neglected. She was almost unrecognizable because her face was hooded behind a shawl, or a veil, or sometimes a feathered hat positioned fashionably low over her forehead. But it was definitely Eula, insisted Bailes. She would step out of the hack and quickly walk to a boardinghouse on that part of the Avenue that was owned by a woman named Mae Tobin.

The men stared at Bailes. They knew all about Mae Tobin. An elderly woman, small and wiry, who wore black dresses, she was known around Austin as "the bawdy housekeeper" because her boardinghouse was not really a boardinghouse at all but a "house of assignation," a sort of a discreet hotel, where Tobin made her rooms available to businessmen either to conduct affairs with Austin women or to meet a high-priced *nymph du pave*. Rooms could be rented by the hour or even the half hour. There was both a front and a back entrance in case an escape was necessary.

Bailes said that he recently had met with Tobin. She had admitted to him that Eula had come to her house on various occasions and went into a back bedroom, where a man was waiting for her. Bailes then dropped his bombshell. He said Tobin had told him that sometime after 11 p.m. on Christmas Eve, Eula had arrived at the house and knocked at her window, asking if there was an available room. Tobin had replied that the house was full. Eula returned to a carriage that was waiting on the Avenue just outside the house, and it disappeared into the night. An hour later, she was found dead.

After Bailes had finished with his tale, a police officer was sent to find Tobin and bring her to city hall. She arrived with her attorney—a man named W. W. Woods. A deal was struck that Tobin would "reveal, make known and tell all she knew as to the murder of Eula Phillips, or information of any kind that she might give, so as to show up the guilty person or persons and convict them." In return, she would "not be prosecuted" for running a house of assignation.

Tobin acknowledged that Eula had indeed come to her house in the weeks before her death—sometimes in the afternoons, and sometimes at night. And it wasn't just to meet one man, Tobin said. She had three lovers who visited her at different times. Tobin cryptically added that none of the men ever told her their names.

When asked about Christmas Eve, Tobin also admitted that Eula did come by the house and quickly had left. Tobin said that she was not sure if Eula was alone or if there was a man in the carriage with her.

Tobin left city hall and Bailes sketched out what he believed had taken place. The way he saw it, Jimmy had sneaked off to one of the saloons, gotten drunk, as was his habit, returned home, and passed out on his bed. Eula tiptoed out of the house and either had taken a hack to Mae Tobin's or was picked up by one of her lovers in his carriage. When she returned home, Jimmy was awake. At first he had done nothing, allowing her to change into her nightgown and put her hair in rollers. But after she had fallen asleep, he had gone outside, grabbed an ax from the woodpile, came back in the room, slammed the ax twice into her skull, and then dragged her into the backyard, where he put pieces of kindling on her body to make the murder look as if it had been done by the crazed black men who had been killing the servant women. Jimmy then returned to their bedroom and hit himself in the head with the back of the ax so that police would believe he had been attacked, too.

III

Bailes left and the city leaders began talking. Had Bailes and Tobin made up the story about Eula in order to get at the reward money? Was Bailes pushing to have Jimmy arrested so that he finally could bask in the fame that had long been denied him?

Then one of the men reminded the others about the odd behavior of Bob, the prison bloodhound that had been brought to the Phillips home on Christmas Day. After sniffing around the backyard where Eula was found, Bob didn't take off down the alley but had gone straight into the house, making his way to Jimmy's bedroom and "rearing up" on Jimmy's bed.

Suddenly, it all made sense. The reason Bob had found no good trail to follow away from the house was because there *was* no trail. Bob had gone after Jimmy because he must have been in that backyard with Eula.

Now everyone was starting to get excited. Eula, they said to one another, their voices rising, had not been murdered by a Midnight

Assassin! What had happened was nothing more than a simple domestic killing.

A hearing was convened before Justice of the Peace William Von Rosenberg, a twenty-five-year-old lawyer, with Bailes as the star witness. Von Rosenberg promptly issued an arrest warrant for Jimmy for the crime of "uxoricide"—the murder of one's wife, which was punishable by hanging. Because Jimmy was barely able to speak or walk due to his own wounds, Von Rosenberg ordered a police officer to stand guard next to Jimmy's bedroom door at the Phillips home, presumably to prevent him from escaping.

When the news broke about Jimmy's arrest, Austin's stunned citizens dissected every nugget of information they knew about him and Eula. In that still very Victorian period, when the merest whisper of a sexual indiscretion could ruin a married woman for the rest of her life, it was almost impossible for anyone to fathom that an exquisite young wife, one who came from such high social standing, would dare to go to a house of assignation to have an affair with a man other than her husband. So why did Eula do it? Was it because she wanted to exact revenge on Jimmy for the way he had treated her? Had she taken money from her lovers and then hidden it away, planning to use it to support herself when she would leave Jimmy for good?

Or had Eula come up with the very radical idea that having sex with another man—engaging in just a few minutes of intimacy—was going to be her only way of obtaining some sense of pleasure, maybe even happiness, in her lonely life?

Residents tossed out the names of men they suspected might have come to Mae Tobin's to engage in "carnal relations" with Eula. According to the newspapers, the names of "both young and middle-aged men" were "bandied about." Someone guessed that the men were probably "gentlemen." Someone else suggested they were members of Austin's "gay gallant," young bachelors who loved having a good time with pretty women.

Doing his best to defend his son and daughter-in-law, Jimmy's father, James Sr., gave an interview to the *Daily Statesman*, claiming that Eula had never slipped out of the house to meet other men. The elder Phillips did admit that Jimmy had gone on a drinking "spree" a few weeks before Christmas, which led Eula to leave and stay with relatives. But, he insisted, Eula had been back within a couple of days after Jimmy had promised to straighten up and go to work. Jimmy did get a job, his father said, helping build the new Fireman's Hall and giving his paycheck to Eula so he wouldn't spend it at the saloons.

According to the elder Phillips, the couple had completely reconciled by Christmas Eve. Jimmy had spent that afternoon buying presents, including toys for his son. He had gone by Booth and Sons, a store on Pecan Street, to make a payment on new furniture he had bought to put in his and Eula's room. Then he had returned home. When Jimmy's mother went to Jimmy and Eula's room at around ten o'clock that night to give them cookies, Jimmy had his head resting on Eula's lap. "They were as happy as any young couple I know of," said Phillips. His son's arrest, he added, was "a grievous outrage perpetrated . . . without the shadow of evidence."

The elder Phillips was at least right about one point: there was no actual physical evidence linking Jimmy to his wife's death. It was impossible, for instance, to know for sure what made Bob the bloodhound go into the Phillips home on Christmas Day. He could very well have been following the trail of Eula's blood and not any scent left by Jimmy. On top of that, there was the statement made by Dr. Cummings, the Phillipses' family doctor who had treated Jimmy that night. He said that "no one could administer to himself the sort of ax blow that he has received to the head." Nor was Eula strong enough, at a mere hundred pounds, to produce such an injury. The blow had to have come from someone else.

Several newspaper reporters made it clear that they too were highly skeptical of the evidence against Jimmy. "The charge that Phillips Jr. murdered his own wife in the city of Austin on Christmas morning is declared to be an outrage of the deepest dye," snapped the *Fort Worth Mail.* "The only charge that can be alleged against Phillips is that he would get on a spree occasionally. And if all men who are guilty of that

The Travis County Courthouse, also known as "the Castle," where all the murder trials were held

charge had to be hanged, a thousand women would be forced to cling to one man's coattail, at least until another generation of men could be raised."

But the city's leaders were not backing down. Citizen's Committee of Safety chairman Wooldridge announced that the committee would be raising funds to hire Taylor Moore, a well-regarded Austin lawyer and former district attorney himself, to "assist" District Attorney Robertson as a "special prosecutor" at Jimmy's trial.

Interestingly, a few days after the Christmas Eve attacks, Moore had given an interview with the *St. Louis Republican* suggesting that he, too, suspected that the murders of Austin's women were probably the work of "a maniac who at regular intervals feels an uncontrollable desire to outrage and murder women." But after accepting the Citizen's Committee's fee, he obviously changed his mind. He now told reporters that he and young District Attorney Robertson were already "up to their armpits" preparing their case against Jimmy. He noted that at least a couple of people who had known Jimmy and Eula were planning to testify that Jimmy had made specific threats to kill Eula if he ever found out she was cheating on him. One man reportedly would be testifying that a drunken Jimmy had come to his home one afternoon in November 1885, holding a small pocket knife, angrily asking if he knew Eula's whereabouts.

Still, for many of Austin's citizens, there was one question to be answered—and it was maybe the biggest question of all. If Jimmy really did murder Eula, then who murdered Susan Hancock?

It didn't take long for them to get their answer. A couple of weeks after Jimmy's arrest, Justice of the Peace Von Rosenberg held another closed-door hearing in his courtroom. When it was concluded, he walked outside and announced that Thomas Bailes of the Capital Detective Association—yes, the very same Thomas Bailes who had come up with the "evidence" to arrest Jimmy—had presented "new evidence" regarding the Hancock case, which had led Von Rosenberg to issue an arrest warrant charging another Austin man with murder.

Everyone leaned forward, eager to hear the man's name. According to the evidence that had just been presented in his courtroom, Von Rosenberg said, Mrs. Hancock's killer was none other than her own husband, Moses.

CHAPTER SEVENTEEN

Once again, when the news reached the Avenue, people stopped in their tracks. Moses Hancock had axed his wife to death on Christmas Eve, right around the same time that Jimmy Phillips had axed Eula? He had dragged Susan into his backyard, just like Jimmy had dragged Eula into his backyard, presumably to make the police think that she too had been attacked by the black killers of the servant women?

Almost everyone shook their heads in disbelief. At the least, they said, Jimmy Phillips had a motive to kill his unfaithful wife. But Susan Hancock had been a quiet, placid woman, with nothing in her personality to cause offense. Most days, she had sat in her home on Water Street overlooking the Colorado River, reading novels and writing letters. (One newspaperman wrote that she possessed "much literary ability.") She had worn unadorned blue dresses with imitation pearl necklaces, perhaps to conceal her somewhat thickening neck.

Moreover, there had been no outward sign that she and her husband had any significant marital problems. According to one of the Hancocks' neighbors, Moses and Susan had "lived peaceably." The idea that this fifty-five-year-old carpenter suddenly would want to rip apart his gentle wife on Christmas Eve was, well, insane.

An editorialist for the *Daily Statesman* was so perplexed by Hancock's arrest that he wrote that Bailes's testimony "will need to be as strong as Holy Writ to convince the people of this murder-ridden community that Mr. Hancock—whatever motives might have existed—was the author of the damnable and hellish crime that sent his wife to the grave." Another reporter stated that Bailes and the prosecutors had better provide some intelligent explanation as to why Hancock and Phillips, two men who reportedly didn't even know each other, would "transform themselves at the same hour into infernal fiends."

It turned out that the key figure in the Hancock case was Mrs. Hancock's sister, Mrs. Mary Falwell, who lived in the town of Waco. After reading about Jimmy's arrest, she had paid a visit to Waco's marshal and told him that she too suspected that Hancock had committed murder. The truth, Mrs. Falwell had said, was that life at the Hancock home had not been peaceful. Her sister, Susan, had grown "nervous" and "uneasy" over Moses's increasing fondness for alcohol. When he drank, he would shout and cuss at his wife until she cried. He had once kicked the family dog. "From my own knowledge I don't think Mr. Hancock and my sister lived together happily for the last two or three years of her life," Mrs. Falwell said.

Mrs. Falwell then had her own bombshell to drop. She had informed the marshal that her sister had begun making plans to "secretly move" with her two daughters to Waco. For proof, Mrs. Falwell pulled out a letter that she said she had come across while cleaning up the Hancock home after her sister's death. The letter, which apparently had been written in November or December 1885, read:

> *Dear Husband,*
>
> *I have lived with you eighteen years and have always tried to make you a good wife and help you all I could. I have loved you and followed you day and night. But you won't quit whiskey, and I am so nervous I can't stand it. It almost kills me for you to drink, and Lena*

[the Hancocks' eldest daughter] *is almost crazy and will lose her mind. If I was to do anything to disgrace you and our children, you would have quit me long ago. Take good care of yourself. Write to me at Waco, and I will answer every letter. Your wife until death, Sue Hancock.*

Perhaps hoping to get in on some of the reward money himself, the Waco marshal had contacted Bailes. Bailes, in turn, had paid another visit to Von Rosenberg's court, claiming that Hancock no doubt had read his wife's letter, gotten angry, and decided to kill her before she left for Waco with the girls.

Yes, Bailes said, it was a coincidence that Hancock, like Jimmy Phillips, not only had chosen to murder his wife on Christmas Eve but deliberately had made the murder look like it had been carried out by one of the servant women annihilators. But the fact was that coincidences did happen. And in all honesty, which scenario seemed more unreasonable—that two uxoricides were carried out around the same time by two unhappy husbands who had decided to copycat the black killers—or that one mysterious man, for unknown reasons, had devised a plan to dismember one prominent white woman he didn't know and then race across town to chop up another white woman he didn't know, all within the space of an hour?

III

After hearing what Bailes had to say, at least a few residents thought Hancock's arrest made perfect sense. One man told the *Daily Statesman* that Mrs. Hancock's letter, combined with Mrs. Falwell's stories, were "of such character as to cast very grave suspicions" upon the carpenter. A story got started about something that had happened to the Hancock family in the 1870s: Hancock supposedly had tried to attack Susan but she had saved herself "by fleeing from the premises and taking refuge with a neighbor." According to another story that made the rounds, Mrs. Hancock had met with her church pastor in San Antonio and told him that she was worried her husband would someday get drunk and kill her. And some newspaper got hold of a story that Hancock had kept a hatchet "concealed" in a wall of his home on Water Street.

A *Daily Statesman* reporter went to see Hancock at the county jail. He was a handsome man with thick, swept-back hair and light-colored eyes, but on this day he looked "haggard and careworn." At first, he wouldn't talk, saying that all the newspapers "have lied enough about me already, and I don't desire to have anything to do with them." But when the reporter asked if he had ever read the letter from his wife telling him she was leaving for Waco, he said, "No sir!" Nor, he added, had he ever kept a hatchet hidden in a wall.

The reporter bore in, asking if he had a drinking problem. Hancock said he had been on a few "sprees" lasting no more than a couple of days.

"Is it not possible, Mr. Hancock, that at such times you abused your wife?" the reporter asked.

"I don't think I ever did," Hancock replied.

"Mr. Hancock, can you prove by anyone that at one time, while drunk, you did not abuse your wife and threaten to kill her and that she went to a neighbor's house for fear you would?"

Hancock said that he did not believe any such thing had happened, and he referred the reporter to several people around Austin "who will say we got along well."

III

Hancock didn't give himself a particularly convincing defense. Still, there were plenty of other Austin citizens who were not persuaded that he, or Jimmy Phillips, were killers. Austin's white women, in particular, remained terrified that there were more killings to come. Walking toward their houses, even before the sun set, they would suddenly swing around with a muted cry, thinking they'd heard footsteps behind them, and they'd run for their lives, kicking up dust, getting their stockings dirty. Late one night, a young single mother who had heard a noise was found by police crouched against a wall with her daughter, both of them "half dead with fright."

Petmecky's continued to do a brisk business selling guns and ammunition. On the Avenue, the salesmen were still pushing electric burglar alarm systems and Atwell's Patent Window Bolts. Druggists sold sleeping potions and tonics that were guaranteed to calm women's "nerves."

In an attempt to make Austin's citizens feel more at ease, Marshal Lucy continued to have Sergeant Chenneville and his officers patrol the neighborhoods at night. Chenneville also purchased two more bloodhounds, which the seller had guaranteed were far better trackers than the two that already lived in Chenneville's backyard. According to the *Daily Statesman*, he kept them out until "the wee hours" so that they would be ready to chase down the killer—or killers—in case another attack occurred.

Meanwhile, the talk about a Midnight Assassin—or, as a writer for the Western Associated Press wire service had begun calling him, "the Talented Sensationalist"—kept getting louder. Some citizens called on Marshal Lucy to station officers around the State Lunatic Asylum to make sure no one was escaping. An editor of the *Waco Daily Express* was so disturbed by the asylum's lack of security that he wrote, "It seems to us that the very first thing to be done would be to have the asylum closely watched day and night, without permitting either the officers or patients to know anything of it."

There were other calls for Lucy to have his officers interrogate all men in Austin of "unsound mind," including the eccentric Dr. Damos, the old man who walked the sidewalks of Congress Avenue, giving speeches about shipwrecks and the end of the world. "It has often been the case that the harmlessly insane, who have been tolerated for years to walk freely about, have suddenly turned into bloodthirsty madmen," noted the editor of the Austin-based *Texas Vorwaerts*, a German-language newspaper written for the state's German immigrants.

Police officers did reinterrogate more suspects from the previous attacks on the servant women just to see what they were up to. One officer went looking for Maurice, the Malaysian cook, at the Pearl House—the man who supposedly had been seen walking through the city "beastly drunk" around the time in late August 1885 when little

Mary Ramey was murdered. But when he arrived at Maurice's boarding-house, the proprietor, Mrs. Schmidt, said that Maurice had just moved. Mrs. Schmidt was not certain, but she thought Maurice had told her he was going to Galveston, where he planned to sail for England on a freighter, working as the ship's cook to pay for his fare.

The officer looked at Mrs. Schmidt. England? Maurice the cook actually had said he was moving all the way to England?

That's what he told me, said Mrs. Schmidt.

As for the newspapers, they continued to run wild with columns of lurid speculation about who the Midnight Assassin might be. A reporter for the *Dallas Mercury* wrote that the killer could be some otherworldly figure straight out of "the weird legends of the dark ages, when ghosts and vampires glutted their fiendish appetites with horrors indescribable." A reporter for the *San Antonio Light* hinted that the attacks could literally be the work of Satan. "Many hitherto have not believed in a personal Devil, but it looks like He has broken loose in the capital of Texas," he wrote.

And then there was George Monroe, the owner of Korman and Monroe, a successful New York publisher, who was so taken with the idea of a Midnight Assassin that he commissioned Kenward Philp, a former New York journalist turned novelist, to write a fictional short story about him. Philp was well-known: in 1870, he had written "The Bowery Detective," which had been called "the first dime novel detective story." Monroe telegraphed newspapers around the country, letting them know that after doing extensive research, Philp had come up with "an original theory" about a white man committing the murders. Monroe offered each newspaper the rights to print Philp's Austin story for a cost of six dollars.

Some newspapers, such as the *Omaha Bee* in the state of Nebraska, quickly agreed to run the story. But the only newspaper in Texas willing to pay for it was the *Fort Worth Gazette*. Other editors, including those at the *Daily Statesman*, didn't want to spend such an exorbitant fee without reading the story first, which Monroe would not agree to do.

In his opening paragraph, Philps described the killings as "a mess of horrors . . . more frightful than Edgar Allan Poe or Victor Hugo or Alexandre Dumas ever conjured up from their romantic brains." He then launched into a rather straightforward narrative about a New York newspaperman named Gerald Shanly coming to Austin and eventually discovering that the murders had been committed by "a gentleman farmer . . . a steely-gray-eyed man of powerful build, sallow complexion, six feet in height, slow-spoken, with bushy, standing-out black eye-brows." Several months earlier, the newspaperman learned, this farmer's brother had been convicted of murder by a jury made up of both black and white men. Enraged over the verdict, the farmer had decided to get revenge by murdering female relatives—wives, daughters, sisters, and nieces—of the male jurors. The farmer rode to and from the home of each woman in a carriage driven by his male black servant—"a gigantic Negro," wrote Philp—who took a circuitous route around the city, crisscrossing over his tracks several times, to confuse the bloodhounds.

Philp's short story was arguably the first piece of American fiction ever written about a serial killer. But his tale was hardly riveting—or even frightening. It didn't have a gruesome opening murder scene or a climactic chase in which the killer tried to get away. The gentleman farmer was quietly arrested at his farm, after which he soon confessed.

The biggest problem with Philp's story, of course, was that it didn't come close to capturing the real mystery of the murders. And on January 31, that mystery only deepened when police in San Antonio, one hundred miles to the south, were informed that the body of Patti Scott, a twenty-eight-year-old black servant woman, had been found in her quarters.

When the police arrived, they discovered Miss Scott had been struck three times in the head with the blade of an ax.

III

This time, there was an obvious suspect: Patti's husband, William, whom she was divorcing. William was known to be a violent man who, according to the San Antonio newspapers, had "brutalized" Patti

192 · SKIP HOLLANDSWORTH

several times and once had attempted to cut her neck with a razor. But after Patti's murder, police didn't find any blood on him, and they couldn't break his alibi of being asleep that night at a local hotel.

Without an arrest, the newspapers immediately began to suggest that the killing was connected to the Austin murders. A *New York Times* reporter actually did a comparison of Patti Scott's wounds with the wounds inflicted on the Austin women. "There was the same deadly cut across the base of her skull that three of the Austin victims bore, and the blow on the crown of her head was identical with that in the Austin tragedies," the article concluded. "It is the general belief that the deed was done by the Austin murderer. This belief has created a perfect panic among the females of the city [of San Antonio]."

Indeed, there was a replay in San Antonio of the very same fear that had taken place in Austin: women hid behind barricaded doors while police officers, "special policemen," and citizens' vigilante groups roamed the streets at night. Editorialists for the San Antonio newspapers added to the fear by writing that one or more of the Austin killers had almost certainly moved to San Antonio, pushed out of Austin by Marshal Lucy as part of his plan to "cleanse" Austin of its criminals. "Is it just for any city, when it fails to manage its own lawless elements, to shove them off to depredate on other cities?" cried an editorialist for the *San Antonio Times*. An editorialist for the *Daily Statesman* came right back with a defense of Lucy. "Right or wrong, that is just what other towns and cities have been doing until they have caused Austin to be over run with thieves and murderers, and Austin now proposes to keep them running, even if it has to run some of them through the gates of Hell," he wrote.

Although Mayor Robertson said nothing about the latest turn of events, he couldn't have been all that displeased. Finally, with Patti Scott's killing, the headlines about murder were no longer focused on Austin. Sensing that this was the perfect time to restore the city's luster—and in the process, restore his own reputation—he met with businessmen to come up with new promotional projects. Sadly for the mayor, it was too late to do anything about the fiftieth celebration of

Texas's independence, which was coming up in a few weeks. The Texas Semi-Centennial Organizing Committee, which he formed, had disbanded in the aftermath of the Christmas Eve murders. (Apparently, none of the committee members were interested in working on such a project while the city's women were being struck down.) Still, Robertson remained upbeat. He and his fellow businessmen decided to put together another pamphlet, this one titled, "Austin—The Healthiest City on the Continent."

The pamphlet claimed that only 331 people had died in Austin in the year 1885—a death rate of "less than 12 per 1,000 inhabitants," which few other cities in America could match. Only a dozen of those deaths "were from violence or unnatural causes." (Of course, the pamphlet did not go into detail about those violent deaths.) The pamphlet went on to call Austin the best city in the country for those who wanted to live long lives. "Austin, the admiration of strangers and the pride of all Texas, is the most beautifully situated and healthful of any city on the continent." "Her elegant residences, broad drives, and clustering groves growing in tropical sunlight; and her modest but picturesque mountains, her changeful landscapes, her flowers and sunshine and balmy breezes, all tell of health and life and ripe old age."

No doubt at Robertson's encouragement, the downtown merchants and shop owners held early spring sales in hopes that people would come inside the stores to shop instead of lingering on the streets to talk about murder. The irrepressible Charles Millett did his part, of course, bringing in New York actress Blanche Curtis—"undoubtedly the greatest actress in her line in America today, perhaps in the world," read his advertisements—to perform the lead role in a play titled *The Farmer's Daughter*. The University of Texas invited all residents to hear a lecture delivered by its physics professor, Dr. Alexander MacFarlane, titled "The Habitation of the Planets." In his talk, MacFarlane concluded that the four large outer planets had "not yet sufficiently cooled down to allow life on their surface such as is seen on the earth," but that someday humans would be living on Mars.

The audience enthusiastically applauded. There will be life on Mars! Robertson, of course, was thrilled—the topic of conversation was changing to more hopeful subjects. Now, all he needed was for Jimmy Phillips and Moses Hancock to be convicted at their trials, and Austin would be able to move past the murders once and for all.

PART FIVE

FEBRUARY 1886 – MAY 1888

"A prominent State officer
and an active candidate for the
Governorship of Texas . . . knows
something about
Eula Phillips' murder."

CHAPTER EIGHTEEN

In late February, Jimmy Phillips was led into the main courtroom of the grand two-story county courthouse, which had been built with gleaming white limestone—it was nicknamed "the Castle"—for a pretrial evidentiary hearing. Jimmy stumbled toward his chair and didn't speak. His doctors said that he was still "delirious" from his severe head wounds.

District Attorney Robertson and special prosecutor T. E. Moore laid out their case against him. They said his parents had lied about Jimmy and Eula reconciling before Christmas and having a happy life. It was also significant, they argued, that no one in Austin had been able to produce the name of any other man who would have wanted Eula dead. Texas District Judge A. S. Wright, an elderly, stern man who was presiding over the case, nodded, tapped his gavel on his desk, and announced that Jimmy's trial would begin in May.

But two days later, the news raced up and down the Avenue that there was, in fact, a new suspect in Eula's murder—and it was the Pinkerton detectives, of all people, who had identified him. After six weeks of work, the private eyes from Chicago had finally made a break-through. According to newspaper accounts, the Pinkertons had received a telegram from a "prominent citizen" alleging that one of the men Eula had secretly met at Mae Tobin's house of assignation was "a distinguished politician." It just so happened, this citizen wrote in his telegram, that the politician was "a prominent State officer and an active candidate for the Governorship of Texas" and that he "knows something about [Eula's] murder."

There was only one man who fit the definition of such a man. It was William J. Swain, the strapping, barrel-chested state comptroller.

III

The newspapermen raced to Swain's office to ask him if he had had sex with young Eula. And what did he know about her murder? And what did he know, for that matter, about all the other murders?

Swain stood behind his desk and declared that he had never met Eula Phillips. He bellowed that he would find "the party" who had gone to the Pinkerton detectives and spread "such underhanded slander," and he vowed that he would hold the person "accountable" in a court of law for such an "indignant and cruel outrage."

It wasn't long before Swain announced that he and his staffers had learned that the telegram from the so-called "prominent citizen" had been sent from the city of Waco, which just happened to be the home of Sul Ross, a slim, balding former war hero who had recently declared that he would be running against Swain for the Democratic Party's nomination for governor.

In 1860, as a member of the Texas Rangers, Ross had led the her-alded rescue of Cynthia Ann Parker, a white woman who had been captured by Comanche Indians when she was a child. During the Civil War, he had fought in 135 battles for the Confederacy. He was definitely well known and very respected around the state. But he wasn't much of a politician. One reporter noted that he was an "atro-cious" orator who spoke in "a camp meeting drawl," and another reporter pointed out that he had no substantial ideas about how Texas should be improved or promoted. (During a two-year tenure he served

The "cohorts" of gubernatorial candidate
Sul Ross (above) were accused of spreading
a rumor that the Midnight Assassin was
Ross's opponent William Swain.

in the legislature, Ross voted against the state appropriating $15,000 to install its exhibit at the World's Industrial and Cotton Centennial Exposition in New Orleans.) Ross's own campaign manager, Waco attorney George Clark, a long-time political operative, admitted that Ross had been "quite timid" about the idea of running for governor because he didn't believe he could win.

In fact, it was hard for anyone to imagine Ross being able to beat the popular Swain, who was already drawing large crowds at his campaign stops around the state. It was assumed that Swain was, in the words of one reporter, a "shoo-in" for governor, unless a major scandal derailed his campaign. And now, fortuitously for Ross, a scandal had hit just at the right time. Around the state, people were reading headlines saying that William J. Swain, the man who wanted to lead Texas into the twentieth century, could very well be one of the most vicious killers in Texas history.

Swain said he would be going to court to ask for a subpoena requiring the telegraph operator in Waco to testify which Ross "cohort" had come into his office to send the telegram to the Pinkertons. Ross's campaign manager Clark heatedly denied Swain's insinuation that anyone involved in the Ross campaign had anything to do with the telegram. Ross's hometown newspaper, the *Waco Daily Examiner*, also came to his defense, claiming he wanted to win the election "fair and square." In a clever bit of writing, another newspaper that supported Ross, *The Balance Wheel*, encouraged voters to do the right thing and pay no credence to the newspaper stories "that attempt to connect Col. W. J. Swain with this horrible, blood-curdling crime by stating that he was known to have been riding with [Eula Phillips] a short time previous to her murder, which was 12 o'clock at night."

Under such headlines as "A Dastardly Outrage" and "The Infamous and Lying Dispatch," the newspapers that backed Swain's candidacy vehemently came to his defense, with a couple of them calling the telegram's author a "cowardly sneak" and a "cut-throat." The *Fort Worth Gazette* described the whole affair as "one of the most damnable and infamous libels ever attempted in Texas." T. E. Moore, the special prosecutor, issued an affidavit stating that he and District Attorney Robertson, during their investigation of Eula's murder, had come across no witnesses who mentioned Swain as her paramour. As for that telegraph operator from Waco, he refused to speak about the source of the Swain telegram, which to Swain's camp was a clear sign that Ross—or someone on his staff—had pulled off the dirtiest of political tricks.

When Ross opened his gubernatorial campaign in Waco just days after the rumor was circulated about Swain and Eula, he didn't mention Swain's name. His speech focused on the issues of the day— taxation, public school funding, and the fencing of the cattle ranges of West Texas—though he did briefly mention the need to bring "dignity" to the governor's office. Swain in turn went on a barnstorming campaign throughout the state, telling his supporters that he was not going to stand idly by while his detractors made "vile," "low," and "dirty" statements impugning his character.

But the allegations about Swain and his "impure life" would not go away. Although the *San Antonio Daily Express* was one of the newspapers supporting Swain, it acknowledged that the allegations about his relationship with Eula, regardless how false, "may not make him governor." Even Governor Ireland postponed endorsing him as his successor. He decided to wait until after Jimmy Phillips's trial before making an endorsement. If Phillips was acquitted, then Swain would still be a suspect, which, for the governor, would be a very big problem.

III

Mayor Robertson was clearly devastated by the havoc the fake Pinkertons had wrought. In early March he brought the detectives to his office, paid them the balance they were owed for their work, and sent them back to Chicago. He then met with the aldermen and told them they needed to pass more ordinances to counter allegations from around the state that Austin was an immoral city. One ordinance they passed established "Sunday laws," in which all businesses would have to be closed from 9 a.m. to 4 p.m.—and saloons closed for the entire day—so that residents would have more time to read the Bible and improve their Christian attitudes.

Meanwhile, out at the State Lunatic Asylum, Dr. Denton was also doing what he could to allay the fears of those who had come to believe it was a dangerous place, teeming with vicious madmen. Speaking to legislators, he said there had only been one escape in the last twelve months. He mentioned that plans were in the works to add more gardens and walking paths to the asylum's grounds to ensure that the patients felt an even deeper sense of tranquility.

Denton, however, didn't seem to be speaking with his usual enthusiasm—and soon everyone in Austin learned why. In February, Denton quietly had gone to a county judge and requested that an Austin citizen, who was suffering from a "very distressing and deplorable" mental condition, be "involuntarily committed" to the asylum and "placed under restraints." The citizen was none other than his own son-in-law, Dr. James P. Given, the asylum's thirty-four-year-old assistant superintendent.

Denton had said nothing to the judge about what had caused Given's insanity. All that the judge was told was that the young doctor was "bereft of his reason." Denton then made a curious request. He asked

that his son-in-law be "removed from the effects of his present association" and moved to the North Texas Lunatic Asylum, a small branch
of the State Lunatic Asylum that had recently opened in the northeast
Texas town of Terrell.

The judge agreed, and Given had been taken to the Austin railroad
depot, put on a train (probably strapped in a private car), and taken to
Terrell. In his admissions report at the new asylum, Given's cause of
insanity was still not revealed. All that was written down was that he
suffered from "Dissipation," which was a vague term that asylum doctors in that era used to describe any number of behaviors, ranging from
alcoholism to "hallucinatory activity."

Upon learning of his fate, Given's friends were inconsolable.
They described him as "a genial and accomplished gentleman," "deserv-
edly popular with all with whom he associated," and one of the city's
best "imports." He possessed "a high sense of honor" and was "upright
and just in all his dealings"—a diligent doctor who had spent long hours
keeping up with the patients' conditions. There had been nothing in his
behavior, said his friends and associates, that suggested he had been
losing touch with reality.

Was it conceivable that, within the space of just a few weeks, Given
had lost his mind? Or had he been hiding his insanity for a very long
period of time? And why, once his "dissipation" was discovered, was it
so important to Denton that his son-in-law be sent to the new branch
asylum in order to be removed from "his present association"? What
did that mean?

One can only speculate, because the records detailing Given's
treatment at the new asylum were never added to the asylum's files—
either that or they were later removed. Perhaps Given had contracted
syphilis, which in that era was untreatable and a major source of insanity, sending parasites burrowing into the brain, and Denton had
wanted to hide that fact from the public to protect Given's sterling
reputation. Perhaps Denton didn't want Given to become the subject
of ugly rumors that his mental condition had transformed him, under
the light of the moon, into a murderous "maniac." Or perhaps Denton

hadn't wanted Given to suffer the same character assassination he had seen Swain endure.

If that was Denton's motive, he was certainly successful: no scandalous rumors about Given ever made the newspapers. But as for the asylum itself, Denton wasn't so lucky. His dreams of making the institution into a perfect paradise—a place of gentle refuge away from the heartless world—had been dashed. The *Daily Statesman* even noted that the editors of the Fort Worth and Dallas newspapers were "congratulating themselves" that they had not won their bids to the state legislature years ago to have the state asylum built in their cities. Indeed, the editors proclaimed, compared to Austin, their cities were blessedly free of madmen.

III

On May 24, Jimmy Phillips's trial began. Hoping to get a seat in the courtroom, spectators were at the courthouse before it opened, the men dressed in their best dark suits and flat-crowned Stetsons, and the women wearing silk dresses and high hats filled with a wilderness of feathers. One reporter described the courtroom as "crowded to suffocation."

Toward the front of the courtroom was a plain oak table for District Attorney Robertson and T. E. Moore. Another table was reserved for Jimmy's defense team, William Walton and John Hancock (no relation to Moses), who were regarded as the best criminal lawyers in Austin. Although neither man liked the other—Walton had been an ardent secessionist during the Civil War and Hancock an outspoken abolitionist who was once deprived of his seat in the state legislature because he wouldn't take the Confederate oath—they were both so outraged by Jimmy's arrest that they had set aside their differences to defend him. There were other tables in the courtroom for representatives of the press: reporters from the state's bigger newspapers, as well as those for the national wire services. The *New York World* and *Chicago Tribune*, among other newspapers, promised their readers to publish "full accounts" of the trial testimony.

Jimmy was at the defense table, where he sat slumped forward, staring absently at the wall. Reporters described him as "pale," "feeble," and "care-worn and haggard, as if he had not yet recovered from his terrible wounds." Judge Walker strode into the courtroom. A bailiff announced, "Court is in session. Hats off except for the ladies!"

For weeks, the newspapers had been predicting that the trial would unfold as a Gothic melodrama of deception, sexual suspense, and gruesome murder—"as exciting, as dark and as implacable, as *The Mystery of Edwin Drood*," declared the *Daily Statesman*, referring to the last novel written by Charles Dickens, which at the time of his death in 1870 was unfinished, leaving the identity of the murderer unknown. In their opening arguments, Robertson and Moore laid out a melodramatic narrative of a young wife who was given to rampant infidelity and a jealous young husband who was given to drink. Walton and Hancock countered with an equally dramatic anti-narrative, telling the jurors that any number of men, from well-heeled ex-lovers to the notorious gang of bad blacks, could have killed Eula.

Over the next three days, a parade of people who knew Jimmy and Eula were brought to the witness stand by the prosecutors to testify about Jimmy's abusive ways. One man, George McCutcheon—he owned the farm near the town of Georgetown where Jimmy and his wife had lived for a few months in order to keep Jimmy out of the saloons—testified that just before the couple returned to Austin, he had told Jimmy to stop drinking, saying, "You are ruining yourself and making your wife miserable." Jimmy had replied that he was worried that Eula was carrying on with other men. McCutcheon said Jimmy then asked him, "Do you think Eula is too fast?" McCutcheon said he replied, "No, I think she is a good and virtuous woman, but she talks a little too much," to which Jimmy said, "If I thought she was not virtuous, I would kill her and then kill myself."

Jimmy's sister Adelia came to the witness stand to testify that Eula was scared of Jimmy—so scared, in fact, that she once had hidden for a few days in the East Austin home of a poor black woman named Fannie Whipple after Jimmy had tried to attack her.

The spectators gasped. Eula was so desperate to get away from her own husband that she stayed at the shanty of a *Negro*?

Adelia set off more courtroom gasps when she testified that she knew that Eula had met at least two men at Mae Tobin's. Adelia insisted that she didn't know the men's names. Nor, she added, did she have any idea about Eula's activities with any particular man on Christmas Eve. But yes, she said, Eula had been "an untrue wife."

Then Mae Tobin, the star witness, walked into the courtroom. According to the newspapers, people "rose" from their seats "on tiptoe" to get a look at her. She sat down in the witness chair and folded her hands in her lap. The room fell silent as she began to talk, and everyone "hung upon her words . . . with breathless attention."

At first, Tobin stuck to the same story she originally had told to Thomas Bailes, the private investigator, acknowledging that Eula had been to her home during the fall of 1885 to meet "young men and other men of uncertain age." But this time, she decided to name names. She said she had recognized three men who had been with Eula. One was John T. Dickinson, the secretary of the powerful state commission that was overseeing the construction of the new capitol. Another was Benjamin M. Baker, the state superintendent of public instruction (the head of Texas's public schools). And the third man was William D. Shelley, a clerk in the comptroller's office whose father just happened to be the law partner of John Hancock, one of Jimmy's defense attorneys.

The spectators gasped for the third time. They waited to see if Tobin would acknowledge that William Swain, the comptroller himself, was also one of Eula's paramours. But all that Tobin would say was that Eula had come to the house with two other men whose names Tobin did not know. Tobin also reiterated that she had not been able to tell if there was a man in the carriage with Eula on Christmas Eve when she came to the house maybe an hour before her death.

In the next day's newspapers were huge front-page headlines: "Austin Agog. A Ten-Inch Bomb Exploded in an Austin Court" and "High State Officials Given Away—and Others Shaking in Their Boots." Tobin herself was described as "The Scarlet Woman," "The Procuress," and "The Shameless Cyprian." The *Houston Daily Post* declared that her testimony had set off "one of the most extensive and profound scandals ever known in Austin."

For their part, Dickinson, Shelley, and Baker expressed the usual outrage, alleging that their political enemies had paid Tobin blackmail money to name them as visitors to her house of assignation. Baker went so far as to pay for a "card" to be published in the *Daily Statesman* in which he declared that he "had no acquaintance with Mrs. Phillips, and never spoke to her in my life." (The card didn't have much impact around his home: his wife soon left with the children for her parents' home in East Texas.)

Interestingly enough, when the trial resumed, Jimmy's attorneys barely cross-examined Tobin about Eula's visits. But they did rip into the prosecutors for presenting no evidence at all indicating that Jimmy knew about his wife's secret life. Nor, they charged, did the prosecutors present any evidence linking Jimmy to Eula's murder. When Robertson brought up the behavior of Bob the bloodhound rising up on Jimmy's bed to sniff him, Hancock the defense attorney got great laughs in the courtroom when he shouted, "I wouldn't hang a dog upon the testimony of a dog!" Additional points were scored in Jimmy's favor when three doctors testified that he physically would not have been able to wound himself so severely with an ax toward the back of his own head.

Jimmy's lawyers then introduced a new suspect. They theorized that George McCutcheon, the man Eula and Jimmy stayed with on the farm near the town of Georgetown, had come to Austin on Christmas Eve to carry out the murder. The attorneys speculated that McCutcheon had been having an affair with Eula and that he once had given Eula money to go to a pharmacy on Congress Avenue and purchase chamomile flowers and extracts of cottonwood and ergot, which if mixed properly could produce an abortion. Maybe, they said, McCutcheon had decided to kill Eula before his own wife found out about his and Eula's relationship.

"Is it true you were in the habit of having carnal intercourse with Eula Phillips while she lived at your house?" defense attorney Walton asked McCutcheon.

"I decline to answer the question," McCutcheon said heatedly, adding that he had an unimpeachable alibi for Christmas Eve: he had been at a "stag party" that night near his farm and had been seen by many other men. Still, McCutcheon was forced to admit that he owned a fine trotting horse that could have quickly carried him on Christmas Eve night from his farm to the Phillips home and back before daybreak.

Jimmy did not testify. But his attorney did have him take off his shoes and socks, place his foot in a bucket of ink, and step on a pine board, making a footprint. That footprint was displayed next to the bloodied footprint that had been found outside Jimmy and Eula's room just after the murder. Jimmy's footprint was clearly smaller.

T. E. Moore told the judge that the demonstration was flawed. He said Phillips was probably carrying his wife when he made that bloody impression, which meant his feet almost certainly would have made flatter prints due to the extra weight. Jimmy's attorney William Walton, who weighed 175 pounds, promptly climbed up on Jimmy's back and asked him to put his foot again in the bucket of ink and step on another pine board. Jimmy's footprint was still too small.

In closing arguments, Walton and Hancock told the jurors that if Jimmy's footprint didn't match the bloodied footprint, then they had no choice but to acquit. They portrayed Jimmy as a loving husband who had been working hard at sobriety and had tragically been attacked by the "same fiend" who had murdered his wife.

After deliberating for a day and a half, the jury came back into the courtroom. Just about everyone in the gallery was assuming a verdict of not guilty. The entire trial had been a travesty, some people were saying. Surely, Jimmy would be going home later that day.

The foreman rose and announced that he and his fellow jurors unanimously found Jimmy guilty of second-degree uxoricide and that he should spend seven years in the state penitentiary.

And once again, the spectators in the courtroom gasped.

CHAPTER NINETEEN

Jimmy was led from the courtroom to the county jail, where he would be staying until the state prison wagon arrived to take him to the penitentiary. Newspapermen headed to the Austin Press Club at the Horseshoe Lounge to type up their stories and try to explain to their readers how such a verdict had been rendered. The *Galveston Daily News* reporter hinted that the jurors had been bribed or, at the least, secretly given some information about Jimmy and Eula that influenced their decision. There was simply no way "to account for the verdict," he wrote, unless "there was some inside business that was made known to the jury privately." The *San Antonio Express*'s man claimed that the decisive factor in the trial was T. E. Moore's powerful courtroom performance, noting: "His eloquence rather than the guilt of the prisoner caused a verdict of guilt." Trying to maintain some sense of balance, all that the *Daily Statesman*'s man would write was that "the majority of Austin's citizens" believed the jury had "erred."

Hancock and Walton announced they would be filing an appeal immediately. Walton was especially furious at District Attorney

Robertson, accusing him of transforming himself from a nice young man into a "veritable thug" who had done anything possible "to win at all costs," leaving "no human contrivance, no trick of the trade, no art untried to secure a conviction."

Robertson replied that he had not resorted to any shenanigans to persuade the jury of Jimmy's guilt. He said no one—such as his own older brother—had asked him to do what he could to get Jimmy behind bars. He and Moore simply had done what the law required them to do: they had laid out the facts to the jurors, and the jurors had decided on their own that no mysterious killer had come after Eula. Robertson then said that he would soon be convening a new jury, as the law required, to hear the case of the State of Texas versus Moses Hancock for the murder of his wife, Susan.

But why, several citizens wanted to know, didn't Robertson and Moore present any testimony regarding the identity of the man who supposedly was with Eula on Christmas Eve? Was it Swain? Or was it someone else "of high position and wealth"? A rumor swept through the Avenue that "a rich cattleman" was actually with Eula and that he had "planked down" blackmail money to Tobin in return for her not mentioning his name in court. Who, people asked, was the cattleman?

Robertson and Moore said they had uncovered no information about any Christmas Eve paramour. As for Swain, he made no public comment at all about the trial or Jimmy's conviction, He believed he didn't have to. For one thing, he still had the endorsements of a vast majority of the state's newspapers—a four-to-one advantage in newspaper endorsements over Sul Ross, one reporter figured. The Democratic Party nominating convention in Galveston was only two months away. Swain could not imagine that he could be brought down in such a short period of time by ludicrous rumors that he had been involved in murder.

To reassure voters that there was nothing about him to fear, Swain went on another barnstorming tour around Texas. In the town of Rockdale, his staffers arranged for the town's ladies to turn out "in full force" and cheer when they saw him. He gave a speech that lasted nearly two hours, his voice never faltering. After hearing Swain speak, one reporter called him "a full-fledged candidate" and went on to say that his opponent Ross was nothing more than a "kindie [kindergartener] beating the brush." The reporter added, "Swain has served Texas and her interests too long and too faithfully to be defeated by an unwarranted effort to pull down and belittle the man."

But the Swain-Eula rumors did not go away. The newspapers that supported Ross noted that Swain had never followed through on his vow to hunt down the author of the telegram that claimed he had been with Eula on Christmas Eve. At the same time, the wily Clark and Ross's other campaign operatives were spreading damaging new stories about Swain: that he had violated state nepotism policies by hiring his two sons to work at the comptroller's office, that he had illegally used state stationery to write campaign letters, that he had put a woman on his payroll even though she did not come to work, and that he was "in collusion" with the men building the new state capitol, taking bribes in return for his help in getting construction materials at a very cheap price.

What made matters worse for Swain was that Governor Ireland never delivered his endorsement: he obviously believed his own political future would be better served if he kept his distance from the comptroller. As a result, when the Democratic convention was convened in August at the gymnasium-size roller rink in Galveston, it was obvious that Swain had lost significant support. Many of the 696 delegates were openly telling reporters that he had too much baggage to be the next governor. What was best for Texas, they said, was a reliable, old-fashioned war hero—not a murder suspect.

On the day of the nominating speeches, the heat was so stifling inside the roller rink that the delegates took off their coats and fanned themselves—"their fans reaching desperately for air," wrote one reporter. Suffering from a fever, Ross spoke for only twenty-five minutes. "He was nervous," noted the *Galveston Daily News*. "His face was flushed and his eyes devoid of their customary luster. . . . His speech was a disappointment to his friends."

Swain then rose to deliver his oration. According to the newspapers, his "friends" broke into applause numerous times. When he finished laying out his positions on the issues, he came to the very edge of the platform and in a voice "trembling with agitation" and "now and again swelling into a roar of rage," he lifted his arms and declared, "This campaign has been the most disgusting in mudslinging and vituperative slander that has ever disgraced the footstool of Deity. I have filled offices for fifteen years in the state. I have turned them over untarnished and I defy any man to find a single blemish in the record that I have made for the state of Texas. But lying and contemptible scoundrels—men who would be thieves if they had the opportunity—have been slandering me from one end of the state to another."

Swain looked at Ross's supporters. "Gentlemen, whatever you say about me, I can go home and make as good a soldier as ever fought in the Democratic ranks," he stated, his voice still trembling. "And you can't touch me!"

When he finished, "hats were tossed aloft" among his supporters, "handkerchiefs waved," and "shouting and cheering lasted for fully two minutes." But it was too late. Swain, in the words of one reporter, was a "doomed duck." Ross received 433 votes on the first ballot to Swain's 99, with two other candidates accumulating the other 164 votes. Amid a "tumult of shouting," Ross was carried on the shoulders of his friends from his hotel room to the roller rink, where he gave a brief acceptance speech. An embittered Swain returned to Austin and announced that upon completion of his term as comptroller, he would be joining an Austin law firm that focused on "land matters." He said he would never again run for public office.

III

For the rest of the summer and fall of 1886, Austin remained quiet. In October, William Frank "Doc" Carver, a former Nebraska dentist and farmer, came to the fairgrounds to put on *The Golden West*, a dramatic spectacle that offered a nostalgic portrayal of life as it once was in the American West. In the mid-1880s, there were probably half a dozen such Wild West shows traveling the country, the most popular put on by former Pony Express rider William F. "Buffalo Bill" Cody. But

Carver was right on Buffalo Bill's heels. Six feet, four inches and 265 pounds, he always wore a broad-brimmed hat and a suit of buckskin, beautifully trimmed and beaded, with thick, hand-stitched leather boots rising to his knees. His hair was very long, brushed behind the ears, and his mustache was enormous. In his promotional material, he called himself "the Champion Rifle Shot of the World" and "the Wizard Rifleman of the West, Conqueror of All America and Europe, and Cynosure of People, Princes and Warriors and Kings."

Carver's show in Austin was a sellout: hundreds of residents were packed tightly together in the grandstands. A brass band began to play, and into the arena came what the *Daily Statesman* later described as "an imposing historical parade" of cowboys, lawmen, outlaws, Indians in war paint, hunters, Mexican vaqueros, and Carver himself, who swept off his hat and bowed as the crowd cheered.

There was a flurry of acts: a horse race between Pony Express riders, a war dance among the Indians in full regalia, a reenactment of the Deadwood Stagecoach ambush, and a gunfight between lawmen and "bad men"—with the lawmen winning, of course. "Wild buckin' broncos" were lassoed by cowboys. "Hunters" pretended to shoot buffalo. Holding a Winchester rifle at his hips, and without taking aim, Carver put on a display of his deadeye shooting skills, first hitting a series of stationary targets, and then hitting dozens of objects that his assistants threw high into the air: blocks of wood, stones, four glass balls at a time, and a dozen silver dollars.

Then came the last act of the show—what everyone had been waiting for. Indians in feathers and war paint, whooping and waving their bows in the air, raced across the arena toward a mother and her children huddled in a small log cabin. The spectators rose in their seats as more Indians, dazzling and fierce, poured into the arena, circling the cabin, preparing to attack.

Suddenly, the announcer shouted into his megaphone, "Here comes Justice!" Riding furiously toward the cabin from the other side of the arena was Carver and his cowboys, firing away at the Indians with his rifle, the gunpowder smoke filling the air. One by one, the Indians fell to the ground, pretending to be dead, and the audience cheered with delight. The frontier mother and her children had been saved from a scalping.

As Carver turned and made his last bows, Austin's residents kept cheering. For those few moments, they were able to remember a time when the men in white hats always won and the bad men always lost—a time, at least, when everyone knew who the bad men were.

It was a feeling that lasted exactly four weeks—until November 10, to be precise. The judges who made up the Court of Appeals of Texas, which was based in Galveston, announced that they had reviewed the appeal filed by Jimmy Phillips's lawyers over his murder conviction, and they agreed that the prosecutors had not presented proof, as they had promised they would at the beginning of the trial, that Jimmy ever knew of Eula's infidelity.

Nor, ruled the judges, had any evidence been presented by the prosecutors tying Jimmy to his wife's murder. The jury's judgment was "reversed and remanded," and Jimmy's case was returned to Austin's district court for a new trial.

III

Jimmy was brought back to the county jail from the state penitentiary, and District Attorney Robertson allowed him to be released on bail to live at his father's home with his young son Tom. Robertson most likely had a strategic reason for establishing bail: he hoped Jimmy would head to a saloon, start drinking, and either tell someone that he had murdered Eula or, at the least, confess that he knew about her trips to Mae Tobin's. Then, with the new evidence, Robertson would have him rearrested and retried.

Jimmy, however, said nothing, and by all accounts, he didn't go on any drinking sprees. Residents who saw him on the Avenue said it just made no sense whatsoever that this young man could have ripped apart his wife and placed firewood on top of her body.

As the Christmas season arrived, some citizens anxiously wondered if the Midnight Assassin—or whoever was doing the killings—would stage another Christmas Eve attack. But Austin remained perfectly peaceful, free even of "petty crime," according to a report in the *Daily*

Statesman. On New Year's Eve, Sul Ross celebrated his inauguration as Texas's new governor with a banquet and a ball at the newly opened Driskill Hotel. He stood on a platform and in his tinny voice told the assembled guests—at least a thousand in all—that he wanted his tenure to be known as "the era of good feeling in Texas."

Governor Ireland was at the ball, already talking about what he would be doing if he were chosen to be U.S. senator later that month. (In that era, prior to the passage of the Seventeenth Amendment to the U.S. Constitution, the members of the state legislature, not the voters, picked the senators.) For his campaign, he had produced a pamphlet titled *The Man of Destiny*, which listed all of his accomplishments, and in an article written for the *North American Review*, he had laid out what he believed Texas would look like in fifty years: "Teeming millions will occupy its soil. . . . Commercial and trade will be at its height . . . and Texas, loved and protected by its gallant sons, and pushed forward in the grand march of improvement by their brave, strong arms, and the prayers and smiles of its beautiful ladies will bloom and blossom!"

Many legislators, however, had been receiving campaign contributions from railroad barons, who had no fondness for Ireland. They called him "Oxcart John" because he had opposed a proposal to give subsidies to railroads to build more tracks through rural Texas. (Ireland said the railroads were already making plenty of money.) When the vote for U.S. senator took place at the end of January, the winner turned out to be a late entry into the race, John H. Reagan, a longtime politician and supporter of the railroads. Ireland returned to his hometown of Seguin, near San Antonio, to practice law. He never ran for office again, and, according to one biographer, lapsed into "depression." Like William Swain, he was destined to become a minor footnote in the state's history.

III

In late March 1887, four months after Jimmy Phillips's release from prison, District Attorney Robertson filed a motion in state district court to have the case against him dismissed. Robertson did not directly comment on the question of Jimmy's innocence: he only said that no new evidence had emerged to support a conviction. But perhaps to save face—or perhaps because he was being pushed by his brother and members of the Citizen's Committee of Safety to get at least one conviction—he said he would be prosecuting Moses Hancock later that year for the murder of his wife.

That trial began in June. Because T. E. Moore was no longer interested in working as a special prosecutor—since the Phillips trial, he had been elected to the legislature—Robertson hired a former U.S. assistant attorney, Jack Evans, to assist him. The prosecutors' first witnesses included neighbors of the Hancocks who testified that they heard no noise whatsoever coming from the Hancock home on Christmas Eve, the implication being that if a man had jumped the fence, axed a woman, and jumped back over the fence, they surely would have heard something.

The prosecutors also called a couple of neighbors who testified that they heard Moses (who had been out of jail on bond since his arrest) tell a completely different story than the one he originally told Marshal Lucy about what had happened in his backyard on Christmas Eve. They said Moses had informed them that there had been two men standing over his wife, and that one of them had pulled out a pistol and threatened Moses to stay back.

The key witness was a man named Joseph Gassoway, who had known Moses for many years. After the Christmas Eve murders, he had been hired by Marshal Lucy, using money provided by the Citizen's Committee of Safety, to work as an undercover officer and keep in close contact with Hancock. Gassoway said that one night while the two men were on a camping trip in West Texas, Moses had gotten very drunk and begun talking about how he wanted to "hang up" Thomas Bailes (the private detective) for having him arrested. Gassoway said Moses had told him, "Them damn sons of bitches down at Austin are trying to work up something on me, but they have not got anything, nor never will, out of me." Gassoway said Moses then had asked him if he thought his daughters would "give him away." If he had to, he said, he would flee to Brazil so that the police and private detectives wouldn't be able to find him.

Hancock's defense attorney was John Hancock, the same attorney who had defended Jimmy Phillips. He was so furious that Moses was being prosecuted that he had taken on the case for free. His cocounsel was an old friend, Bethel Coopwood, a rather eccentric lawyer who raised camels on his ranch outside the city, several of which he had sold to the Barnum & Bailey circus. The two defense attorneys portrayed Moses as a man who had turned to alcohol after the murder of his wife to deal with his grief. He had told his contradictory stories about Christmas Eve only after imbibing large amounts of whiskey. The defense attorneys also accused Gassoway of inventing the story about his camping trip with Hancock, claiming he was only after part of the reward money.

Hancock didn't testify. But his eldest daughter, Lena, came to the witness stand to say her parents had "lived happily together." Yes, she admitted, her mother had found fault with Moses's drinking, but he had "never laid a hand" on her and certainly hadn't touched Lena or her younger sister. And yes, she continued, her father got angry, but he was still a good man.

Lena then testified that her mother had not worked up the courage to show her father the letter she had written telling him that she was going to leave him and move to Waco. Instead, she had put the letter in the bottom of a box of artificial flowers, which was where Mrs. Hancock's sister had found it. The authorities were wrong, Lena said. Her father had no motive to murder her mother.

At the very end of the trial, the defense attorneys presented a surprise witness. They had Travis County sheriff Malcolm Hornsby testify about an event that took place on February 9, 1886, a little more than a month after the Christmas Eve killings, when Sheriff's Deputy William Bracken was called to a saloon in Masontown, a black community located just east of the Austin city limits. Bracken learned that a customer at the saloon named Nathan Elgin—a young black man in his early twenties—was "quite drunk" and "raising Hades in general." He had gotten into an argument with a black woman, knocked her down, and dragged her to a nearby house, where he had begun to "thump her." When Bracken arrived at the house, he tried to place some "nippers" (handcuffs) on Elgin's wrists, but Elgin quickly turned and struck the deputy "severely" on the head. Bracken pulled out his pistol and shot Elgin in the chest, killing him.

Sheriff Hornsby testified that when he arrived at the scene, he saw that Elgin was missing a little toe on the right foot. Hornsby said he remembered that one of the bloody footprints found outside Eula and Jimmy's room on Christmas Eve looked as if it had a little toe missing. Suspicious, he had ordered that a plaster cast of Elgin's foot be made, which was later compared to the Phillips footprint. Hornsby said it was his opinion that the two footprints matched.

Hornsby also testified that he believed footprints discovered in the alley behind the house where Mary Ramey had been murdered also seemed to indicate the little right toe was missing. Although that footprint had not been preserved, Hornsby speculated that it too probably matched Elgin's.

It was a startling piece of testimony: the sheriff of Travis County was suggesting that Elgin was definitely involved in at least two of the Austin murders and that he could very well be the Midnight Assassin.

Elgin had grown up in Austin, and he was known during his teenage years as "a kind of bad citizen." In July 1881, according to the *Daily Statesman,* he and another young black man named Green Alexander had carried on "a row" not far from the governor's mansion, "cursing each other for some time" before Alexander drew a pistol and fired three shots at Elgin, "none of them taking effect." One year later, Elgin had been arrested and briefly jailed after he allegedly wrote a note threatening to kill a deputy sheriff.

But since then there had been no reports of Elgin being arrested. At the time of his death, he was married with two children, and he worked as a cook at the city's finest restaurant, Simon and Billeisen's, on Congress Avenue, helping the chef prepare such dishes as quail, venison, and "fine chops."

Was there a possibility that Elgin's four-toed footprint matched the footprint at the Phillips home? Harry White, a deputy U.S. marshal who had studied and measured the footprints at the Phillips home, never mentioned a missing toe when he testified at Jimmy's trial. He would say only that "the impressions of the heel and toes" were so light that they were "indistinct." Nor did Thomas Wheeless, a notary public who also made measurements of the bloody footprints at the Phillipses', make any statement at Jimmy's trial suggesting there was a missing toe. As for the footprints found in the alley behind the Weeds' house, five toes had clearly been seen, with one of those toes "peculiarly shaped." All in all, a *Daily Statesman* reporter had written, "the rumors relative to Elgin and the crimes . . . are false in every particular."

In fact, at Jimmy's trial, John Hancock never once brought up Elgin's name. So why was he doing it now? Had he come to believe that Elgin really was the Midnight Assassin—or, at the least, part of the gang of bad blacks who had murdered Austin's women? Or was he so determined to get his client Moses Hancock acquitted that he had decided to use every card at his disposal—even if it meant using flawed testimony from a mistaken county sheriff?

The lawyers made their closing arguments, and after a couple of days of deliberations, the vote among the jurors was six for acquittal and six for conviction. A day later, the vote changed to eight for acquittal and three for conviction, with one "doubtful." The foreman went to Judge Walker and said no one was budging, and Walker called a mistrial.

It was now June 6, 1887. After nearly two and a half years of investigations and dozens of arrests, not one man had been convicted for any of the murders of Austin's women.

And in the early morning hours of July 13, the attacks resumed.

CHAPTER TWENTY

In the town of Gainesville, 250 miles to the north of Austin, eighteen-year-old Genie Watkins, the daughter of a wealthy cattleman in nearby Dallas, was visiting her friend Mamie Bostwick, also the daughter of a wealthy cattleman. The newspapers would later describe Genie and Mamie as "handsome girls" who "possessed very loveable dispositions" and who were "quite popular in society." Genie was "a pupil at Dallas High School and stood high in her classes." Mamie attended an all-girls' boarding school in Tennessee.

In the middle of the night, Mamie's mother heard "a scuffling sound" coming from Mamie's bedroom. (Mr. Bostwick was in Chicago on business.) She rose and walked into the bedroom just in time "to see the form of a man jump through the east window." On the bed lay Genie and Mamie "weltering in their blood." The bright light of the full moon "revealed gaping wounds upon the faces of both girls."

Genie had been struck by a hatchet or an ax over the right eye, the force of the blow so strong that it "penetrated both frontal bones" of her forehead. Her right eye itself had been "driven from its socket" and was "lying upon her cheek, hanging only by a slight thread." Mamie had been struck just under her right eye, struck again in the right temple, and struck a third time in the face, from the right corner of her nose to the center of her mouth. Her upper lip "was almost entirely severed."

Mrs. Bostwick began screaming and neighbors came running. Within minutes, the whole town "was in a state of confusion and excitement." Every officer in the city was summoned to the home. One officer took off his hat and fanned the girls. The police department's lone bloodhound was brought to the Bostwicks' backyard, where he sniffed around and quickly took off into the night, running toward a creek bed. But he soon came to a baffled stop.

The next morning, none of the town's stores or banks opened. A "citizen's meeting" was convened at city hall, where the first order of business was to start a reward fund. It quickly reached a total of $200. All of the men at the meeting were "deputized" by Gainesville's sheriff. Some were sent to the railroad depot to look for any suspicious-looking man with bloodied clothes trying to board a train. Others were ordered to "scour the countryside." Still others did home-to-home searches, looking for a killer hiding in a back room.

That afternoon, the son of the Fort Worth sheriff showed up on the train with his bloodhounds. By then, "large footprints" had been found in the Bostwicks' garden. The bloodhounds sniffed the tracks, but because "the ground around the house had been trampled by the many curiosity seekers," they were unable to find any scent worth following.

Although Mamie Bostwick never lost consciousness, her brain was so damaged that she could not remember anything about the attack. Genie Watkins stayed alive for about twenty-four hours before she took her last breath. After a jury of inquest ruled that she had been murdered "by a party or parties unknown," the police released Genie's body to her family, who had it transported by train back to Dallas. According to the newspaper accounts, "at each town along the way people turned out to show their sympathy for the fallen young lady." A procession "stretching several blocks" followed Genie's casket from the Dallas railroad depot to the Floyd Street Methodist Church, where her funeral was conducted. Many of the mourners carried "wreaths and garlands to place upon the bier." Those who couldn't get inside the packed sanctuary stood by the open windows to hear the Rev. G. W. Briggs deliver the eulogy.

Over the next several days, the Gainesville police questioned nine local men—"two Negroes and the rest Mexicans," the *Dallas Morning News* reported. The evidence against them was "so slight" that they were detained for only a short time. With the police investigations going nowhere, the same fear began to sweep through much of North Texas that had swept through Austin. Residents in Gainesville and surrounding towns, and even as far away as Dallas and Fort Worth, slept with their doors closed and their windows "doubly secured." Bands of "armed men" walked the streets from midnight to sunrise. The newspaper in the town of Sherman, thirty-five miles from Gainesville, called on the state legislature to pass a law that would "make it justifiable" for every homeowner "to kill a man or any person upon his premises at night upon sight if he be attempting to hide his actions, no matter whether the object be theft or murder."

Of course, the reporters arrived. Under such sensational headlines as "Two Young Ladies Horribly Mangled While Asleep" and "A Fiend from the Depth of Hades Murders Girls in Their Bed," they left no doubt that the Gainesville attacks were connected to the Austin murders. Just as the *New York Times* had done with Patti Scott's killing in San Antonio, the *Daily Statesman* put together a kind of forensic analysis of the Austin and Gainesville attacks, noting that "Misses Bostwick and Watkins" were both struck in "nearly the same anatomical region" (the right eye) as the "women and girls who were assassinated in Austin." The same correspondent from the *New York World* who had come to Austin after the Christmas Eve 1886 murders soon showed, and he concluded that the two girls had been attacked by the "Intangible Nemesis." In his article, the *World*'s correspondent wrote that "the time of night, the time of the moon, the fact that the victims in each case seemed without an enemy, the similarity of the wounds and the impenetrable mystery which overshadowed each of the crimes, all point to the same bloody hand in the awful work."

Sensing that the state's reputation was taking a serious public relations hit—other newspapers in the East were beginning to call the killer "the Texas Jekyll"—an anxious Governor Sul Ross announced that he would be adding $1,000 to the reward fund that had been raised by Gainesville's citizens. People hurried to their local post offices to mail letters to the governor naming men they believed had done the killings. Someone reported that a traveling salesman was the culprit. Someone else wanted the authorities to check into the whereabouts of a stonecutter who was known to be violent with women. At least one tipster resurrected the old Indian theory, claiming the killer was a crazed Comanche "hiding out" in Indian Territory just north of Texas in Oklahoma (which was not yet a state).

But no arrest was made, which only set off more waves of fear, even in Austin. Convinced the Midnight Assassin still lived among them, biding his time, waiting for the perfect opportunity to carry out his next attack, many homeowners continued to make sure their houses were secure. More "electric burglar alarm systems" were purchased and installed. One woman told the *Daily Statesman* that it was a scientific fact that the last image a murdered person saw remained permanently upon the retinas of his or her eyes. She suggested that a photographer be hired to take a close-up photo of the eyes of the next victim of the Austin killings. When developed, she said, the photo would reveal the face of the killer, and the police could finally solve the murders.

For his part, Mayor Robertson refused to mention any connection between the attacks in Gainesville and Austin. Instead he continued his booming. In one of his speeches, which he gave just after the Gainesville axings, he described Austin as "orderly and prosperous, with a growing moral development and a future promising everything that is good and great." He announced that Austin was growing more rapidly "in wealth and population" than Atlanta, which was considered the greatest city of the South. When the members of the Texas Medical Association arrived in Austin for their annual convention, he gave a welcoming speech in which he actually bragged that Austin had become one of the safest cities in the country. "In Austin, there is freedom from disorder and wrong-doing which would excite red-hot envy in the breast even of a St. Louisan," he proclaimed.

But Robertson's days as a politician were numbered, and he knew it. The news finally broke that he had not hired the famed Pinkerton National Detective Agency of Chicago back in early 1886. William Pinkerton, the co-owner of the agency, had received a letter from relatives of either Eula Phillips or Susan Hancock asking what his detectives believed had happened regarding their loved one's death. He had sent that relative a letter of his own, which was eventually published in the newspapers, saying he had never sent anyone from his agency to Austin. Although an investigation by the aldermen found that Robertson had acted "honestly and squarely"—and that it was not his fault that the detectives he had hired were "of little account"—many residents were furious to learn that he had gone ahead and paid out $3,328.27 in city funds to the fake Pinkertons just to avoid embarrassment.

That fall, Robertson announced he would not be running for reelection in December. He returned to his law practice, his dreams of being known as the man who led Austin into a golden new era permanently dashed. His longtime rival Joseph Nalle quickly declared his candidacy for mayor, calling himself "the people's candidate." He described his platform as one of "sound business and fiscal reform." And he said that unlike the previous administration, he would keep Austin "safe and secure."

This time around, Nalle won the election in a landslide vote. To make sure citizens did feel safer and more secure, he proposed to the aldermen that the Austin Water, Light and Power Company be authorized to set up twenty-five electric lamps on poles twenty to thirty feet high in order to light up more parts of downtown. (The aldermen agreed.) Meanwhile, Marshal Lucy asked Sergeant Chenneville to establish a mounted patrol division: a team of five to ten officers who constantly rode through the city on horseback, ready at any moment to race to the scene of a crime.

By the spring of 1888, Austin had returned again to its "pitch of gaiety." The Driskill Hotel was filled almost every night with visiting businessmen and politicians. (To impress its customers, the hotel's restaurant had begun printing its menus in French.) Charles Millett expanded the stage of his opera house so that he could bring in larger opera companies to perform. Several new downtown businesses opened, including another tobacco shop, another ice-cream parlor, and a hardware store that sold everything from porcelain toilets to wallpaper. And William Radam was selling so much Radam's Microbe Killer that he had announced he would be building factories around the country to manufacture his potion so that all of America's citizens could experience "the greatest discovery of the age." Indeed, Radam was about to get so rich that he would soon leave Austin and move to New York to live in a mansion on Fifth Avenue.

On May 16, the new state capitol building, which had finally been completed after six years of work, was opened with a formal dedication ceremony. The building was, as advertised, a "noble edifice," the biggest statehouse in the union, a Romanesque palace of polished red granite covering three acres of ground, with 392 rooms, 924 windows, twenty-two-foot-high ceilings, and seven miles of wainscoting carved in a variety of woods. On top of the capitol's dome, the Goddess of Liberty smiled placidly, her head crowned in laurel and a sword in her hand. Her facial features had been exaggerated by the stonecutters to make them discernible to everyone on the ground, 311 feet away.

The ceremony for the new capitol was described by one reporter as "one of the highlights of the century in Texas." Dignitaries from around the state came to participate. "Splendid carriages swung up Congress Avenue, through the pink granite gateposts, and up the drive that circled the capitol to discharge party after party of well-dressed officials and observers," wrote another reporter.

During the ceremony itself, six bands alternately played. A chorus sang patriotic songs. Governor Ross rose and gave what a reporter described as "an eloquent and feeling address" about Texas's "unbridled future." Among those in attendance were ten Chicago businessmen— led by contractors Abner Taylor, Charles B. Farwell, and his younger brother John V. Farwell—who had made an agreement with the state

Workmen standing beside the Goddess of Liberty before she was placed atop the capitol's dome in May 1888

legislature back in the early 1880s to build the capitol in return for 3,050,000 acres of raw land, an area the size of the state of Connecticut, located in the Texas panhandle. Already, the Chicago men were transforming their acreage into the largest cattle ranch in the world. They had named the ranch the XIT, which, depending on who one talked to, was either an acronym for the ten Chicago men in Texas or for the fact that the ranch was spread over ten Texas counties. So far, 781 miles of the ranch had been fenced with barbed wire to hold 150,000 head of cattle, and a ranch manager named B. H. "Barbecue" Campbell out of Wichita, Kansas, had been hired. Old-time Texans shook the Chicago men's hands and just laughed. Who would have thought, they said, that the biggest ranch in Texas would be funded and operated by a bunch of non-Texans?

The completed state capitol building

The celebration went on for another five days, with each day marked by parades, concerts, grand balls, and fireworks. Military drill teams came from as far away as Montgomery, Alabama, to perform. The famous Battle of Gettysburg Cyclorama, a giant, 360-degree panoramic painting on the inside of a cylindrical platform that depicted Pickett's Charge, was shipped down from Pennsylvania and set up on the capitol grounds. One afternoon, there was a moment of silence at the capitol for the fallen heroes of the Alamo.

At least 50,000 out-of-town visitors witnessed the week of festivities, and it is probably safe to say that a few of those visitors couldn't help themselves: they hired hacks to drive them past the quarters of the murdered servant women and then past the Hancock and Phillips homes. The visitors swapped shivery stories about the way all the women had been axed and bludgeoned, and they talked in nervous tones about the possibility that the Midnight Assassin was still somewhere in Austin—a man hiding in the shadows.

III

But he never emerged. There were no more ax attacks on any woman in Texas. It seemed that the Midnight Assassin, if there ever was such a man, had indeed moved on to conduct his attacks somewhere else. But where had he gone?

In the first week of September, a story came over the news wires. In the lower-class Whitechapel district in the East End of London, 4,295 miles away from Austin, a man had come across what he believed was a dead animal lying in a poorly lit alley. When he had looked again, he realized he was looking at a woman's body.

She was cut up and drenched in blood.

PART SIX

SEPTEMBER 1888 – AUGUST 1996

"I would suggest that the same
hand that committed the
Whitechapel murders committed
the Texas murders."

CHAPTER TWENTY-ONE

The dead woman's name was Mary Ann "Polly" Nichols, a London prostitute who made so little money that she often was seen begging for food and drink. She had been slashed twice in the throat with a knife, the wounds so deep that she was nearly decapitated. Her skirt had been pushed up to her waist and she had been stabbed as many as thirty-seven times in the abdomen, including twice in the genitals.

Prostitutes had been killed before in London—a metropolis of 5.6 million—but this killing was so gruesome that it had attracted the attention of the press. According to the wire service story, the lead suspect was an unknown man who wandered through the district at night, coming out of the fog to extort money from the prostitutes and beating those who refused to give him what pennies they had. Although none of the women had been able to give a detailed description of the man, other than to say that he wore a leather apron, the police reassured the public that it would only be a matter of time before he was apprehended. Already, they said, they had a suspect they were looking for: a "Jewish immigrant" named Pizer who was a slipper maker by trade and who was known to walk the Whitechapel streets.

It seemed like nothing more than a one-day story. But a *Daily Statesman* reporter who read the wire service dispatch immediately saw a connection—"a striking similarity," he wrote for the newspaper's September 5 edition—between "the murders across the water and the servant girl murders in Austin." He noted that the Whitechapel and Austin murders had been "perpetrated in the same mysterious and impenetrable silence." He also pointed out that the Whitechapel prostitutes had described the man who had attacked them as "a short, heavy-set personage," which was the same description given by Irene Cross's nephew regarding the man who had come into her quarters to murder her in August 1885.

A few days later, on the morning of September 8, the severely mutilated body of another Whitechapel prostitute, Annie Chapman, was found in the back alley of a dilapidated lodging house less than a quarter-mile away from where Polly Nichols's body was discovered. Chapman had a deep knife wound to her neck and more wounds to her abdomen. Her small intestines had been ripped out and thrown to the ground. Part of her uterus was missing.

After Chapman's murder, a letter purportedly from the killer signed "Jack the Ripper" was received by a London news agency. In the letter, which began "Dear Boss," the writer stated that he was "down on whores" and wouldn't "quit ripping them" until he was caught.

The letter set off a panic in the East End. At night, according to one reporter, Whitechapel was "saturated" with police officers. Blood-hounds raced up and down the fog-enshrouded alleys. The Whitechapel Vigilance Committee, made up of a group of volunteer East End citizens, patrolled the streets, looking for suspicious characters.

When it turned out that Pizer, the slipper maker, had a perfect alibi proving that he was not in the Whitechapel area the nights of Nichols's and Chapman's murders, dozens of new tips poured into the Metropolitan Police Service about who this Jack the Ripper could be. Among the suspects was a lunatic butcher, a "fanatical vivisectionist" (a person who injures living animals for scientific and medical research), a mad Polish hairdresser, and a couple of "Jewish paupers."

The police investigation, however, hit nothing but dead ends. On September 30, at 12:45 a.m., a third Whitechapel prostitute, Elizabeth "Long Liz" Stride, was found dead, the victim of a single incision by a knife that severed the main artery on the left side of her neck. Less than an hour later, a fourth prostitute, Catherine Eddowes, was found in a corner of Whitechapel's Mitre Square. Her throat had been cut, and her face, stomach, and pelvic areas slashed. Her intestines were missing, as was her left kidney and uterus.

The London police investigated more suspects, including a Russian con man, an abortionist, and even the actor playing the dual role of Jekyll and Hyde in the stage version of Robert Louis Stevenson's novella, which was being performed that very month at London's Lyceum Theatre. Back in Austin, the *Daily Statesman* was churning out more stories suggesting that Scotland Yard was looking for the wrong man. The murders of the Whitechapel prostitutes, the newspaper said, were almost certainly the work of the Midnight Assassin, who also committed two murders within the span of an hour. "The peculiar mutilation of the bodies, the silence in which they are slain—no outcry—the impenetrable mystery that envelopes the assassin—all tend to make a case almost entirely similar to the series of Austin women murders," the *Daily Statesman* concluded in one of its stories.

Under such headlines as "America's Whitechapel" and "Is the London Monster from Texas?" other American newspapers began pushing the London-Austin connection. The *New York World* weighed in, concluding that "it is by no means impossible that the perpetrator of the Austin murders and the Whitechapel fiend are one and the same . . . a man gratified at the gush of blood, the warm quiver of the flesh and the crunch of cold steel into the bones." The *Atlanta Constitution*, the leading newspaper of the South, also argued that it was perfectly logical that "the man from Texas" would have moved to London:

"The fact that he is no longer at work in Texas argues his presence somewhere else," the *Constitution* explained. "His peculiar line of work was executed precisely in the same manner as is now going on in London. Why should he not be there? In these days of steam and cheap travel, distance is nothing. The man who would kill a dozen women in Texas would not mind the inconvenience of a trip across the water, and once there he would not have any scruples about killing more women."

The fact was that significant differences existed between the Austin and Whitechapel attacks. The victims in Texas had been slaughtered with axes, knives, steel rods, and bricks. Only a knife had been used on the Whitechapel women. What's more, the Texas victims did not have their organs carried away. And there had been no letters written by anyone in Texas claiming credit for the murders or hinting at more attacks to come.

Nevertheless, the idea that Jack the Ripper was a Texan made for sensational copy, and soon the newspapers in England were in on the frenzy. "A Texas Parallel!" cried the *Woodford Times* of Essex. "The monster has quitted Texas and come to London!" trumpeted the *London Daily News*, a newspaper that circulated around the country.

No doubt because they didn't want to have to face the possibility that one of their own would want to dismember prostitutes with such relish, many of England's citizens eagerly embraced the idea that a less civilized American was doing the Whitechapel killings—someone who had grown up surrounded by what one London writer described as "more pernicious cultural influences." It was especially easy to imagine that this American was, as one letter writer put it to London's *Daily Telegraph*, "a Texas rough."

And surely, declared other letter writers, a sophisticated, self-controlled Englishman wouldn't have written that "Dear Boss" letter. The letter's crude grammar and syntax "most certainly" suggested "an American background."

Incredibly, even detectives for the London Metropolitan Police were intrigued by the Texas theory—so much so that they decided to hunt down "three persons calling themselves Cowboys" who had come to England in May 1887, more than a year earlier, as members of Buffalo Bill Cody's Wild West show. Cody had been asked to bring his show to England to perform at the American Exposition, a kind of trade fair designed to promote the United States' latest industrial, mechanical, and agricultural advancements, and he and his entire cast—209 people in all, including the famous female sharpshooter Annie Oakley and 90 "real Indians"—had sailed from New York on the *State of Nebraska* steamship, along with 180 horses, 18 buffalo, 10 elk, 5 Texas steers, 4 donkeys, and 2 deer belowdecks.

At Earl's Court in the heart of London, Cody's Wild West show had played to standing-room-only crowds—as many as 30,000 had come to each performance. One afternoon, Queen Victoria, who was celebrating her Golden Jubilee, arrived. It was reportedly the first time since her husband's death a quarter of a century earlier that she had appeared in person at a public event. The queen was so impressed that she returned to watch a second show on the eve of her Jubilee Day festivities, this time with an assortment of Europe's kings, princes, and princesses. At one point, the Prince of Wales and the kings of Denmark, Greece, Belgium, and Saxony had hopped aboard the Deadwood Stagecoach and, with Buffalo Bill in the driver's seat, ridden around the arena.

During their time in London, however, many of Cody's men who played pistol-waving cowboys had developed rather rowdy reputations. One of the cowboys, Jack Ross, had been charged with "willfully" breaking a plate-glass window at a pub. Another, Richard Johnson, who was billed in the show as "the Giant Cowboy," had been charged with assault at another pub after getting into a fight with two police constables, one of whom had to be hospitalized. Ross and Johnson had been released from jail and allowed to return to Cody's company, which went on to perform in other English cities before heading back to the United States in May 1888. But for unknown reasons three other men who played cowboys had remained in England. Maybe, the police detectives surmised in October, one of those cowboys was not just rowdy but an utterly deranged Wild West killer. And maybe he had come from Austin, Texas.

The detectives found the three men, subjected them to lengthy interrogations, and eventually released them after they "satisfactorily accounted for themselves." The detectives learned that at least four

Lakota Indians from the show had been inadvertently left behind in London and were still wandering the streets. One of them was Black Elk, who had fought at Little Big Horn as a young teenager and in Buffalo Bill's show performed as an Indian chief—"reserved and dignified," the show's announcer called him. The London police were curious to find out if Black Elk had grown so angry over being left behind in London that he had allowed his savage side to take over.

When Black Elk and his fellow Lakota tribesmen were found, however, they too "satisfactorily" accounted for their whereabouts on the dates of the Jack the Ripper murders. As an act of generosity, the English government transported the four Lakota tribesmen to yet another western show that was traveling through Europe—this one run by a promoter named Mexican Joe, who gladly hired them to be his token Indians until they earned enough money to pay for their trips back to their reservations in America, as far away from the civilized white world as possible.

III

At this point, London police detectives figured the "Texas parallel" had hit a dead end. But it hadn't. One afternoon, a detective talked to an English sailor by the name of Dodge who said he recently had gone to have a drink at the Queen's Music-Hall, a working-class pub. There he had encountered a man "of about 5 feet 7 inches in height, 130 pounds in weight, and apparently thirty-five years of age," who was a native of Malaysia.

According to Dodge, the Malay said he had been working as a cook on steamers that came in and out of English ports, and that he recently "had been robbed by a woman of bad character" in Whitechapel. The man had said that "unless he found the woman and recovered his money he would murder and mutilate every Whitechapel woman he met."

The story made the wire services and was cabled to America. One of the reporters at the *Daily Statesman* ripped the story off the telegraph machine and started reading. A Malaysian cook in London? Wasn't there a Malaysian cook at the Pearl House named Maurice? A man who just after the Christmas Eve killings of Susan Hancock and

Eula Phillips had suddenly decided to leave Austin, telling people he was headed for Galveston in hopes of finding a job on a steamer to take him to England?

In the next day's edition of the *Daily Statesman*, there was a long article under the headline, "A WONDERFUL COINCIDENT. Bloody Links Connecting Whitechapel with the Austin Assassinations. A Strange Story Graphically Told of the Crimes with a Malay Cook as the Central Figure." The article reminded readers that "nothing was known" about Maurice's past and that during his time in Austin, he "rarely had been seen about town." It mentioned that "three of the most bloody and cruel of the Austin murders"—those of Eliza Shelley, Mary Ramey, and Susan Hancock—had occurred "three or four blocks away" from the boardinghouse where "this Malay is said to have slept." For a few weeks, Maurice had been "kept under detective eyes, hoping that something definite would be found to warrant his arrest," yet he had done nothing suspicious until he left Austin "during an unguarded moment."

An accompanying editorial stated that it was not just coincidence but "a strong possibility" that the Malay cook at the Pearl House and the London Malay cook on the steamer were "one and the same." The editorialist also speculated that "this inhuman wretch, wandering demon and bloody fiend" could very well be a member of "the secret order of thugs, in the East, who worship Bhavani, the goddess of crime, whose business and occupation is murder, with the cord and the silent knife."

The *Daily Statesman*'s reports were quickly picked up by the wire services and cabled across the ocean. The London newspapers published a number of articles and letters from readers that concluded it made perfect sense that a Malaysian was behind both the Texas and Whitechapel murders. According to a couple of the articles, Malay men were bred to commit such vicious killings. One London writer actually concluded that the mutilations of the Whitechapel prostitutes were all done according to "peculiarly Eastern methods" designed "to express insult, hatred, and contempt."

Sir Charles Warren, chief of the Metropolitan Police, ordered his officers to begin "searching everywhere" for the Malay cook. But they couldn't find him. Nor did any other witness come forward to say that he too had met a Malay who told a story about murdering prostitutes. Eventually, Sir Warren was forced to acknowledge that Dodge, the seaman, probably had invented the entire tale about a Malay killing Whitechapel prostitutes. "The Malay story cannot hold," Warren told a newspaper reporter.

III

Yet even then, the idea of a Whitechapel-Texas connection continued to intrigue people around the world, even those who belonged to the highest circles of academia. On the evening of December 14, 1888, a little more than a month after one more Whitechapel prostitute, twenty-five-year-old Mary Jane Kelly, was discovered eviscerated—her face had been cut, her throat severed down to the spine, and her abdomen emptied of almost all its organs—Dr. Charles Edward Spitzka, America's most famous alienist, arrived at the Academy of Medicine on West 43rd Street, just across the street from Bryant Park, for the monthly meeting of the New York Society of Medical Jurisprudence, made up of a group of the city's most esteemed lawyers and doctors. Although the society's meetings were usually devoted to technical issues regarding medical testimony at criminal and civil trials, the title of this evening's discussion was "The Whitechapel Murders: Their Medico-Legal and Historical Aspects." Spitzka, the society's vice president, had agreed to deliver a long speech laying out his theories about Jack the Ripper.

Spitzka, who was thirty-six years old, was a brilliant doctor—"a man of tremendous intellectual heft," another doctor had once said about him. Raised in New York City, he had gone overseas to study at the medical schools at the University of Leipzig and the University of Vienna, specializing in the field of alienism, the study of people whose minds had become "alienated" from reality. When he returned to New York, he joined the city's Post-Graduate Medical School as a professor of nervous and mental diseases. In 1881, he had been asked to conduct a lengthy examination of Charles Guiteau, the assassin who had shot President James Garfield, and he had made national head-lines when he testified at Guiteau's trial that he was a "moral mon-strosity" who had been driven to kill for reasons beyond his mental control.

In 1883, Spitzka had authored a textbook, *Insanity, Its Classification, Diagnosis and Treatment*, which was immediately hailed as the stan-dard of psychiatric writing in that pre-Freudian era. In articles he penned for such high-flown medical journals as *Alienist and Neurologist* and the *American Journal of Insanity*, he had written that it was a grave mistake to believe that the criminally insane were nothing more than "idiots" or depraved half-human "beasts." Even in the depths of their delusions, they possessed what Spitzka had described as a "reasoning mania."

That evening at the Academy of Medicine, Spitzka walked into the packed lecture hall carrying a sheaf of papers. His red hair was brushed straight back from his brow and his thick mustache ran across his entire face and intersected with long, triangular sideburns. Affixed to the bridge of his nose was a pince-nez.

Spitzka started off with some general comments about other great mass murderers of ancient history. He mentioned the Roman emperor Tiberius, who according to myth killed children and kept their heads for relics, and he brought up the folk talk of Bluebeard, the fifteenth-century French nobleman who supposedly had murdered his many wives. He told the story of the Marquis de Sade, the aristo-crat who tortured women in the late 1700s, and he summarized a few cases of men who found a "voluptuous exaltation" when they com-mitted murder—among them a young Parisian named Louis Menes-clou, "the lilac murderer," who in 1880 had enticed a young girl with lilacs before cutting her into pieces.

Spitzka then spent several minutes expounding on the behavior of Jack the Ripper, describing how he would slaughter a woman without being seen, slip away, and emerge weeks later to slaughter again. Spitzka told his audience that the Ripper's killings were so expertly carried out that he must have honed his technique somewhere else before coming to Whitechapel.

And that very place, Spitzka said after a pause, had to be in Austin, Texas, which had experienced murders that were "terribly similar in every detail" to the Whitechapel killings, in which the victims were "so mutilated that they fell apart on being lifted up."

Spitzka continued, "I would suggest that the same hand that committed the Whitechapel murders committed the Texas murders." He went on to describe this man as having possessed "Herculean strength, great bodily agility, a brutal jaw, a strange, weird expression of the eye—a man who has contracted no healthy friendships, who is in his own heart as isolated from the rest of the world as the rest of mankind is repelled by him."

Perhaps most disturbing, Spitzka added, was that there was no telling where this Texan was today. Spitzka speculated that he may have already "discontinued his work" in London and moved to another city to create his "bewildering horror." Perhaps, said Spitzka, he had returned to the United States and was right there in New York City.

Spitzka even suggested that the murderer of the Texas and Whitechapel women "could be sitting among us at this moment" so that he could hear all the speeches being made about him!

There was a silence. Some of the men in the hall broke out into nervous laughter. But the great Spitzka did not crack a smile.

CHAPTER TWENTY-TWO

In February 1889, just two months after Dr. Spitzka's speech, the *New York Sun* printed a startling story from the city of Managua, the capital of Nicaragua. According to the newspaper, the bodies of six women had been found in that city over a period of ten days.

"Like the women of Whitechapel, they were women who had sunk to the lowest degradations of their calling," stated the *Sun*. "They have been found murdered just as mysteriously, and the evidence points to almost identical methods. Two were found butchered out of all recognition. Even their faces were most horribly slashed, and in the cases of all the others their persons were frightfully disfigured. There is no doubt that a sharp instrument, violently but dexterously used, was the weapon that sent the poor creatures out of the world."

The *Sun*'s story was picked up by the wire services and reprinted in newspapers everywhere, from the London *Times* to the *Taranaki Herald* in New Zealand to the *Daily Republican* in Mitchell, South Dakota. Reporters eagerly speculated that, as Dr. Spitzka had predicted, the Herculean man was on the move. In Austin, under the headline, "Is It the Foul Fiend Himself?," the *Daily Statesman* wrote, "From the surrounding circumstances, does it not seem possible that one and the same person—some wandering, bloody demon, who, after finishing his dreadful tasks, seems to vanish with supernatural skill—may be the author of the Austin homicides, the Whitechapel butcheries and the Central American assassinations?"

It was soon discovered, however, that the entire story was a hoax: police in Nicaragua had not issued any report about prostitutes being killed. Apparently, the *Sun*'s editors had made up the tale just to sell more newspapers. They had learned, as had other newspapers, that any scoop involving Jack the Ripper would give them whopping newsstand sales for that day.

Spitzka continued to push his Herculean-man theory. He published a paper for the *Journal of Mental and Nervous Disease* that reiterated the points he'd made in his New York speech, claiming that one killer had used a small city in Texas as his training ground, honing his skills until he was ready to travel to London, the world's greatest metropolis, to become Jack the Ripper. He went into more detail about the killer, describing him as a man driven by either "singular antipathies" or "romantic notions of revenge."

Yet other alienists found Spitzka's scenario just too hard to swallow. For one thing, the Herculean man's travel itinerary—Texas straight to England—didn't make much sense. If he was obsessed with ripping apart women, wouldn't he have stopped somewhere in between Texas and England to do a few killings? After carrying out the seven murders in Austin between 1884 and 1885—which was followed by the murder in San Antonio of Patti Scott a month later, which was followed by the Gainesville attacks of July 1887—would this Herculean man really have stayed hidden away for a year before reemerging in Whitechapel, of all places, in late August 1888?

Maybe, as one New York reporter wrote, a literate but very disturbed man in London had "read about the Austin murders," which in turn had inspired him to become "the gory slasher of Whitechapel." But that would be about the only connection. The most likely scenario was that the Texas killer was still in Texas.

III

But if that was the case, what had happened to him? At this point, more than three years had passed since an Austin woman had been assaulted or murdered. Marshal Lucy was no longer conducting an official investigation into any of the murders. All of the leads had dried up. There were no more phone calls from tipsters, and no one was coming forward to say he had overheard someone making a drunken confession at one of the saloons. As far as Lucy was concerned, there was nothing more to do.

Similarly, District Attorney Robertson had given up attempting to prosecute anyone for any of the murders. By then, he had decided not to retry Moses Hancock, just as he had earlier decided not to retry Jimmy Phillips, and he had decided to stop pushing his grand jury to come up with new indictments.

Was there a reason Robertson had backed off taking anyone to trial? Had he known all along that he had lacked the evidence to secure a conviction? Robertson wouldn't say. He seemed perfectly content just to forget about the murders altogether. As long as they had stopped, why stir the pot?

Besides, he was hoping to be appointed to the office of state district judge to replace Judge Walker. The last thing he needed was a rival accusing him of botching the prosecutions of the Austin killings.

On Congress Avenue, at restaurants and in the saloons, some citizens continued to swap theories about what had happened to their city. Interestingly, there were plenty of people who were still of the opinion that there never was a Midnight Assassin. They adamantly believed the murders had been committed by uneducated "bad blacks." A few even stuck with the mystical "killing mania" theory. The *Daily Statesman* printed a long interview with a detective from Memphis who was visiting Austin. He said he had been studying the Austin murders and had concluded that both lower-class black criminals and well-regarded white men had been affected by some mystical "suggestion" to murder their girlfriends or wives.

At least some of Austin's residents had to have been comforted by the fact that only a couple of men who had been suspects in the original murders were still living in Austin in 1889. Walter Spencer, Mollie Smith's boyfriend, remained at his mother's home, working at the brick factory, and Anastazio Martinez, the mentally unbalanced Mexican ragpicker, continued to reside at the State Lunatic Asylum. According to a staffer's report, Martinez quietly spent his days "cultivating flowers in the front yard."

As for Oliver Townsend, the infamous chicken thief, he had been sent away to the state prison to serve out a ten-year sentence on what appeared to be a trumped-up burglary charge. Not wishing to suffer the same fate as Townsend, other black suspects like Dock Woods had packed up and left Austin for good.

The white suspects were also gone. Moses Hancock had given up his carpentry business, sold his home on Water Street, and moved to Waco, where people didn't stare at him on the streets. Jimmy Phillips had moved with his young son to the town of Georgetown, forty miles north, where he had found a job at a chair factory. He rarely mentioned the events of 1885 except to complain about his recurring headaches from his ax wound. He met and married a young woman who lived across the street, raised four more children, taught all of them to play musical instruments, and started the Phillips Family Band, which performed at local events.

And William Swain had moved to Houston. After his loss in the 1886 gubernatorial race, he had never been able to build a successful law practice in Austin. Nor had he been able to overcome the rumors that he had been Eula Phillips's lover and perhaps was involved in her murder. In 1888, according to a story in the *Daily Statesman*, when a young woman named Maria Dowd, who had rented a floor of a home owned by Swain's son Walter, got into a dispute over her lease and was evicted, she strode up to Walter and snapped, "Your whole family is just as low as can be. Your father before you was a midnight murderer, and you are no better!" Once he left for Houston to join another law firm, Swain was rarely seen in Austin again.

Mae Tobin was also nowhere to be found. Despite the deal she had made with Mayor Robertson's administration allowing her to maintain her house of assignation off Congress Avenue in exchange for her testimony in Jimmy Phillips's trial, new mayor Joseph Nalle unapologetically had ordered Marshal Lucy to have Tobin escorted out of town. Her house had then mysteriously burned to the ground. "When the last flames were extinguished and the smoking remains were examined," a *Daily Statesman* reporter wrote, "it was plain to be seen that no more scandals would be hatched within its walls; no more victims to murder would be selected from those who frequented its confines; and that all that would be left of it was a charred and blackened mass of weatherboarding, odiferous carpets and ruined second-hand furniture."

Nalle seemed determined to do everything he could to erase all memories of the killings. He proved himself to be as worthy a boomer as his predecessor Robertson, declaring in one speech, "Crimes of a serious nature are almost totally unknown in our midst. A sense of security dwells among the humblest as well as the highest, and a general observance of the law among all classes is a conspicuous virtue that is not passed unnoticed by those who come among us."

Yet the memories—and the fear—were never completely extinguished. Residents were still coming to the Avenue to buy electric burglar alarms, door locks, sleeping potions, and tonics for the nerves. At night, before going to sleep, men set their rifles and pistols beside their beds. One widow, Mrs. Delores Johnson, who was described as among the city's "kindest and most charitable ladies," kept a pistol under her pillow. She and her husband, Dr. Lucian Johnson (who had died earlier that year from natural causes), had been the employers of Eliza Shelley, the servant woman who had been murdered in her quarters behind the Johnsons' home back in May 1885. Mrs. Johnson had been so horrified by what had happened—and so determined that nothing like that would ever happen to her—that she had kept the pistol as close to her as possible.

But that July, while Mrs. Johnson was changing the sheets of her bed, the pistol fell to the floor, discharged, and sent a bullet into her abdomen, almost instantly killing her. The news devastated Austin's residents. It was a cruel twist of fate, they said, that Mrs. Johnson had become one more victim of the Austin killings.

III

Throughout that year of 1889, Alexander P. Wooldridge, the president of the City National Bank who had led the Citizen's Committee of Safety in the aftermath of the 1885 Christmas Eve killings, had been meeting with members of Austin's Board of Trade (the precursor to the Chamber of Commerce) to discuss an idea that he believed would restore Austin's reputation as one of America's great new cities. He wanted the city to build a sixty-foot-high dam on the Colorado River, upstream from Austin, and send the runoff water through an adjoining power station—or "dynamo," as it was then called—to create low-cost electricity.

Wooldridge had originally come up with the idea of a dam one year earlier, claiming that farmers around Austin would be able to use the runoff water to irrigate farmland and grow more crops. But the idea was tabled by a majority of the board members, who wanted instead to promote Austin's religious and social institutions and its temperate climate. Now, with his new proposal for a dynamo, Wooldridge had a better argument. Not only would the owners of factories and manufacturing plants want to move to Austin to take advantage of the dynamo, there would be enough electricity left over for the city to power electric streetcars and to install as many streetlights as it wanted.

Mayor Nalle opposed Wooldridge's proposal, claiming that the cost to build a dam, which was estimated to be at least $1.4 million, would send the city into "ruinous" financial circumstances. Furthermore, he said, there was no telling what the dynamo would cost.

To Nalle's surprise, however, the Board of Trade was thrilled with Wooldridge's idea—and so were Austin's citizens. At the December 1889 city elections, they voted Nalle out of office and voted in John McDonald, a building contractor and unabashed supporter of the dam. A new set of candidates for aldermen, all of them dam supporters, also won their elections, and they quickly agreed to hold a bond election to raise the money to build the dam and the dynamo.

The election was not held for another year; it took place on May 6, 1890. Nevertheless, public support for the project did not waver. The bond package passed by an overwhelming margin, and several hundred citizens gathered on Congress Avenue to celebrate. "A band played and rockets were sent high up to the heavens. Great crackers were fired and Roman candles and colored lights illuminated the whole city," wrote the *Daily Statesman*, which also pointedly noted that among those on the Avenue were "scores of ladies, all in high feather and rejoicing with exceeding great joy."

Were the women celebrating the dam? Or were they celebrating the fact that lights were coming that would allow them, for the first time in at least five years, to walk the streets at night without fear? Was it because they believed the Midnight Assassin would no longer want to live in a city that never went dark?

The *Daily Statesman* did not say. It did not refer at all to the murders. Its reporter simply concluded his story with the line, "Things are brighter and more hopeful for us than ever before in the history of Austin. . . . It is hurrah and huzzah and tol-de-roll loll!"

III

It took three years for the dam to be completed, after which work began on the dynamo. Mayor McDonald and the aldermen met and agreed to spend $153,000 on a "citywide lighting system." Instead of choosing a more modest plan involving more electric streetlights on top of twenty-foot-high poles, like the ones Mayor Nalle had installed when he first took office, McDonald and the aldermen decided to go with the arc lamps, set on very tall towers. With such towers, there not only would be plenty of light, but drunk cowboys leaving the saloons on Saturday nights wouldn't be able to shoot out the lamps the way they had been shooting out the electric lights that had been stationed on the downtown streets.

Ironically, in 1893, there was only one American city—Detroit,

Michigan—that was still using the taller arc lamps, and officials there were preparing to take them down and return to streetlights. Like other cities that had tried them, Detroit officials had found the lamps too expensive to maintain. Indeed, arc lamps no longer captivated the country the way they once had—except in Austin. McDonald and his staff cut a deal with Detroit officials to buy thirty-one of their towers. Made of wrought iron and cast iron, they looked like miniature Eiffel Towers. Each of them was 165 feet tall and weighed approximately 5,000 pounds. To keep them from falling over in a windstorm, guy wires were connected from their triangular frameworks to the ground. On top of each tower, a ring of six high-powered carbon arc lamps were installed.

As opposed to other cities that had put their arc lamps only above railroad depots and downtown shopping districts, Austin's officials placed their lamps across the city to cover as much ground as possible. Finally, on May 5, 1895, everything was ready. At 8 p.m., a switch was flipped at the dynamo, and the turbines started churning, sending electricity racing toward Austin as the engineers gave the lights a ninety-minute test. "There was a sudden blinding flash and the town was in a blaze of white light that hid the rays of the moonlight with its brilliancy," observed a *Daily Statesman* reporter. "In every nook and corner the brilliant lights sent their shooting rays and the whole face of creation was transcendent."

Startled, everyone poured out of their houses to stare at the light. It was so strong, shooting out from each tower in every direction for more than 3,000 feet, that people could read the time on their watches and recognize their neighbors three or four houses away.

"From every section of the city loud shouts of joy were heard," the *Daily Statesman* reporter wrote. "All up and down the Avenue gentlemen were sauntering along, meeting, shaking hands and congratulating one another on the successful outcome of their long cherished scheme."

Once again, the newspaper did not directly connect the arc lamps to the murders. But the reporter did happen to write that Austin's residents had spent years "groping around in that darkness that threatened the life and safety of all." They had been forced to nervously walk streets

THE MIDNIGHT ASSASSIN • 249

In the 1890s Austin erected giant "moonlight towers," which some residents hoped would keep the Midnight Assassin away for good.

that were "steeped in utter darkness." Now, he declared, the people of Austin had "every cause for rejoicing" because the fear of the night was gone forever. "For an hour and a half, the citizens were permitted to gaze at that which might justly be said to be the dawn of a new era in Austin's history . . . the hour of Austin's triumph . . . the realization of Austin's golden dream."

Indeed, he concluded, "The brilliant day of prosperity is now near at hand."

CHAPTER TWENTY-THREE

As the weeks passed, there were, predictably, some residents who didn't like the lamps. They complained about the buzzing sound the lights made. They were bothered by the ash from the carbon that drifted down onto their heads, singeing their hair. The city's gardeners were worried that the constant light would cause their corn and bean stalks to grow around the clock, which would require them to use saws to cut the plants down, and owners of chicken coops feared their chickens would ceaselessly lay eggs twenty-four hours a day until they dropped dead from exhaustion. The drunken cowboys who came to town on Saturday nights were not deterred at all by the tall towers. They circled them on their horses, firing their pistols at the lights, whooping with glee.

Nevertheless, the members of the Board of Trade were so delighted with the lamps that they decided to change Austin's official nickname from "City of the Violet Crown" (in honor of Austin's stunning sunsets) to "The City of Eternal Moonlight." The board published a pamphlet encouraging all Texans to move to Austin to enjoy the benefits of "the greatest illumination of electric light" ever seen in the state. Exuberant real estate developers began building more homes under the moonlight towers, telling potential buyers that they would never again have to worry about crime. One developer, Monroe Martin Snipes, told customers that the upper-class neighborhood he had built on a swath of land in north Austin, which he was calling Hyde Park, was unsurpassed in America. It not only had a moonlight tower, he said, it had "the coolest weather in Austin, the best streets, and absolutely no dust, mud, tenants, liquor or Negroes."

In 1898, three years after the moonlight towers had been erected, Marshal Lucy retired, saying his work was done. He went into private business, taking a job as a vice president of the American Surety Company. The new marshal, Robert Thorp, asked for Sergeant Chenneville's resignation, saying it was time for the old cop to go, his body worn out from all the years he had spent chasing criminals. But Chenneville wasn't able to give up law enforcement completely. He went to work for a private detective agency in Austin called the Merchant Police and Southern Detective Agency, and he kept his bloodhounds in his backyard, in case they were ever again needed.

Even after they had left the police department, neither Lucy nor Chenneville spoke to the newspapers about what they believed had happened in Austin in 1884 and 1885. They never revealed their opinions about the attacks—whether they had been carried out by one man or many. They never speculated—at least not in public—about the existence of a Midnight Assassin.

They weren't the only ones who stayed quiet. After he left office, Mayor Robertson did not speak about the murders, either. His brother James, who did become a state district judge, also said nothing. And the once effusive Dr. Denton of the State Lunatic Asylum never addressed the rumors that one of his own patients had been slipping out at night to chop up women.

What's more, as far as can be determined, Denton never again spoke about his son-in-law, Dr. Given, the asylum's former assistant superintendent who had been legally declared insane six weeks after the Christmas Eve murders. Only a few months after Given had been sent to the branch asylum in the North Texas town of Terrell, he had died of what asylum officials in Terrell described only as "paralysis." Did it turn out that he had been stricken with a bout of syphilis that had made its way to his brain? Denton would never say. He obviously wanted to put that part of his life behind him. By the time the moonlight towers were turned on, he had left the asylum to open the Austin Sanitarium for Nervous and Mental Diseases, a small private hospital filled mostly with wealthy women who suffered afflictions ranging from headaches to hysteria.

A lot of people were ready to put the murders behind them. At least a half-dozen histories of Texas were published in the decade between 1885 and 1895, and not one of them made any reference to the story that Austin had been terrorized by a Midnight Assassin. The California historian Hubert Howe Bancroft, who had sent his researcher and ghostwriter J. W. Olds to Austin in August 1885, right at the height of the killings, had decided the murders were not significant enough to fit into his lofty 841-page opus, *History of the North Mexican States and Texas: 1531–1889*. In his two-volume *History of Texas from 1685 to 1892*, the well-known Texas newspaperman and historian John Henry Brown also ignored the murders, preferring instead to focus on such heroes as Sam Houston, who led Texas in its fight for independence from Mexican rule. Needless to say, Mrs. Anna Pennybacker, the very proper schoolteacher who wrote a textbook in 1888 for the state's public schools, *A New History of Texas*, did not think it was appropriate for the children of Texas to be reading about women being chopped to pieces.

Even the young writer William Sydney Porter, who had written a letter to a friend back in May 1885 about the "Servant Girl Annihilators," never returned to the subject. In 1894, when he started an Austin humor magazine that he titled *Rolling Stone*, he didn't make one reference to the murders, and he didn't write about them when he moved to New York City—after having served a three-year prison stint for embezzling money from an Austin bank, where he had briefly worked as a teller. In New York, he published nearly five hundred short stories under his pen name O. Henry. Several of his characters were based on people he had met in Texas or in prison. He wrote about bums, swindlers, kidnappers, and safecrackers. He wrote stories about a stagecoach robber named Black Bart and an Old West outlaw named the Cisco Kid. But he didn't use the killings as fodder for any of his writing. He didn't create his own fictional version of a Midnight Assassin. Apparently he had concluded that the entire saga was far too grisly for his more lighthearted literary temperament.

At least for a while, the Austin killings did remain a topic of interest among the country's alienists. When they met at New York's Academy of Medicine—the very place where Dr. Spitzka had delivered his infamous speech claiming that the Midnight Assassin and Jack the Ripper were the same "Herculean" man—they periodically discussed the issue of "moral insanity," which at the time was considered to be a medical condition, no different than a physical illness, afflicting those who in almost all ways were normal except that they were unable to control certain emotions. At one meeting, several alienists declared the servant girl assassinations were a prime example of the damage that a morally insane man could inflict on society with his "abnormal conduct." In this case, he couldn't control his ingrained hatred of women.

The alienists came up with a list of factors that they believed would lead seemingly normal human beings with "unimpaired mental facilities" to come down with moral insanity and go on a killing rampage. Some declared that the morally insane were obviously the offspring of "intermarriage among criminals and drunkards." Others said they must have suffered some sort of childhood injury, such as a blow to the head or a mental shock that destroyed part of their mental capabilities. There were alienists who argued that certain people had been born with "impaired or defective nervous tissue" that led them to a life of crime. Dr. Graeme M. Hamfriend, a professor of nervous and mental diseases at the New York Post-Graduate Medical School and Hospital, declared in one speech, "As the artist and musician get their power of artistic creation from some brain conformation that was born in them, so this criminal gets his life tendency in the same way."

And there were a few alienists who advocated a theory that had first been formulated by the German alienist Richard von Krafft-Ebing.

In 1886, he had published a scholarly work titled *Psychopathia Sexualis*, which was regarded as the first-ever academic study of sexual perversion: page after page of information about pederasts, satyrs, rapists, sadomasochists, masturbators, homosexuals, child molesters, and fetishists (people obsessed with certain parts of the body or with objects like handkerchiefs). After the Jack the Ripper murders, Krafft-Ebing had updated his book to include a section on men who committed what the Germans called *Lustmord:* lust murder. Krafft-Ebing was convinced that these men found ultimate physical pleasure—"a state of exaltation, an intense excitation of the entire psycho-motor sphere"—in the murder of women, followed by savage postmortem mutilations on their bodies. For some alienists, the Midnight Assassin was the perfect embodiment of Krafft-Ebing's "lust murderer."

At their meetings, the alienists did try to come up with ways to identify and stop a morally insane "monstrosity" like the Midnight Assassin before he wreaked his particular havoc. Dr. Allan McClaine Hamilton, the attending physician at the New York Hospital for Nervous Disease, who was often described in the press as a "famous insanity expert," advocated for a nationwide sterilization program that he hoped would prevent such men from ever being born in the first place. "The state should have the right to forbid the marriages of habitual criminals, or persons of insane heritage and of consumptives," he declared. "Further than that, habitual criminals should be prevented from having children altogether. . . . The least that can be said is that society has the right to protect itself from [the morally insane] just as it has the right to protect itself from mad dogs."

But Hamilton and the other alienists did not have to be told that they had little chance of protecting innocent citizens from men who were able to conceal their depraved personalities behind masks of normality. In October 1895—five months after Austin's moonlight towers had been erected—the news broke that Dr. Henry Howard Holmes, a wealthy and well-educated graduate of the University of Michigan's medical school, had been accused of murdering at least twenty women he had met at a hotel he had built in Chicago to house out-of-town visitors for the 1893 Chicago World's Fair. Holmes had killed his victims in windowless rooms, usually by asphyxiation, and then had whisked their bodies down a secret chute into the basement, where he had dissected them and later sold their organs and skeletons to medical schools.

What was perhaps most disturbing about Holmes's murders was that he had carried them out over a period of six months without arousing the slightest suspicion. It wasn't until he was arrested in Boston for other murders that his scheme in Chicago was discovered.

The ghastly tale was splashed on the front pages of newspapers around the country, including the *Daily Statesman*. At least, some of Austin's residents must have said after reading the story, the city of Chicago had been able to find its killer. At least Chicago had some sort of ending.

III

As the nineteenth century gave way to the twentieth, the Midnight Assassin was still being ignored by Texas historians. But people in Austin hadn't forgotten about him—not completely. Children had devised their own nickname for the Midnight Assassin: they called him the "Axe Man." They raced for their homes as the sun was setting, shouting to one another that the Axe Man was hiding in the shadows just beyond the light of the moonlight towers, waiting for them to come close so he could grab them.

"We all heard stories that he had never left, that he was walking the streets," said Mrs. Myrtle Callan, who was born in Austin in 1902 and after college taught history for many years at the city's Texas School of the Deaf. In the last years of her life, Mrs. Callan compiled forty-six scrapbooks about Austin's history and she frequently received guests in her little gray-painted home who wanted to know more about the city's past. "I'd ask my parents what he did to those women, but they wouldn't talk about it," she told a visitor in the spring of 2002, a few years before her death at the age of 105. "They didn't want me to have nightmares. But I did. He was like a ghost."

He wasn't the only ghost. Some residents swore that they saw a young woman, dressed in a white gown, her complexion like marble, walking the grounds of the new state capitol late at night. Others said they had seen her at the foot of Congress Avenue, near the spot where Mae Tobin had run her house of assignation. It was the ghost of Eula Phillips, they believed—warning other women to live chaste lives, else they would be killed, too.

And there were days when an elderly black woman would be seen hobbling along the Avenue. But she was no phantom. It was Rebecca Ramey, the mother of young Mary, who had been slaughtered in V. O. Weed's backyard shed. Rebecca now lived at the home of another daughter, Minnie. Because of the blows she herself had received during the long-ago attack, her brain was damaged and her face still disfigured. Whenever she walked the Avenue with her family, pedestrians passing by turned their heads so they didn't have to look at her.

Rebecca died in 1910. As far as can be determined, she was the last female survivor of the attacks—at least the last one who was in Austin. It is not clear what happened to Lucinda Boddy and Patsy Gibson, the two young servant women who had suffered severe head injuries after being assaulted in Gracie Vance's servants' quarters. Because Lucinda and Patsy had been unable to work or care for themselves, they were most likely taken to the County Poor Farm, where many infirm and elderly blacks were sent to live out the rest of their lives. Without medical treatment, it's hard to imagine they lived for very long. They would have been buried in unmarked graves at the back of the farm—two more victims of the killings.

For years, the murders had a long, lingering effect on Austin's black population. Jim Crow policies came early to Austin because of the white residents' fear—and distrust—of the "bad blacks." Just after the turn of the century, the city aldermen passed an ordinance that required the separation of blacks and whites on streetcars. There were also proposals to move all the black residents to East Austin. If kept in one place, said many whites, the police would have less trouble keeping tabs on all the city's worst black characters.

The city's black leaders were routinely ignored by the white establishment. In truth, for a long time, there were no black leaders at all. After Albert Carrington's loss to a white man in the aldermen's race in

able on the January 1886 killing of the San Antonio servant woman Patti Scott. I drove to the library in the north Texas town of Gainesville to see what information it had on the 1887 ax attacks on the two white teenagers, Mamie Bostwick and Genie Watkins.

Was the Midnight Assassin involved in those two incidents? I could not say for certain. But just like that, I was back on the hunt again, convinced that there was no way he simply could have *stopped* killing.

I looked into a rumor that Henry Holmes, who had carried out the grisly 1893 World's Fair killings in Chicago, had spent time in Texas in the 1880s. It wasn't true. (Holmes had come to Texas for a brief period *after* the Chicago killings.) I investigated another rumor that Eugene Burt, the son of Dr. William Burt, the staff physician of the City-County Hospital, was the Midnight Assassin. In 1896, at the age of twenty-six, Eugene had murdered his wife and two children with a hatchet and thrown their bodies down a cistern in the basement of their home. He was soon arrested, found guilty at trial, and executed. His relatives described him as a young man who had lost his mind.

Was it possible, I wondered, that Eugene's desire to kill had started back in 1885, when he was only fifteen years old? I remembered that he had been one of the townspeople who had come to the Hancocks' on Christmas Eve and that he had found the ax in the backyard that had been used to kill Mrs. Hancock. Did Eugene know all along where the ax was because he had put it there?

But at Eugene's trial, his relatives said he was a mostly normal teenager until his father died in 1886, nearly a year after the Austin murders had come to an end. At that point, Eugene began to show "marked depravity." Surely, I thought, if that depravity had emerged at a much younger age, someone would have noticed. And surely, if he had killed the Austin women, he would not have been able to wait a decade before killing again.

Although I seriously doubted that there was any connection between the Midnight Assassin and Jack the Ripper, I figured I had nothing to lose by traveling one weekend to Galveston's library to see if the name of Maurice, the Malaysian cook, was listed on any of the ships that had left Galveston's port for England between 1886 to 1888. His name was nowhere to be found. On another day, I called the senior curator of the Buffalo Bill Historical Center in Wyoming to ask if he had any information on the "three American cowboys" from Buffalo Bill's Wild West show who had stayed in London after the show ended and who had been questioned during the Jack the Ripper murders by London police detectives. Was it possible, I asked, to find out the names of those cowboys in hopes of learning if any of them had been living in Austin from 1884 to 1885? The curator lightly coughed and told me he would call me back. Needless to say, he did not.

I was able to trace the life of the Lakota Indian Black Elk, the other Buffalo Bill cast member who had been interrogated by the London police after he had accidentally been left behind by the show. When Black Elk returned to the United States in 1889, he went straight to his homeland: the Pine Ridge Indian Reservation in South Dakota, where he was named one of the tribe's medicine men. In December 1890, the U.S. Cavalry attacked the Lakotas in what would become known as the Battle of Wounded Knee. Black Elk rode out to the battlefield, hoping to take of care of survivors and end the bloodshed, and he was grazed in the side by a soldier's bullet. Black Elk lived until the age of eighty-seven, trying until the end of his life to promote harmony between white men and Native Americans. He published a famous autobiography, *Black Elk Speaks*, which is now considered a classic of Native American literature. In his book, he wrote that he had joined Cody's show and come to England because "I wanted to see the great water, the great world and the ways of the white men." But the legendary medicine man never wrote about those strange days when he was taken to Scotland Yard, suspected of having carried out savage attacks on women in Whitechapel.

Finally, I spent an hour talking to Shirley Harrison, a London "Ripperologist"—an amateur researcher obsessed with the Jack the Ripper killings—who believed that James Maybrick, a well-to-do English cotton merchant, had come to New Orleans in late 1884 for the beginning of the World's Industrial and Cotton Centennial Exposition, slipped over to Austin to do the killings, and then returned to London to become Jack the Ripper. Although Harrison admitted to me

1885, during the height of the murders, it would not be until 1971 that a black man was again elected to the city council.

III

By the 1930s, all of the homes and servants' quarters where the attacks had occurred were gone, demolished in the name of progress, replaced by bigger homes, office buildings, a bank, a restaurant, and, at one point, a parking lot for automobiles. New residents arrived and the city grew far beyond the light of the arc lamps. A couple of towers were dismantled because they were considered unstable, and others were taken down to make way for construction projects. One was knocked over by an errant vehicle. During World War II, city officials ordered that a central switch be installed at the city's electric department that could be used to immediately turn off all the lamps in case there was a Nazi or Japanese air raid. But the switch was never used. The lamps on top of the towers kept burning, night after night, still symbolically protecting Austin's citizens from the dark.

Of course, even with the lamps, Austin wasn't spared from evil—at times, unimaginable evil. On a sunny morning in August 1966, a twenty-five-year-old architectural engineering major named Charles Whitman, who had been complaining of searing headaches and depression, took an elevator to the observation deck of the 307-foot-high University of Texas Tower, which had been built in 1937. According to one newspaper's description, Whitman was "a good son, a top Boy Scout, an excellent Marine, an honor student, a hard worker, a loving husband, a fine scout master, a handsome man, a wonderful friend to all who knew him—and an expert sniper." He pulled out an M-1 carbine rifle, aimed at the pedestrians below, and in the space of ninety-six minutes shot forty-three people, killing thirteen, before he himself was gunned down by an Austin police officer. One reporter later wrote that the tower killings "introduced the nation to the idea of mass murder in a public space."

Whitman, of course, was chronicled in an array of history books. He was analyzed by psychiatrists, the new name for alienists, who used such modern terms as "psychopath" instead of "morally insane" to explain his behavior. Numerous journalists studied his childhood, his years in the military, and even his brain chemistry. They noted the impact Whitman's shootings had made on Austin's ordinary citizens, leaving them trembling with terror, haunted for the rest of their lives.

And what about the Midnight Assassin, who eighty-one years earlier had introduced the nation to the idea of serial murder?

Incredibly, he remained forgotten by historians. It was as if he had walked out of history altogether. It was as if he had never existed.

EPILOGUE

"If no one could catch the killer back when he was alive, what makes you think you can catch him now?"

Austin in the 1890s, seemingly a city at peace

Today, Austin is 271 square miles in size with a population of nearly one million residents. More than 55,000 students attend the University of Texas and another 50,000 citizens work for the state government. The city has become renowned as a haven for technology companies, research consortiums, advertising agencies, and filmmakers. Because there are nearly a hundred bars and nightclubs that feature musical groups, Austin's official nickname has now become "the Live Music Capital of the World."

A few landmarks remain from 1885: the granite-pink state capitol, of course, as well as the governor's mansion; the Driskill Hotel; the Corinthian-columned administrative building of the State Lunatic Asylum, which is now known as the Austin State Hospital; Millett's Opera House, which has become a private dining club; a few other downtown buildings; and a handful of private homes that had been built for the city's wealthiest residents.

And scattered around the city are fifteen moonlight towers. They are essentially useless, the pale glow of the lamps barely visible above the harsher glare coming from hundreds of electric and mercury lights closer to the streets. But they are not going anywhere. In the 1970s, city officials were able to get the towers designated as state and national historical landmarks. In their written applications to obtain such designations, the officials never mentioned the murders. They didn't explain that Austin residents in the late 1880s had wanted the towers erected because they were still very anxious about what lurked in the dark. The towers were simply described as quaint, nostalgic relics of a time gone by, as much a part of Austin as the streetcars are of San Francisco.

In 1998, when I first heard about the murders, I had trouble believing the story was true. A lone man called the Midnight Assassin was wandering the streets of Austin with an ax, a knife, and an icepick, slaughtering women at will? And the famous moonlight towers had supposedly been built to keep him away? I couldn't help but laugh out loud. The whole tale seemed like something straight out of bad fiction. Besides, I said, if these murders had taken place, shouldn't I have read about them in the history books?

Still, I was intrigued enough to head to the Austin Public Library and to the Dolph Briscoe Center for American History at the University of Texas to read the tiny, faded newsprint of nineteenth-century Texas newspapers preserved on microfilm. And it wasn't long before I discovered that the Midnight Assassin was not only very real, he was unlike any killer in history—a sadistic but remarkably cunning monster who on some nights only wanted to scare women, who on other nights only wanted to assault them, and who, on seven nights between December 1884 and December 1885, decided to unleash all of his rage, tearing apart his victims so quickly that they didn't have a chance to scream.

I actually found myself marveling at the audacity and the execution of his Christmas Eve killings: axing Susan Hancock just before midnight in the southern end of downtown, dragging her out to her backyard, and immediately racing to the northern end of downtown, only a couple of blocks from the police department, where he axed Eula Phillips and dragged her into her backyard.

What I found most astonishing about the Christmas Eve rampage was that the killer allowed Susan's and Eula's husbands, as well as Eula's infant son, to live, just as he had allowed someone to live at the scenes of all of his other murders. He seemed utterly confident that he would not be seen—or, at least, identified. In that regard, he was absolutely correct. Of the eight people who were left alive at his various murder scenes, only two got a fleeting glimpse of him, and both of them were children: the seven-year-old son of Eliza Shelley, who thought the man was white, and the twelve-year-old nephew of Irene Cross, who thought the man was black.

The more I read, the more I was determined to get to the bottom of what Mayor Robertson had described as "the mystery of the murders." I began digging through barely legible city records and police files, pored over more newspaper articles, and tried to decipher handwritten transcripts of inquests and examining trials. I held magnifying glasses over sepia-toned photographs, the edges of the photos disintegrating, the albumen in some places completed absorbed by the paper, and I looked for victim's tombstones at the former city cemetery.

I also hunted down grandchildren and great-grandchildren of Austin residents who were affected by the murders, asking if any family stories had been passed down over the years about the Midnight Assassin. Almost everyone I contacted—including descendants of Grooms Lee, James Lucy, Sergeant Chenneville, Mayor Robertson, District Attorney Robertson, and Alexander P. Wooldridge—knew next to nothing about the murders. I placed a call to Dorothy Larson in California. Mrs. Larson is the granddaughter of Eula Phillips's sister Alma. I told her that I was investigating the Austin murders of 1884 and 1885. There was a silence. Mrs. Larson said, "What murders?"

I asked Mrs. Larson if she knew how her great-aunt Eula had died. There was another silence, this one even longer. She finally said, "Eula? You know about Eula?"

She told me that her grandmother had rarely mentioned Eula during her lifetime, saying only that she had been found dead in an alley. "And now you are telling me she was murdered?" she asked.

I recounted what I knew of Eula: her marriage to the abusive Jimmy, her trips to Mrs. Tobin's house of assignation, and her mutilated body discovered in the backyard. When I was finished, Mrs. Larson seemed to be holding back tears. She said, "So that explains why my grandmother would always say to me, 'Honey, don't ever do anything that would make you ashamed to see your name in the newspaper.' It was her favorite phrase."

We ended our conversation. A few days later, the phone rang. It was Mrs. Larson. She told me had searched through her garage and found a tattered photo album that her grandmother had kept throughout her life. Next to a photo taken of Alma as a young woman was a photo of another young woman. "I always wondered who the other girl was and why my grandmother had her photo," Mrs. Larson said. "Now I realize it was a photo of Eula. All these years, Alma kept these memories of her sister—her beautiful, doomed sister." She asked me to talk about Eula some more—what she looked like and how she had acted. "She must have been so lonely," Mrs. Larson said when I finished. And then there was another very long silence.

III

As the months passed, I searched through even more Texas newspapers looking for details about the murders, and I traveled to the New York Public Library to read the *New York World*'s stories. I wrote an article about the Midnight Assassin for *Texas Monthly* magazine, hoping other descendants would read it and contact me with more clues. I did speak to Peyton Abbott, the grandson of V. O. Weed, who had been the employer of Rebecca and Mary Ramey. A resident of Colorado, Abbott told me that his grandfather had bought a police whistle in late 1885 to blow in case the killer came around a second time. "I've got the whistle in a little box if you want to come up here and look at it," Abbott said. "But that's about all I know."

Months passed. On a map of Austin made in the 1880s, I marked where every murder had taken place. I tried to guess what escape route the killer would have taken and where he would have hidden. On a sheet of paper I wrote down the names of all the homeowners whose servant women were murdered, and I attempted to find out if there was any connection among them. Maybe they attended the same church. Maybe they went to Turner Hall on Tuesdays for its roller-skating night. On another sheet of paper I wrote down all the possible links between Mrs. Hancock and Eula, thinking there had to be some particular reason the Midnight Assassin targeted those two women.

But nothing turned up. Maybe, I said, completely reversing myself, it was pure coincidence that the Christmas Eve double murders ever took place at all. Maybe, after killing Mrs. Hancock, the Midnight Assassin had raced away on horseback, headed toward downtown, seen Eula leaving Mrs. Tobin's house of assignation, and followed her home to kill her, too.

I decided to look through state prison records for information on the original black suspects who had been arrested in 1885 to try to find out if any of them had committed murder later in their lives. I came up empty. I did learn that Oliver Townsend, the chicken thief who had been sent to prison on a burglary charge in 1886, reportedly escaped from a prison chain gang in 1895, when he was in his midthirties. Yet there were no records indicating where he went or what he did.

I filed an open records request with the state attorney general's office to review patient records from 1884 and 1885 at the State Lunatic Asylum, my goal being to find some notation that suggested one of the patients had been slipping out of the asylum at night. When the records were made available a year later, I read about a man who was obsessed with drinking his own urine and another man who was so convinced he was Napoleon Bonaparte that he wore a bicorne and an epaulet on his shoulder. I read about a teenager who believed that he had swallowed a stick of dynamite and was afraid he was about to explode, and I read about Lombard Stephens, the deranged patient in the Cross Pits who had sent Governor Ireland several letters vowing that he would eat the governor's brains if he was not paid $500,000.

But there was no indication that any patient had been under suspicion for making his way to Austin to assault women. Nor was there any hint that a staffer, such as Dr. Given, the asylum's assistant superintendent, had engaged in such behavior. I was so obsessed with Given that I contacted the University of Edinburgh in Scotland, where he had been a medical student in the 1870s. During those years, one of his classmates was Robert Louis Stevenson, who later would write *The Strange Case of Dr. Jekyll and Mr. Hyde*. I wondered if Given exhibited any behavior during his years in Edinburgh that would have inspired Stevenson to start formulating a story about a doctor whose mind seemed to be occupied by two seemingly opposite personalities, each striving for the upper hand. But once again, I came across nothing.

Like so many of Austin's citizens back in the 1880s, I kept saying there was no way that the Midnight Assassin could have gone for an entire year killing women in such a small city and remaining unnoticed. He had to have done or said something that would have drawn at least a little suspicion. Nevertheless, my list of suspects was narrowing. At one point, I learned that Grooms Lee, the young man who had been named Austin's marshal in December 1884, had never married and rarely associated with women. I came up with a theory that he harbored a secret but unrepentant hatred of women, which led him to become the Midnight Assassin. When I actually said this out loud to one of Lee's descendants, a sweet, elderly woman named Lois Douglas who lived outside of Austin, she gave me a confused look and said, "I was always told that Grooms was a nice boy, a very nice boy with a good smile." She pointed out that Lee had lived out the rest of his days in Austin, never causing a bit of trouble before he died in 1923. "He never wanted to hurt people," Mrs. Douglas said politely. "I think you are very mistaken."

III

Eventually, some friends and family members suggested that the time had come for me to move on. They seemed to be worried that I was following one too many rabbit trails. A man I knew pulled me aside at a party and said that I reminded him of one of those amateur researchers who had become obsessed with solving the mystery of President Kennedy's assassination.

For a few years, I did stop researching the murders. I tried not to think about them. But one afternoon, when I was in San Antonio, I found myself visiting its public library to see what reports were avail-

that she had little proof whatsoever to back up her claims—and I could find no evidence Maybrick ever came to Texas—she chuckled and said that her theory "makes as much sense as anything you've come up with."

In all fairness, I couldn't argue with her. Because there are so many unanswered questions about what exactly had happened on those dark Austin streets in 1884 and 1885—so little in the way of physical evidence, or police records—no suspect can be dismissed entirely. Even the most sober scenario regarding the identity of the Midnight Assassin holds no more water than the most hare-brained.

And maybe that is why, all these years later, the story remains so haunting. We are as fascinated by what we do not know as by what we do know. Indeed, in many ways, the rampage of the Midnight Assassin is the perfect crime story—a rip-roaring whodunit of murder, madness, and scandal, replete with the sorts of twists and shocks that give a page-turner its good name.

Except there is one catch. There is no dramatic last-act revelation, no drum-roll finale. Everything ends up precisely where it started, in a gray limbo of unknowing. The trail of clues just stops, like bewildered bloodhounds baying in the night.

III

I've often been asked what would happen if the Midnight Assassin were operating today. The answer is that he most likely would have been caught after the first murder, of Mollie Smith. Police detectives would have at their disposal an array of forensic tools—DNA tests, fingerprints, and blood typing—to find their man. They would be able to study security footage from cameras along city streets, and they would have dozens of patrol officers following up on citizens' tips. If they got stuck, they would be able to call the Federal Bureau of Investigation to ask for a team of agents trained in behavioral science to fly in from Quantico.

But then, who knows for sure? As that *New York World* reporter wrote in 1886, the Midnight Assassin did indeed "give to history a new story of crime." He was a performance artist with a signature style, apparently operating without any apparent motive, destroying his victims for nothing more than the pure pleasure it brought him. He sent a city spiraling into chaos—and then, improbably, he disappeared forever, faceless and elusive, without even taking a bow.

And more than a century later, we still do not know his name.

Was the Midnight Assassin a barefoot black man from an impoverished neighborhood? Was he a lunatic from the asylum? Was he some sort of itinerant madman who spent a year in Austin before moving on? Or was he a gentleman who wore a Stetson and a fine suit and whose daily demeanor gave no indication that he possessed any talent for crime?

I remain convinced—or perhaps it's better to say that I remain full of hope—that the answer is still out there, locked up inside some musty filing cabinet in the Austin police archives or buried in someone's attic among long-forgotten letters that have grown moldy with age. I continue to beg anyone who has any information about the killings—any theory at all—to contact me. But, I have to admit, I have never forgotten a conversation that I had with Peyton Abbott, the grandson of V. O. Weed, who had bought the police whistle to blow whenever the Midnight Assassin returned.

"The old man kept that whistle with him for the rest of his life, waiting to blow it, knowing the killer was out there," Abbott told me. "But he never blew that whistle—not once."

After a pause, Abbott asked me a question. "If no one could catch the killer back when he was alive, what makes you think you can catch him now?"

When I wasn't sure what to say, he chuckled softly. "Sometimes, you just have to accept the fact that some mysteries are never solved," he said, and chuckled again. "That's why they are mysteries, you know."

NOTES AND SOURCES

Much of this book is based on hundreds of articles from more than thirty nineteenth-century newspapers. Sometimes the articles were a few hundred words long—the *New York World*'s feature story was the exception. Sometimes they lasted no more than a couple of sentences. Each anonymous author tended to add a detail or two about whatever was happening: a murder, an investigation into a murder, or the arrest of a suspect. I often felt that I was putting together a giant jigsaw puzzle, made up of thousands of pieces—and there were still so many pieces missing. In my mind, I kept urging those nineteenth-century reporters to ask follow-up questions of city officials and police officers, to do more investigations into particular suspects, to find out if a man did, in fact, accompany Eula Phillips to Mae Tobin's house of assignation on Christmas Eve. I wished one of those reporters had gone to Marshal Lucy or Sergeant Chenneville toward the end of their lives and persuaded them to reveal all they knew. Alas.

At the same time, however, I came across a rich seam of material that captured the pulse of a young city as it was making its way into the modern age. I read dozens of books, dissertations, manuscripts, letters, journals, and yes, more newspaper articles about Austin. In many ways, Austin became the most interesting character in the book, an intoxicating mixture of the Old South, the Old West, and the new Gilded Age. Because the murders affected every level of Austin society—from the most privileged members of white society to desperately impoverished African-Americans—I had a rare opportunity to create a portrait of race, class, gender, urban life, and, most significantly, the nature of American violence. Indeed, the Midnight Assassin's rampage was a freakish foretaste of what was to come in American life, especially in the rapidly growing, behaviorally volatile cities. That is why, at least for me, his story is so important.

One side note: there has been a long debate among Austin history buffs over the role the murders played in the erection of the city's "moonlight towers." When the idea of the towers was first proposed, three and a half years had passed since the last murder had taken place. What's more, there is no evidence that any city leader publicly declared that the towers would keep away the Midnight Assassin. On the other hand, the question still has not been answered as to why the towers were erected at the very time that other cities were taking them down. Why didn't Austin's leaders just erect regular streetlamps—lots of them? And why did they want the towers spread throughout the city and into the white neighborhoods, instead of just putting them around downtown like other cities had done?

I keep wondering about the reporter for the *Austin Daily Statesman* who, on May 4, 1895, when the lamps in the towers were first turned on, speculated about the possibility that the light would end Austin's fear of violent crime at night, which he claimed had lingered for many years. Was the reporter making a reference to the Austin killings of 1884 and 1885? I tend to think he was, but I'm not sure we will ever know.

PROLOGUE

"London police officials were speculating" comes from Hudon's "Leather Apron; or, The Horrors of Whitechapel," p. 10.

The *New York World* article ran on January 1, 1886.

"The Midnight Assassin" was reported in the *San Antonio Daily Express*, September 8, 1885.

Women being given guard dogs comes from the *Austin Daily Statesman*, December 29, 1885. The proposal for electric lights comes from the *Austin Daily Statesman* on March 21, 1886.

Coverage of the New York Academy of Medicine meeting was reported in the December 20, 1888, issue of the *Boston Medical and Surgical Journal*; the January-June 1889 issue of the *Weekly Medical Review*; and the *New York Herald*, December 14, 1888. "The most extensive and profound scandal" was reported in the *Houston Daily Post*, May 26, 1886.

The Kenward Philp short story was reported in the *Austin Daily Statesman* on January 13, 1886, and the *Fort Worth Gazette* on January 18, 1886.

CHAPTER ONE

Details on the late December cold front are taken from the *Austin Daily Statesman, San Antonio Daily Express, Dallas Daily Herald,* and *Bastrop Advertiser* between December 12, 1884, and January 20, 1885. Also see Gard's *Rawhide Texas,* p. 4; and the diary of Austin resident Eugene Bartholomew, p. 146.

Details on the Hall family and its Austin residence come from the *Austin Daily Statesman* on November 13, 1881, December 25, 1883, January 1, 1885, and January 2, 1885. Information on Tom Chalmers comes from the *Austin Daily Statesman* on April 29, 1884. Details on the Texas Rangers are from Robinson's *The Men Who Wear the Star: The Story of the Texas Rangers,* pp. 168–79.

Information on Walter Spencer comes from the 1880 U.S. Census records and the *Austin Daily Statesman* on August 7, 1881, and June 19, 1884. Details on Butler's brick factory come from William Owens's interview in *Mann's Slave Narratives*, pp. 7–8.

Biographical detail on Mollie Smith comes from the 1880 U.S. Census; the *Austin Daily Sun* (a short-lived newspaper that closed in March 1885), on January 1, 1885; the *Austin Daily Statesman* on July 7, 1882, January 1, 1885, January 2, 1885, and January 3, 1885; the *Fort Worth Gazette* on November 15, 1885; and the *Frederick News* of November 20, 1888. Mollie's life and duties as a servant was taken from accounts in the *Austin Daily Statesman*, January 3, 1883; *Lippincott's Monthly Magazine*, March 1, 1883; the *Christian Messenger*, May 27, 1885; and Sutherland's *Americans and Their Servants*, pp. 12–122. Mollie called a "yellow girl" comes from the *Austin Daily Statesman*, May 26, 1885.

The accounts of the late-night conversation between Spencer and Chalmers are taken from the *Austin Daily Sun*, *Austin Daily Statesman*, *Galveston Daily News*, *Houston Daily Post*, and *Fort Worth Gazette* of January 1, 1885.

CHAPTER TWO

Estimates of Austin's population in 1885 vary, ranging from 11,000 to 23,000. The lower number was usually thrown out by Austin's critics and the 23,000 was trumpeted by Austin's boosters. A more unbiased estimate of 17,000 comes from Moffatt's *Population History of Western U.S. Cities and Towns, 1850–1900*.

Description of the police department comes from the *Austin Democratic Statesman*, a forerunner to the *Austin Daily Statesman*, March 19, 1876; from the Sanborn Fire Insurance Maps of Austin from June 1885; from photos of Austin City Hall, gathered by the Austin History Center of the Austin Public Library; and from Barkley's *History of Travis County*, pp. 222–29.

Winds tangling telephone lines is based on reports in the *Austin Daily Statesman* from March 22, 1884, and May 16, 1970; and the *San Antonio Daily Express* from January 22, 1884, and January 24, 1884. More on police departments and telephones comes from Harring's *Policing a Class Society: The Experiences of American Cities*, p. 49; and *Victorian America: Transformations in Everyday Life, 1876–1915*, pp. 188–89.

The report of Steiner's call to the police department is found in the Austin Police Department's *Record of Police Calls and Arrests*, October 21, 1879, to May 31, 1885, p. 85.

Number of police officers is from the *Austin Daily Statesman*, May 19, 1885; and from Barkley's *History of Travis County*, pp. 222–29.

Grooms Lee afflicted with the dengue is from the *Austin Daily Sun* on January 1, 1885, and January 5, 1885.

Austin having five to six murders a year is from the Austin Police Department's *Record of Police Calls and Arrests*, October 21, 1879, to May 31, 1885.

Officer Howe descriptions and duties is from the *Austin Daily Statesman* on December 28, 1883, February 24, 1884, July 27, 1884, August 21, 1884, and June 27, 1885. Also see Tracy's "A Closer Look at O. Henry's Rolling Stone," p. 30.

Howe's uniform description is from the *Austin Daily Statesman*, January 9, 1884.

Howe's duties are described in the *Austin Daily Capitol* (an Austin newspaper that went defunct in late 1884) on November 27, 1884; and in the *Austin Daily Statesman* on July 30, 1880, February 25, 1883, February 7, 1884, February 12, 1884, March 9, 1884, December 18, 1884, January 4, 1885, February 2, 1885, February 4, 1885, October 10, 1885, and March 24, 1885.

The descriptions of the murder scene throughout the rest of the chapter, the activities of the police, and the arrest of Lem Brooks are taken from the *Austin Daily Statesman, Austin Daily Sun, Dallas Daily Herald, Dallas Morning News, Fort Worth Gazette, Galveston Daily News, Houston Daily Post, San Antonio Light, San Antonio Daily Express, Waco Day,* and *Waco Daily Express* from January 1–6, 1885. More stories were later written about Mollie's murder in the *Austin Daily Statesman,* December 10, 1885; the *New York World,* December 29, 1886, and January 1, 1886; and the *National Police Gazette* on July 30, 1887.

Details on Sergeant Chenneville are taken from the author's interviews in 2002 and 2004 with his grandchildren Louise Davis and Jack Chenneville and his great-granddaughter, Dr. Tiffany Chenneville. Descriptions of Chenneville come from Streeter's *Ben Thompson: Man with a Gun,* pp. 168–69; Chenneville's handwritten "Application for Appointment as Special Texas Ranger" on March 11, 1889; and Chenneville's biographical file at the Austin History Center. Many descriptions of Chenneville were found in the *Austin Democratic Statesman,* among them March 9, 1878, March 13, 1877, March 16, 1878, November 3, 1878, April 2, 1879, and April 15, 1879, and in the *Austin Daily Statesman* on February 27, 1880, August 3, 1880, February 5, 1882, March 11, 1882, July 19, 1882, July 6, 1883, January 16, 1884, October 2, 1884, January 13, 1885. "Pals" is from the *Austin Daily Statesman,* December 12, 1884. "Most industrious officer" is from the *Austin Daily Statesman,* November 29, 1881. "Untiring vigilance" is from the *Austin Daily Statesman,* December 16, 1884.

Chenneville's previous arrests is from the *Austin Daily Statesman* of November 20, 1881, November 29, 1881, January 3, 1882, February 16, 1882, April 20, 1882; and see the *Austin Daily Sun* on August 3, 1882.

Sources for the lack of criminology available to a police officer in 1885 include Cole's *Suspect Identities,* pp. 1–78; Friedman's *Crime and Punishment in American History,* p. 208; Beaven's *Fingerprints: The Origins of Crime Detection and the Murder Case That Launched Forensic Science,* pp. 86–87; Lane's *Murder in America: A History,* pp. 200–211; Lane's *Policing the City, Boston, 1822–1885,* pp. 14–150; and Robinson's *Science Catches the Criminal,* pp. 19–21.

The life of newspaper reporters in Austin is from the *Austin Daily Statesman,* January 6, 1885, October 17, 1885, January 2, 1886, January 8, 1886; and also from the *Fort Worth Gazette* on July 28, 1895, and August 11, 1885. The Austin Press Club scenes are from the *Austin Daily Statesman* on July 15, 1883, and July 2, 1884. More information was taken from Busfield's "History of the *Austin Statesman, 1871–1956*"; Nalle's "The History of the *Austin Statesman*"; and Lang's "A Study of Texas Newspapers from 1876–1890." The actual title of Mark Twain's December 1884 *Century* magazine story was "An Adventure of Huckleberry Finn," p. 268.

The Indian attacks on Texas settlers were later compiled in Wilbarger's *Indian Depredations in Texas.* Accounts of the last of the Comanches were taken from Gwynne's *Empire of the Summer Moon,* pp. 4, 17, 174, 230–70.

Brooks's history and life in Austin is from the *Austin Daily Statesman* on January 1,

1885, January 2, 1885, and January 3, 1885. The "figures" at black dances called by Brooks are described by Hunter in *To 'Joy My Freedom: Southern Black Women's Lives and Labors After the Civil War*, pp. 169–76.

Life of black undertakers is from Mear's *And Grace Will Lead Me*, pp. 108–9; Rice's *The Negro in Texas: 1874–1900*, p. 269; Byrd's *J. Mason Brewer, Negro Folklorist*, p. 20; and McQueen's *Black Churches in Texas: A Guide to Historic Congregations*, pp. 1–27.

Mollie Smith's body falling apart when put in the coffin is from the *National Police Gazette* on July 30, 1887.

CHAPTER THREE

Mollie Smith in the "dead room" of the City-County Hospital is from the *Austin Daily Statesman*, January 1, 1885. The description of the "dead room" (it was also called the "dead house") is taken from the *Austin Daily Statesman*, June 24, 1885, and August 5, 1885; and Barkley's *A History of Travis County and Austin, 1839–1899*, p. 243.

Details about the city's gas lamps are from the *Austin Daily Statesman*, January 11, 1883. Henry Stamps is found in Morrison and Fourmy's *General Directory of the City of Austin, 1885–1886*; and Barkley's *A History of Travis County and Austin, 1839–1899*, p. 246.

Incandescent lamps in Austin is from the *Austin Daily Statesman* on November 10, 1883, and February 9, 1884; also see Southwell's "A Social and Literary History of Austin from 1881 to 1896," p. 16.

Details about New Year's Eve are from the *Austin Daily Statesman* on December 30, 1884, December 31, 1884, January 1, 1885, and January 2, 1885; and the *Austin Daily Sun* on January 1, 1885, and January 2, 1885. Histories of masquerade balls in Austin were found in the *Austin Daily Statesman* on January 8, 1971, and February 28, 1976. Additional information on the Brunswick Hotel comes from the *Austin Daily Statesman* on January 5, 1884, and Tracy's "A Closer Look at O. Henry's Rolling Stone," p. 85. The Gold Room shotgun raffle is mentioned in the January 6, 1885, issue of the *Austin Daily Statesman*. More details on the various Austin saloons can be found in the *Sunday American Statesman Magazine*, January 10, 1926; Humphrey's *Austin: An Illustrated History*, pp. 112–14; *The Industries of Austin Commercial & Manufacturing Advantages, 1885*, p. 95; and the *Austin Daily Statesman* on September 1, 1883, July 2, 1884, and June 3, 1885.

Biographical details on Mayor Robertson come from the *Austin Daily Statesman* of June 13, 1884, June 15, 1884, June 22, 1884, and October 7, 1884; and from the *Austin Daily Sun* on February 18, 1885. Also see Daniell's *Types of Successful Men of Texas*, pp. 421–28; Johnson's *History of Texas and Texans*, p. 1867; and Robertson's obituary in the *Austin Daily Statesman* on July 1, 1892.

The "chili con carne" statement was in the June 15, 1884, edition of the *Austin Daily Statesman*. Robertson's booming and his plans for the future were in the *Austin Daily Statesman* on June 13, 1884, June 15, 1884, June 22, 1884, November 11, 1885, and December 8, 1885. More information on Robertson's work comes from Suhler's "Significant Questions Relating to the History of Austin, Texas, to 1900," pp. 357–62.

Among the sources for the section on Austin's history in this chapter are Fehrenbach's *Lone Star*, pp. 257–60, 320, 419, 422, 434, and 603–4; Humphrey's *Austin: An Illustrated History*, pp. 1–80; Haley's *Texas: From the Frontier to Spindletop*, pp. 99–104, 135;

Jones's *Search for Maturity*, pp. 2, 35–36, 51–52; Barkley's *History of Travis County and Austin: 1839–1899*, pp. 12–13, 84–97; Wheeler's *To Wear a City's Crown: The Beginnings of Urban Growth in Texas, 1834–1865*, pp. 3–141; Gwynne's *Empire of the Summer Moon*, pp. 72–77, 97–135; Streeter's *Ben Thompson: Man with a Gun*, pp. 26–28; Robinson's *The Men Who Wear the Star: The Story of the Texas Rangers*, p. 106; White's *Texas: An Informal Biography*, pp. 130–67; and Orum's *Power, Money and the People*, pp. 23–24. Elizabeth Custer's quote comes from *Tenting on the Plains; or, General Custer in Kansas and Texas*, p. 260.

Reference to the new University of Texas is made in Humphrey's *Austin: An Illustrated History*, pp. 93–100, and Berry's *The University of Texas: A Pictorial Account of Its First Century*, pp. 61–115. Among the sources for the section on the size and design of the state capitol are *The Texas Capitol, Symbol of Accomplishment*, p. 45; *The Texas Capitol: A History of the Lone Star Statehouse*, p. 27; and Humphrey's *Austin: An Illustrated History*, pp. 87–89.

New York City's population is from Cox's *West from Appomattox: The Reconstruction of America after the Civil War*, p. 96. Stories of cattle drives through Austin on what was known as East Road (which is now Interstate 35) come from the *Dallas Daily Herald* on July 4, 1885, and the *Austin Daily Statesman* on June 5, 1976. "Turn of a kaleidoscope" comes from Humphrey's *Austin: An Illustrated History*, p. 76.

The details about specific Austin businesses, street life, and characters were compiled from the *Austin Daily Statesman* between January 1883 and January 1886. The *Daily Statesman* printed a story about J. C. Petmecky on November 15, 1884, and Mrs. Barker on December 11, 1884. The *Austin Daily Capitol* carried a story about Julian Prade on June 19, 1884, and the *Daily Statesman* contained a story about the Austin Roller Coaster on August 23, 1884, August 24, 1884, and August 28, 1884. Other details of Austin businesses and street life were taken from Morrison and Fourmy's *General Directory of the City of Austin, 1885–1886*; Sanborn Fire Insurance Maps; *The Industries of Austin Commercial & Manufacturing Advantages, 1885*; *Historical and Descriptive Review of the Industries of Austin Together with Sketches of the Representative Business Houses, 1885*; Austin's size is from Sanborn Fire Insurance Maps.

More details on life in Austin were found in Robinson's "O. Henry's Austin"; O'Quinn's "O. Henry in Austin"; Barkley's *History of Travis County and Austin: 1839–1899*; Humphrey's *Austin: A History of the Capital City*; Humphrey's *Austin: An Illustrated History*, pp. 68–118; Southwell's "A Social and Literary History of Austin from 1881 to 1896"; Weems's *Austin: 1839–1989*; Swisher's *History of Austin, Travis County, Texas, with a Description of Its Resources*; Manry's *Curtain Call: The History of the Theatre in Austin Texas: 1839–1995*; O'Neal's *The Texas League 1888–1987: A Century of Baseball*; Sweet and Knox, *On a Mexican Mustang Through Texas*; Manaster's "The Ethnic Geography of Austin, Texas: 1875–1910," pp. 41–9; Jones's *Search for Maturity*, pp. 86–87; and Kerr's *Austin, Texas, Then and Now: A Photography Scrapbook*, p. 74.

Berninzo, the organ grinder, was reported in the *Austin Daily Statesman* on May 20, 1885, and Madame Stanley was profiled in the *Austin Daily Capitol* on April 15, 1884. Specific details on Dr. Damos were taken from the *Austin Daily Statesman* on June 11, 1880, February 12, 1881, and January 1, 1886, as well as the *Austin Daily Capital* on February 12, 1884.

Information about O. Henry comes in part from Langford's *Alias O Henry: A Biography of William Sidney Porter;* O'Connor's *O. Henry: The Legendary Life of William S. Porter;* Robinson's "O. Henry's Austin"; and O'Quinn's "O. Henry's Austin."

The Austin Athletic Association's rope-jumping contests were in the *Austin Daily Capitol* on July 11, 1884. The Austins' baseball games were reported in the *Austin Daily Statesman* on June 22, 1884, and June 24, 1884. The chess tournaments were reported in Southwell's "A Social and Literary History of Austin from 1881 to 1896," and John L. Sullivan's boxing exploits were reported in the *Austin Daily Statesman* on April 2, 1884. Mollie Bailey's circus visit to Austin was noted in the *San Antonio Express* on November 11, 1884, and the boy tightrope walker's trek was covered by the *Austin Daily Statesman* on December 7, 1884. The New Year's Day calling parties are from the *Austin Daily Statesman,* December 1, 1885, and December 26, 1970; and the *Galveston Daily News,* January 2, 1885. The reference to Hartzfield can be found in Tracy's "A Closer Look at O. Henry's Rolling Stone," p. 32. Governor Ireland's open house and the governor's activities for that day come from the *Austin Daily Statesman* of December 30, 1884, January 1, 1885, and January 2, 1885; the *Austin Daily Sun* of January 1, 1885; the *Galveston Daily News* of December 31, 1884; the *San Antonio Daily Express* of December 31, 1884; and from Gov. John Ireland's "Inventory of Records, 1879–1887."

Information on the governor's mansion comes from the National Register Information System's *National Register of Historic Places.*

Biographical information on Governor Ireland comes from Seale's "John Ireland and His Times," pp. 1–200; Smith's "The Administration of Governor John Ireland, 1883–1887," pp. 7–77; Daniell's *Types of Successful Men of Texas,* pp. 239–441; Daniell's *Personnel of the Texas State Government,* pp. 138–53; Wooten's *A Comprehensive History of Texas, 1685–1897,* pp. 25–265; Jones's *Search for Maturity,* pp. 46–8 and 56; Campbell's *Gone to Texas,* pp. 303–4 and 318–31; and the *Austin Daily Statesman,* March 30, 1884, and June 27, 1884.

Biographical information on William Swain is taken from Speer and Brown's *Encyclopedia of the New West,* pp. 403–4; "Compt. Swain's Administration," in the *Texas Review,* pp. 466–75; Loughery's *Personnel of the Texas State Government for 1885,* pp. 68–69; and Burke's *Texas Almanac and Immigrant's Handbook for 1883,* pp. 54–56. Newspaper accounts of Swain come from the *Austin Daily Statesman,* March 27, 1884, and July 6, 1884; the *Austin Daily Sun,* January 29, 1885; the *Waco Day,* January 2, 1885; the *Waco Daily Examiner,* March 5, 1885, March 26, 1885, and May 21, 1885; and the *Fort Worth Gazette,* October 2, 1884, and March 31, 1885.

Afternoon train schedules come from the *Austin Daily Statesman,* November 16, 1884, January 1, 1885, and January 17, 1885, and from Morrison and Fourmy's *General Directory of the City of Austin, 1885–1886.*

CHAPTER FOUR

Inquests and justice of the peace responsibilities are from Holden's "Law and Lawlessness on the Texas Frontier, 1875–1890," pp. 188–203; and from Gammel's *Special Laws of the State of Texas, 1822–1897,* pp. 12, 31, and 345.

The testimony of the Mollie Smith inquest jury was covered from January 1 to

January 10, 1885, by the *Austin Daily Statesman, Fort Worth Gazette, Austin Daily Sun, Bastrop Advertiser,* and *Galveston Daily News.*

Mollie Smith's burial was reported in the Cemetery Record for Oakwood Cemetery. The description of the cemetery comes from the *Austin Daily Statesman* on June 1, 1886.

Dr. Humphrey's speech at the University of Texas is from the *Austin Daily Statesman* on January 10, 1885. The Clara Morris play is from the *Austin Daily Statesman* on January 3, 1885, January 13, 1885, and January 20, 1885. The Cattleman's Ball was reported in the *Austin Daily Statesman* on January 11, 1885, January 14, 1885, January 16, 1885, and January 18, 1885. Ida St. Claire was written about in the *Austin Daily Statesman,* February 27, 1885. Blanche Dumont was profiled in Humphrey's "Prostitution and Public Policy in Austin, Texas, 1870–1915," p. 484; Zelade's *Guy Town by Gaslight,* pp. 68 and 138; Williamson's *Texas Pistoleers,* p. 96; and Butler's *Daughters of Joy, Sisters of Misery,* pp. 57–58. Guy Town prostitution is also mentioned in the *Austin Daily Statesman,* December 16, 1880, June 12, 1933, and January 10, 1926, and in Williamson's *Texas Pistoleers,* p. 96.

Brooks's release is from the *Austin Daily Statesman* on January 26, 1885, and March 31, 1885. "Pastor Grant would serve his race better" is from the *Galveston Daily News,* January 4, 1885.

"Onion sociable" is from the *Bastrop Advertiser* on February 21, 1885. The Austin Press Club concert was reported in the *Austin Daily Statesman* on January 25, 1885, and January 27, 1885. Louise Armaindo was reported in the *Austin Daily Statesman* on February 18, 1885, February 20, 1885, February 21, 1885, and February 22, 1885.

The meetings of the state legislature and the vote for women clerks were reported in the *Austin Daily Statesman* for January 15, 1885, January 25, 1885, January 27, 1885, and January 28, 1885.

Descriptions of the old State Lunatic Asylum are from the *Austin Democratic Statesman* on May 7, 1879, and December 9, 1879; and from the *Austin Daily Statesman* for July 20, 1880.

More details of the asylum in earlier days can be found in Sitton's *Life at the Texas Lunatic Asylum, 1857–1997,* pp. 2–5 and 10–30. Also in Brownson's "From Curer to Custodian: A History of the Texas State Lunatic Asylum, 1857–1880," pp. 1–7.

The State Lunatic Asylum under Dr. Denton can be found in Sitton's *Life at the Texas Lunatic Asylum, 1857–1999,* pp. 30–39. Further information is in Denton's *Report of the Superintendent of the Texas State Lunatic Asylum for 1884,* pp. 1–13; Denton's *Report of the Superintendent of the Texas State Lunatic Asylum for 1885,* pp. 1–11; and Denton's *Report of the Superintendent of the Texas State Lunatic Asylum for 1886,* pp. 1–15. Descriptions of the State Lunatic Asylum under Dr. Denton are in the *Galveston Daily News* for September 4, 1885; the *Austin Daily Capitol* for April 17, 1884; the *Austin Daily Sun* for April 23, 1884; the *San Antonio Daily Express* for August 9, 1884, and October 7, 1884; and the *Austin Daily Statesman* for January 10, 1883, January 23, 1883, April 23, 1883, June 23, 1883, March 3, 1884, June 26, 1884, August 18, 1885, and November 27, 1885. More biographical information on Denton comes from Daniell's *Personnel of the Texas State Government for 1885,* p. 72.

The wedding at the State Lunatic Asylum was reported in the *Austin Daily States-*

man on February 12, 1885, and February 28, 1885; and in the *Austin Daily Sun* on February 12, 1885. Descriptions of Dr. Given appear in the *Austin Daily Statesman* on August 27, 1886, and August 28, 1886; and in the *San Antonio Daily Express* on August 28, 1886.

CHAPTER FIVE

The "pitch of gaiety" is from the March 2, 1885, issue of the *Waco Daily Express*.

Details of the cornerstone ceremony come from Lambert's "Report of the Ceremonies of Laying the Corner Stone of the New Capitol of Texas"; Barkley's *History of Travis County and Austin: 1839–1899*, p. 204; and reports from the *Austin Daily Statesman* and the *Galveston Daily News* on March 1, 1885, March 2, 1885, and March 3, 1885. The "harbor of big ships" line is from the *Austin Daily Statesman* on March 6, 1884. More on the state of the capitol's construction comes from the *Austin Daily Statesman* on March 10, 1885.

The attacks on the servant women were detailed by the *Austin Daily Statesman*, *Austin Daily Sun*, *Galveston Daily News*, *Fort Worth Gazette*, *San Antonio Daily Express*, and *Waco Daily Express* between March 10, 1885, and March 21, 1885. More details come from the "Record of Arrests, Oct. 21, 1879–May 31, 1885." The Major Stewart speech on the Old South was reported in the *Galveston Daily News*, August 7, 1885.

"Anticipated lively times" is from the *Austin Daily Sun*, January 10, 1885. The thief stealing "eatables" is from the *Austin Daily Sun*, January 18, 1885. The burglary at Mrs. Cope's is from the *Austin Daily Statesman* on January 10, 1885, and January 18, 1885.

Austin's white citizens blaming the attacks on black men was reported by the *Austin Daily Statesman* on March 14, 1885, and March 20, 1885; the *Austin Daily Sun* of March 14, 1885; the *Galveston Daily News* on March 20, 1885; and the *Fort Worth Gazette* on March 22, 1885.

Sources for Austin's black population, homes, and neighborhoods are Mears's *And Grace Will Lead Me Home*, pp. 11, 26–28, and 64; Manaster's "The Ethnic Geography of Austin, Texas: 1875–1910," pp. 54–5, 70, and 89–91; and Humphrey's *Austin: An Illustrated History*, p. 67.

Austin's black illiteracy: Mears's *And Grace Will Lead Me Home*, p. 113. Descriptions of black male employment are from Rice's *The Negro in Texas, 1874–1900*, pp. 13–14, 38–94, and 184–87. Among the sources for black servant women's work are Hunter's *To 'Joy My Freedom: Southern Black Women's Lives and Labors After the Civil War*, p. 12; Jones's *Life on Waller Creek*, p. 53; Winegarten's *Black Texas Women*, pp. 151–53; Litwack's *Trouble in Mind*, pp. 17–18; Sutherland's *Americans and Their Servants*, p. 30; Smallwood's *Time of Hope, Time of Despair*, p. 48; and the *Austin Daily Statesman* for February 7, 1970, and October 25, 1975.

Black persecution in Austin during slavery: Wormser's *The Rise and Fall of Jim Crow*, p. 11; Mears's *And Grace Will Lead Me*, pp. 9 and 27; *Texas Slave Narratives*, p. 93; and Lack's "Slavery and Vigilantism in Austin, Texas, 1840–1860," pp. 1–20.

Stories of Rev. Grant's church come from the *Austin Daily Statesman* of February 18, 1884, June 17, 1884, and January 20, 1885. Stories about Tom Hill come from the *Austin Daily Statesman* on August 3, 1885, and October 3, 1886. The East Austin business district is identified in the Sanborn Fire Insurance Maps of Austin and Morrison and

Fourmy's *General Directory of the City of Austin, 1885–1886*. The business district is also described in Mears's *And Grace Will Lead Me Home*, p. 158. On black schools: Manaster's "The Ethnic Geography of Austin, Texas," p. 92; and Barkley's "History of Travis County and Austin," p. 176; and the *Austin Daily Statesman* on June 27, 1885. Also, the *Catalogue of the Tillotson Institute, 1884–1885*, pp. 1–84; and Heintze's *Private Black Colleges in Texas, 1865–1954*, pp. 26–28.

Black entertainment in Austin is from Smallwood's *Time of Hope, Time of Despair*, p. 119; Sweet and Knox's *On a Mexican Mustang*, p. 110; Rice's *The Negro in Texas, 1874–1900*, pp. 260–62; Southwell's "A Social and Literary History of Austin from 1881 to 1896," pp. 123–24; Enstam's *Women and the Creation of Urban Life*, p. 188; and the *Austin Daily Statesman*, August 4, 1880, September 30, 1884, February 17, 1886, and June 19, 1976.

Julia Pease's black Christmas parties, the *Austin Daily Statesman*, December 6, 1969. Pressler's Juneteenth celebration is from Manaster's "The Ethnic Geography of Austin, Texas," p. 93. Albert Carrington's biography is from "Carrington Family" vertical files, Austin History Center, and the *Austin Daily Statesman*, December 9, 1884. Millett's not allowing blacks at operas from Manry's *Curtain Call*, p. 9.

Generic white discrimination against blacks in the late 1880s is documented in Worsmer's *The Rise and Fall of Jim Crow*, p. 7; Litwack's *Trouble in Mind: Black Southerners in the Age of Jim Crow*, pp. 91 and 247–65; and Dray's *At the Hands of Persons Unknown*, pp. 94–103. Also from Manaster's "The Ethnic Geography of Austin," pp. 115–122; and the *Austin Daily Statesman*, September 13, 1883, November 27, 1884, and May 14, 1885. "Raucous" noises is from the *Austin Daily Statesman*, January 1, 1884, and the *Galveston Daily News*, January 4, 1885. Loitering on street corners is from the *Austin Daily Statesman*, February 21, 1883.

Fear of black men not having experienced slavery, committing crimes, and "retrograding" comes from Waldrep's *The Many Faces of Judge Lynch*, p. 100; Hale's *Making Whiteness: The Culture of Segregation in the South, 1890–1940*, pp. 73–74; Litwack's *Trouble in Mind: Black Southerners in the Age of Jim Crow*, pp. 2, 99, 178, 211, 302, and 408; Dray's *At the Hands of Persons Unknown: The Lynching of Black America*, p. 147; and Vann's *Origins of the New South: 1877–1913*, pp. 197–200, 210–16, and 302.

"Idleness and drink" is from the *Austin Daily Statesman*, September 30, 1885.

Grooms Lee's history in law enforcement is from the *Austin Daily Statesman* on February 29, 1880, May 21, 1880, and December 12, 1883. Also see the Texas State Archives, listing of "Frontier Battalion of Texas Rangers," December 23, 1874.

Previous Austin marshals is from Barkley's *History of Travis County and Austin: 1839–1899*, pp. 222–27. Ben Thompson's biography is from Walton's *Life and Adventures of Ben Thompson: The Famous Texan*, pp. 151–52 and 191–93; and Askins's *Texans, Guns & History*, pp. 76–86. More stories on Thompson are from the *Austin Daily Statesman* on January 6, 1881, January 13, 1884, February 2, 1884, February 23, 1884, and March 12, 1884.

Lee as a teetotaler is from the *Dallas Daily Herald*, December 14, 1883. Descriptions of Lee's father are taken from *Biographical Encyclopedia of Texas*, pp. 226–27; and from Speer and Brown, *Encyclopedia of the New West*, pp. 418–19. Descriptions of Lee as marshal are from the author's interview with Grooms Lee's grandniece Lois Douglas in 2002; the *Austin Daily Sun* of January 17, 1885; and the *Austin Daily Statesman* of March 3,

1884, March 5, 1884, March 13, 1884, March 25, 1884, December 10, 1884, January 9, 1884, and January 16, 1884. Chenneville's salary increase is from the *Austin Daily Statesman* on December 11, 1883.

Information on the end of the outlaw era, John Wesley Hardin, and Belle Star was taken from Prassel's *The Great American Outlaw*, pp. 26–142; Trachtman's *The Gunfighters*, pp. 176–82; Jones's *Search for Maturity*, pp. 8 and 14; Lewis's *The Mammoth Book of the West*, pp. 334–35 and 479; and Hendricks's *The Bad Man of the West*, pp. 70–85.

Austin Police Department size is from the *Austin Daily Statesman* on May 1, 1884, October 5, 1884, May 15, 1884, June 6, 1885, and June 27, 1885. Also see Barkley's *History of Travis County*, pp. 222–29; Biggerstaff's "Austin Police Force, 1851–1962"; Sweet and Knox's *On a Mexican Mustang Through Texas*, p. 653; and Schlesinger's *The Rise of the City, 1878–1898*, pp. 259–60.

Details about particular Austin officers come from the *Austin Daily Statesman* on March 26, 1884, and January 29, 1885. Details about the black officers are from the *Austin Daily Statesman* on July 3, 1884, and from White's "A Pictorial History of Black Policemen Who Have Served in the Austin Police Department, 1871–1982," pp. 1–12.

March city aldermen meeting for "special policemen" was reported in the *Austin Daily Statesman* on March 21, 1885, March 22, 1885, and March 23, 1885. Mrs. Chenneville fires at prowler, the *Austin Daily Statesman*, April 8, 1885.

CHAPTER SIX

Details on the New Orleans Exposition come from "Guidebook Through the World's Cotton and Industrial Centennial Exposition at New Orleans," pp. 1–24; and Ezell's *The South Since 1865*, pp. 331–32. Details on the Texas exhibit and on Ireland's Texas Day speech come from the *Austin Daily Statesman, New Orleans Daily Picayune, Dallas Daily Herald, Fort Worth Gazette,* and *Galveston Daily News* from April 20, 1885, to April 28, 1885. Details on Ireland's wife are from Seale's "John Ireland and His Times," pp. 156–57; and Farrell's *First Ladies of Texas: A History*, p. 176.

Details about Jefferson Davis's post–Civil War life and beliefs come from Fleming's "Jefferson Davis, the Negroes and the Negro Problem," pp. 407–27.

Details on Radam come from Walters's *Scientific Authority & Twentieth-Century America*, p. 58; Radam's self-published autobiography, *William Radam's Microbe Killer*; and from the *Austin Daily Statesman* on August 28, 1887, August 28, 1888, November 7, 1888, April 2, 1889, and April 24, 1976.

Robertson as author of the *Industries of Austin, Texas* catalogue is indicated in the "Publisher's Note," p. 1.

Details of the servant women attacks and the arrests of suspects in late April and early May come from the *Austin Daily Statesman, Dallas Daily Herald, Galveston Daily News,* and *San Antonio Daily Express*, April 30, 1885, to May 5, 1885.

Stories detailing Eliza's murder come from the *Austin Daily Statesman, Waco Daily Examiner, Fort Worth Gazette, Dallas Daily Herald, Galveston Daily News, San Antonio Daily Express,* and *St. Louis Post Dispatch* of May 7 and 8, 1885. The story of William Shelley's horse theft are reported in the January 4, 1884, and April 23, 1884, *Austin Daily Statesman*.

CHAPTER SEVEN

Stories detailing the police investigation into Eliza's murder and the arrest of Ike Plummer come from the same newspapers listed in the preceding note from May 8 to May 17, 1885. Further information is from the *Fort Worth Gazette* on November 15, 1885; the *New York World* on December 29, 1885, and January 1, 1886; and the *National Police Gazette* on July 30, 1887. Dr. Johnson's Roman coin comes from the *Austin Daily Statesman*, February 23, 1885. O. Henry's "Servant Girl Annihilators" comes from *O. Henry's Rolling Stones*, p. 265.

Black residents terrorized and black voodoo practices are from the *Austin Daily Statesman* on December 12, 1884, May 8, 1885, and May 9, 1885; the *Galveston Daily News* on May 9, 1885; the *National Police Gazette* on July 30, 1887; and the *New York World* on January 1, 1886. More on hoodoo from Dray's *At the Hands of Persons Unknown*, p. 40; and from Meier and Rudwick's *From Plantation to Ghetto*, pp. 79–80.

Stories detailing Irene Cross's murder are from the *Austin Daily Statesman*, *Fort Worth Gazette*, *Dallas Daily Herald*, *Galveston Daily News*, *San Antonio Daily Express*, and *St. Louis Post Dispatch*, May 23 through May 26, 1885. Also see the *Fort Worth Gazette* on November 15, 1885; the *New York World* on December 29, 1885, and January 1, 1886; and the *National Police Gazette* on July 30, 1887. Description of Scholz's beer garden is from the *Austin Daily Statesman*, March 21, 1937.

CHAPTER EIGHT

Stories detailing the next day's scene at the Weyermann home and the police investigation into Cross's murder come from the same newspapers listed in the preceding note from May 23 to May 26, 1885.

Descriptions of the men on the Avenue and their theories about the servant women killings come from the *Austin Daily Statesman* on May 9, 1885, May 10, 1885, May 11, 1885, and September 29, 1885; the *Dallas Daily Herald* on May 8, 1885, and May 14, 1885; the *St. Louis Post Dispatch* on May 7, 1885; and the *Fort Worth Gazette* on June 12, 1885, and November 18, 1885. (Although a couple of the theories were published weeks after the murder of Irene Cross, I am assuming that these theories were already being debated.)

Details of the Tallichet attack are from the *Austin Daily Statesman* and *Fort Worth Gazette* on June 3, 1885.

Details on Oliver Townsend come from the *Austin Daily Statesman* on January 25, 1880, July 27, 1884, January 7, 1885, February 6, 1885, January 27, 1885, March 24, 1885, and July 17, 1885. The "hard time with hemp" is from the *Austin Daily Statesman* on June 7, 1885.

The attacks coming to a stop in June is from the *Fort Worth Gazette* on June 12, 1885, and from the *Austin Daily Statesman* on June 30, 1885.

Howe's arrest of Ireland is from the *Austin Daily Statesman* and the *Fort Worth Gazette* on June 17, 1885, and June 18, 1885. Also see the *Austin Daily Statesman* on August 5, 1885.

Details on the Fourth of July celebrations and the Driskill Hotel ceremony come from the *Austin Daily Statesman* on July 1, 1885, July 2, 1885, July 4, 1885, July 5, 1885, July 7, 1885, and July 15, 1969. More details are from Franz's *The Driskill Hotel*, p. 15; Wheeler's

The Old West: The Townsmen, p. 39; and Schlereth's *Victorian America: Transformations in Everyday Life*, p. 212. The *Austin Daily Statesman* reported the building plan of the Driskill on March 12, 1884, May 11, 1884, October 17, 1885, December 17, 1886, May 25, 1970, and January 27, 1973.

Details on Olds's visit come from the *Austin Daily Statesman* on August 11, 1885, and from Olds's "Texas Notes," housed at the Bancroft Library, University of California, Berkeley, pp. 1–13, as well as *History of North Mexican States and Texas*, pp. 527–29.

Information on the construction of the capitol comes from the *Austin Daily Statesman* on July 10, 1885, July 11, 1885, July 18, 1885, and August 6, 1885. Also see *The Industries of Austin, Texas*, pp. 54–57; *The Texas Capitol: Symbol of Accomplishment*, pp. 36 and 48–52; and Greer's "The Building of the Texas State Capitol, 1882–1888."

Austin's heat comes from the *San Antonio Daily Express*, August 4, 1885. Chenneville on vacation was reported in the *Austin Daily Statesman* on August 9, 1885. "Fishing frolic" was reported in the *Austin Daily Statesman* on August 14, 1885. The baseball game was reported in the *Austin Daily Statesman* on August 29, 1885, and August 30, 1885.

CHAPTER NINE

Stories detailing Mary Ramey's murder, the police investigation, and the arrest of suspects are from the *Austin Daily Statesman, Fort Worth Gazette, Dallas Daily Herald, Galveston Daily News, Houston Daily Post, San Antonio Light, San Antonio Daily Express, New York World*, and *St. Louis Post Dispatch* from August 31 to September 6, 1885. Also see the *Fort Worth Gazette* of November 15, 1885; the *New York World*, December 29, 1885, and January 1, 1886; and the *National Police Gazette*, July 30, 1887.

More details on the Weed family are from the author's interviews in September 2002 and September 2011 with Weed's grandson Peyton Abbott; and from the *Austin Daily Statesman* on October 24, 1895, July 26, 1921, and February 7, 1926. Details on Mary Ramey's schooling come from the "Austin Public Schools Teacher's Daily Register Primary Department Session, 1884–1885."

Details of Aleck Mack's life are from the *Austin Daily Statesman* on January 1, 1884, December 9, 1884, January 29, 1885, and July 18, 1885.

"Desperadoes in the open street" is from the *Austin Daily Statesman* on September 3, 1885; "loafing, shiftless, vagrant Negroes" is from the *San Antonio Daily Express* on September 9, 1885.

Criticism of Grooms Lee is from the *Austin Daily Statesman* on September 2, 1995, September 9, 1885, and from the *San Antonio Light* on September 9, 1885.

Austin's black leaders speaking about murders, trying to meet with the governor and mayor, is from the *Austin Daily Statesman*, September 3, 1885.

Joseph Nalle's history is from Jones's "Joseph Nalle," in *Historical and Descriptive Review of the Industries of Austin*, p. 80; the *Austin Daily Statesman*, June 14, 1884, and March 19, 1911; and the *San Antonio Daily Express*, September 15, 1885. The story of Nalle earlier running for mayor is from the *Austin Daily Capital*, March 3, 1884, and from the *Austin Daily Statesman* on June, 14, 1884. Nalle running again for mayor is from the *San Antonio Light*, October 22, 1885.

CHAPTER TEN

Description of the Capital Detective Agency is from Starr's *History of Travis County and Austin*, p. 228. The history of private detectives comes from Robinson's *The Men Who Wear the Star*, p. 33; Friedman's *Crime and Punishment in American History*, pp. 204–7, and Prassel's *The Western Peace Officer: A Legacy of Law and Order*, p. 134.

Details on the Noble Agency and its detectives is from the *Houston Daily Post* on February 2, 1885, August 11, 1885, September 18, 1885, January 1, 1886, January 17, 1886, May 25, 1886, and September 30, 1886. Also see the *San Antonio Daily Express* of October 7, 1885, and October 8, 1885; and the *San Antonio Light*, October 17, 1885. The *Austin Daily Statesman* carried stories about the agency on January 3, 1885, January 4, 1885, October 1, 1886, October 3, 1886, and October 4, 1886. Also see "The Houston Police: 1878–1944," pp. 10–12, and Marchiafava's *The Houston Police: 1878–1948*, pp. 1–5.

Information on the Pinkertons was gleaned from Thorwald's *The Century of the Detective*, pp. 91–92; Lewis's *The Mammoth Book of the West*, p. 37; Moran's *The Eye That Never Sleeps*, p. 132; and Horan's *The Pinkertons: The Detective Dynasty That Made History*, pp. 1–24.

Details on Hennessey's investigation come from the *Austin Daily Statesman* on September 30, 1885, October 3, 1885, October 4, 1885, and October 7, 1885; the *Fort Worth Gazette* on September 18, 1885; the *San Antonio Daily Express* on October 7, 1885; the *San Antonio Light* on September 22, 1885; and the *Houston Herald* on October 4, 1885.

Details on the attacks of September 28 and 29 culminating in the murder of Gracie Vance, the investigation into her murder, and the arrests of the various suspects are culled from the *Austin Daily Statesman, Fort Worth Gazette, Dallas Daily Herald, Galveston Daily News, Houston Daily Post, San Antonio Light, San Antonio Daily Express, New York World, St. Louis Post Dispatch*, and *Waco Daily Gazette*. Further coverage of the story of the Vance attack and the botched investigation comes from the *Fort Worth Gazette* on November 15, 1885; the *New York World* on December 29, 1885, and January 1, 1886; and the *National Police Gazette* on July 30, 1887.

Dunham's biographical information comes from the *Austin Daily Statesman* on May 7, 1885.

Many of the details about the silver watch come from the *National Police Gazette* on July 30, 1887, along with the *Fort Worth Gazette* and *Austin Daily Statesman* of September 30, 1885.

CHAPTER ELEVEN

The various newspapers accounts of Hennessey's return and his announcement of Jonathon Trigg's eyewitness "statement" are often inconsistent. It seems that some of the reporters mistakenly attributed Hennessey's actions to Austin police officers, and other reporters mistakenly attributed the actions of police officers to Hennessey. My timeline of Hennessey's actions is my best guess as to what probably happened, based on flawed stories. I use the newspapers and the dates listed above for the Vance murder as my source material for Hennessey's investigation, his press conference on the capitol steps, and the controversy over his key witnesses, Jonathon Trigg and Lucinda Boddy.

The Noble Agency's explanation of why Woods had stolen the watch to give to Gracie Vance was reported in the *Houston Daily Post* on January 1, 1886.

Information on Mack's arrest and the accusations that he was nearly lynched, along with Lee's denial, comes from the *Austin Daily Statesman* on October 6, 1885, October 10, 1885, and October 16, 1885.

Detective Himmel arrested is from the *Galveston Daily News* on October 18, 1885.

The city aldermen meeting and the $250 reward is from the *Austin Daily Statesman* on October 7, 1885, and October 10, 1885.

Other October arrests were summarized in the *Austin Daily Statesman*, October 17, 1885. James Thompson's arrest was reported in the *San Antonio Daily Express* and the *Austin Daily Statesman* on November 15, 1885.

Maurice, the Malaysian cook, was not written about in the newspapers until the Jack the Ripper killings in 1888. That is when the story was finally told about his behavior after Mary Ramey's murder and his later disappearing after the Christmas Eve murders. Among the newspaper stories that discussed Maurice's life in Austin in 1885 were the *Austin Daily Statesman* on November 7, 1888; the *St. Louis Post Dispatch* on November 16, 1888; the *Washington D.C. Evening Star* on November 20, 1888; and the *East London Observer* on October 20, 1888.

"Detection of killers is as far off as ever" is from the *Galveston Daily News*, October 25, 1885.

"If a radical change is not made" is from the *Fort Worth Gazette*, September 6, 1885.

"At least fourteen rounds of ammunition" is from the *Austin Daily Statesman* on September 29, 1885.

"The servant girl will soon become one of the rarest and costliest of capital luxuries" is from the *Dallas Daily Herald* on October 1, 1885.

Aunt Tempe's death is from the *Austin Daily Statesman* on November 4, 1885; the *San Antonio Daily Express* on November 4, 1885; and the *San Antonio Light* on November 6, 1885.

Mayor Robertson's speech is from the *Austin Daily Statesman* on November 11, 1885.

That the murders were "carefully directed" and no "ordinary" Negro criminals were involved comes from the *Austin Daily Statesman*, September 2, 1885, and the *San Antonio Daily Express*, September 2, 1885.

The correspondent for the *San Antonio Daily Gazette* first mentioned the killer as "one of the most remarkable ghouls" on September 2, 1885. He used the "Midnight Assassin" moniker for the first time on September 8, 1885, and repeated the phrase on September 29, writing, "The hand of the midnight assassin has resumed his bloody work in Austin."

Among the sources mined for an analysis of the history of serial killings are Wilson and Seamon's *The Serial Killers: A Study in the Psychology of Violence*; Ramsland's *The Human Predator: A Historical Chronicle of Serial Murder and Forensic Investigation*; Hickey's *Serial Murderers and Their Victims*; and Norris's *Serial Killers: The Growing Menace*.

The types of serial killers known in late-nineteenth-century America are from Wilson's *The Mammoth Book of the History of Murder*, p. 34; Hickey's *Serial Murderers and Their Victims*, p. 34; Prassel's *The Great American Outlaw: A Legacy of Fact and Fiction*, pp. 50–84; and Yadon and Anderson's *Ten Deadly Texans*, pp. 53–83. Hardin's autobiography is *The Life of John Wesley Hardin as Written by Himself*.

Spencer's indictment is reported in the *Austin Daily Statesman*, the *Galveston News*, the *San Antonio Light*, and the *San Antonio Daily Express* on November 22, 1885; and more details were provided in the *Austin Daily Statesman* on November 25, 1885.

CHAPTER TWELVE

Biographical information on District Attorney Robertson comes from Daniell's *Types of Successful Men of Texas*, pp. 421–28; Johnson's *A History of Texas and Texans*, p. 1719; Brown's *Indian Wars and Pioneers of Texas*, pp. 286–87; and Robertson's "Life of James Harvey Robertson," pp. 1–15.

Sheeks's arrest is from the *Austin Daily Statesman*, July 3, 1884.

Robertson's court record comes from the *Austin Daily Statesman* on March 16, 1885, and April 11, 1885.

Details of the mayoral campaign come from the *Austin Daily Statesman* on November 3, 1885, November 16, 1885, November 19, 1885, November 21, 1885, December 1, 1885, December 8 1885, December 9, 1885, and December 15, 1885. Also see the *San Antonio Light* on October 22, 1885, November 2, 1885, November 3, 1885, November 11, 1885, November 18, 1885, and November 20, 1885; and the *San Antonio Daily Express* on December 1, 1885, December 13, 1885, and December 15, 1885.

Carrington's loss as alderman comes from Humphrey's *Austin: A History of the Capital City*, p. 35.

Spencer's trial was covered by the *Austin Daily Statesman* on December 8, 1885, December 9, 1885, December 10, 1885, December 11, 1885; and by the *San Antonio Daily Express* on December 10, 1885, and December 11, 1885. Blocker's history is from Hunter's *The Trail Drivers of Texas*, p. 390.

Marshal Lucy's history is taken from the *Austin Daily Statesman* of February 6, 1927, February 11, 1927, February 12, 1927, and March 14, 1927; also see Starr's *History of Travis County and Austin*, pp. 228–29. Lucy being named marshal and his first actions is from the *Austin Daily Statesman*, December 15, 1885.

Grooms Lee's last days in office is from the *Austin Daily Statesman* on December 15, 1885. Lee's report about fines is from the *Austin Daily Statesman* on November 11, 1885.

The high school football game was covered by the *Austin Daily Statesman* on December 19, 1885. Details about Austin during the Christmas season are taken from reports in the *Austin Daily Statesman* between November 19, 1885, and December 26, 1885. More details about Austin during Christmas in the late 1800s come from the *Austin Daily Statesman* on December 7, 1968, December 18, 1971, December 22, 1973, and December 13, 1975.

Lee turning over his badge is from the *Austin Daily Statesman*, December 22, 1885.

The moon on Christmas Eve at its "most effulgent" comes from the *Austin Daily Statesman* on December 26, 1885.

CHAPER THIRTEEN

Details of Christmas Eve murder scenes, town panic, and Christmas Day come from numerous newspapers, including the *Austin Daily Statesman*, *Dallas Morning News*, *Dal-*

las Daily Herald, Fort Worth Gazette, Fort Worth Mail, Galveston Daily News, Houston Daily Post, New Orleans Picayune, Missouri Republican, New York Times, New York Tribune, New York World, San Antonio Light, San Antonio Daily Express, San Antonio Times, St. Louis Post Dispatch, Texas Vorwaerts, and *Waco Daily Express* between December 25, 1885, and January 1, 1886. Other details, not initially reported, also come from the newspapers' coverage of the February 1886 testimony in the preliminary trial of Jimmy Phillips (February 13 to 17, 1886), the May 1886 testimony of the Phillips murder trial (May 25 to June 7, 1886), and the June 1887 testimony in Moses Hancock's murder trial (May 30 to June 8, 1887). The detail about Burt's son finding the ax in the Hancocks' backyard, for instance, was not revealed until June 1, 1887, in the *Austin Daily Statesman* during Moses Hancock's trial.

Besides the sources listed above, other details on Susan Hancock come from the *New York Times* on December 26, 1885; the *New York World* on December 29, 1885; the *Missouri Republican* on December 26, 1885; the *Fort Worth Gazette* on December 26, 1885; and the *Fort Worth Mail* on December 26, 1885.

Other details about Eula Phillips come from the *Waco Daily Express* on June 6, 1885; the *Fort Worth Gazette* on May 26, 1885; and the Texas Court of Appeals summation of the case, *The State of Texas vs. James O. Phillips.*

CHAPTER FOURTEEN

Although the *Austin Daily Statesman* was able to remake its front page for the December 25 editions, the other newspapers didn't print their stories on the Christmas Eve murders until December 26. The information about life in Austin during the week after the Christmas Eve murders, from December 26, 1885, through January 1, 1886, is taken from the same newspapers listed in the preceding note.

Eula Phillips's funeral account is in the *Austin Daily Statesman,* December 27, 1885. More details on how funerals and burials at that time were conducted comes from the *Austin American Statesman,* August 18, 1991. Eula Phillips's burial record comes from the Oakwood Cemetery records. Descriptions of Monroe Miller come from the *Austin Daily Statesman* on April 27, 1880, April 27, 1880, November 4, 1885, November 16, 1968, and September 18, 1976. The account of the shooting at the Southern Hotel in the early morning hours of December 27 was reported only in the *Missouri Republican,* December 28, 1885.

The newspaper accounts of the brief arrests of the Norwood brothers are contradictory. I relied on the December 27, 1885, December 28, 1885, and December 29, 1885, stories in the *Fort Worth Gazette* and *Austin Daily Statesman.*

Some of the citizens' proposals to protect themselves were reported throughout the week. The woman's letter asking for all Austin females to be given dogs was published, for instance, in the *Austin Daily Statesman* on December 29, 1885, and the man's response to her letter was published on December 30, 1885. Governor Ireland's fire alarm proposal was reported on December 27, 1885. The description of the electric burglar alarm salesman was reported in the *Austin Daily Statesman* on January 16, 1885. The "100 policemen" comes from the *Austin Daily Statesman* on December 29, 1885. For concision and clarity, I grouped all of the citizens' proposals in one section in this chapter. Besides being reported in the *Austin Daily Statesman,* the arrival in Austin and the performances at Millett's Opera House of Abbott and the English Opera Company were later reviewed in the *Texas Vorwaerts,* a weekly newspaper for the state's German immigrants, on January 1, 1886.

The citizen's letter about the electric lights was reported in the *Austin Daily Statesman* on January 2, 1886. Other stories and letters asking for electric lights were printed in the *Daily Statesman* on January 22, 1886, and March 21, 1886.

The story of the "fake Pinkertons" was not initially reported in the newspapers. Based on a study of train schedules and a report in the December 27, 1885, *Missouri Republican*—"Experienced detectives are on the way here again to try their skill," read the story—I am using my best estimate as to the date of their arrival in Austin.

CHAPTER FIFTEEN

The revelation about "fake Pinkertons" was first reported on February 22, 1887, in the *Fort Worth Gazette* and the *Austin Daily Statesman* when an investigation was begun by the aldermen over the amount Mayor Robertson had paid the detectives. On February 26, 1887, William Pinkerton wrote a letter to an Austin citizen laying out the entire story about how Austin's mayor had hired the wrong Pinkerton agency. The letter was printed in the *Austin Daily Statesman* on March 4, 1887.

Details about Matthew Pinkerton's agency come from Andreas's *History of Chicago,* p. 119, and Pinkerton's *Murder in All Ages: The History of Crime,* pp. 10–14. Further information comes from the *New York Times* on November 14, 1884, March 16, 1886, March 17, 1886, March 18, 1886, and October 11, 1889; the *Fort Wayne Gazette* on September 14, 1894; and the *Marion Daily Star* of Indiana on December 9, 1895. Details about Matthew Pinkerton's "correspondence school" come from the Pinkertons' National Detective Agency files, Box 9, at the Library of Congress. More about the history of Matthew Pinkerton's agency was found in the *Chicago Daily News* on May 1, 1897, and February 19, 1918.

The Citizen's Committee meetings and reward information were detailed in the *Austin Daily Statesman* on December 29, 1885, January 2, 1886, January 3, 1886, and January 8, 1886.

Governor Ireland's reward comes from the *Fort Worth Daily Gazette* and the *Austin Daily Statesman* on December 31, 1885.

Echols's arrest was reported in the *Austin Daily Statesman,* the *Houston Daily Post,* the *Galveston Daily News,* the *Fort Worth Gazette,* and the *San Antonio Light* on December 30, 1885, and December 31, 1885.

Dallas City marshal Arnold's theory is from the *Dallas Morning News* on January 9, 1885.

Martinez's arrest was reported in the *Austin Daily Statesman* on December 31, 1885, and January 1, 1886; the *Fort Worth Gazette* on December 31, 1885; and the *Washington Critic-Record* on December 31, 1885.

Lucy's policy toward tramps and vagrants is from the *Austin Daily Statesman* on December 27, 1885.

Calling parties, the governor's open house, and Fireman's Hall celebration were reported in the *Austin Daily Statesman* on January 2, 1886; the *San Antonio Daily Express* on January 3, 1886; and the *Galveston Daily News* on January 2, 1886.

The theory that the killer was a patient from the lunatic asylum was reported in the *Austin Daily Statesman* on December 29, 1885; the *Houston Daily Post* on December 29, 1885; and the *Galveston Daily News* on December 29, 1885.

The moonlight madness theory was reported in the *Austin Daily Statesman* on January 15, 1886, and January 17, 1886; and in the *Texas Vorwaerts* on January 15, 1886. The Frank Einstein story was reported in the *Fort Worth Gazette* on December 26, 1885.

The *New York World* stories ran on December 26, 1885, December 29, 1885, and January 1, 1886. Details on the newspaper itself come from Juergen's *Joseph Pulitzer and the New York World*, pp. vii, viii, ix, x, and 22–39.

The "eye to the upper crust" letter was printed in the *Austin Daily Statesman* on December 30, 1885.

The London physician's letter was printed in the *Austin Daily Statesman* on December 29, 1885.

Residents wanting to leave comes from the *Austin Daily Statesman* on December 27, 1885, December 30, 1885, and January 1, 1886. Blacks moving from Austin was also reported in the *Daily Statesman* on January 21, 1886.

The Laredo story was originally published in the *Laredo Times* and reprinted in the *Austin Daily Statesman* on January 1, 1886.

Out-of-town Texans being warned to stay away and female students not coming to the University of Texas are from the *Austin Daily Statesman* on December 30, 1885.

"The dark and bloody ground" is from the *San Antonio Times*, December 29, 1885. "Criminal city" is from the *Dallas Daily Herald* on January 20, 1886. "Worse than Babel" is from the *Fort Worth Gazette* on January 17, 1886.

The *Temple Times* editorial appeared on January 2, 1886.

Rumors about Jimmy Phillips were initially reported in some of the newspapers, including the *Austin Daily Statesman* on January 2, 1886.

CHAPTER SIXTEEN

Details about Eula Phillips's history are from *Austin Daily Statesman* on January 14, 1883; the *New York World* on December 27, 1885; Travis County deed records for 1878; U.S. Census for 1880; Day's *The Heroes of San Jacinto by Sam Houston*, p. 427, and "Post Office Papers of the Republic of Texas, 1836–1839," p. 48.

Information on Bailes was taken from the *Austin Daily Statesman*, March 3, 1885, April 17, 1885, June 3, 1885, February 2, 1886, February 5, 1886, June 5, 1886, October 28, 1886; the *San Antonio Light* on January 4, 1886; the *Bastrop Advertiser* on June 26, 1886; the *Texas Vorwaerts* on January 8, 1886, and February 19, 1886; the *Waco Day* on February 20, 1886; and the *Galveston Daily News* on February 25, 1886.

Mae Tobin's talk with Bailes and later with city officials is reconstructed from accounts in the *Austin Daily Statesman* on February 12, 1886, February 13, 1886, February 14, 1886, May 26, 1886, and May 27, 1886; and the *San Antonio Daily Express* on May 4, 1886. The description of Tobin's house is from the *Austin Daily Statesman* on November 30, 1888.

Details about city leaders, curious about behavior of the bloodhound, are from the *New York World* on January 1, 1886, and the *Austin Daily Statesman* on January 28, 1886.

Details about the uxoricide arrest are from the *Austin Daily Statesman* of February 12, 1886, and February 14, 1886.

Reaction by citizens and family to Phillips's arrest was reported in the newspapers listed above between January 3, 1886, and January 18, 1886.

Prosecutors claiming they had evidence of Jimmy Phillips's violent nature is from the *Austin Daily Statesman*, February 12, 1886, February 14, 1886, May 26, 1886, and May 27, 1886.

T. E. Moore hired as special prosecutor is from the *Austin Daily Statesman* on January 22, 1886, and January 23, 1886. His previous statement about a maniac comes from the *Austin Daily Statesman*, reprinting the *St. Louis Republican* article of January 8, 1886.

Hancock's arrest is from the *Austin Daily Statesman* and the *San Antonio Daily Express* on January 28, 1886, and January 29, 1886.

CHAPTER SEVENTEEN

Reaction to Bailes's evidence on Hancock is from the *Austin Daily Statesman* on January 31, 1886; and from the *Waco Day* on January 30, 1886, and February 2, 1886.

More criticism of the arrest is from the *Texas Vorwaerts*, January 29, 1886. "Men into infernal fiends" and "strong as Holy writ" are from the *Austin Daily Statesman* on January 28, 1886.

The description of Mrs. Hancock's letter is from the *San Antonio Daily Express* on January 28, 1886; the *Houston Daily Post* on January 30, 1886; the *Fort Worth Gazette* on January 30, 1886; and the *Austin Daily Statesman* on January 31, 1886, and June 2, 1887.

The Moses Hancock interview is in the *Austin Daily Statesman*, January 29, 1886.

Maurice, the Malaysian cook, leaving for England was first reported in the *Austin Daily Statesman*, November 7, 1888, November 14, 1888, and November 17, 1888.

"Talented sensationalist" was first used in wire service stories on January 4, 1886. Other newspapers, such as the *Fort Worth Gazette* on December 27, 1885, were using the "Midnight Assassin" moniker.

As for the proposals made to stop the "lunatic," they were printed throughout late December and to the end of January 1886. For concision purposes, I again compiled these stories into one section. Among the sources are the *Waco Daily Express* on December 31, 1885, and January 8, 1886; the *New York Times* on December 26, 1885; the *Texas Vorwaerts* on January 15, 1886; and the *Austin Daily Statesman* on January 18, 1886. Dr. Damos was mentioned specifically in the *Austin Daily Statesman* on February 6, 1886.

Philp's story is discussed in the *Austin Daily Statesman* on January 13, 1886; the *Waco Day* on January 20, 1886; and the *Fort Worth Gazette* on January 13, 1886, January 14, 1886, January 15, 1886, and January 16, 1886. The story itself was published in the *Gazette* on January 18, 1886.

The Patti Scott murder comes from the *San Antonio Light* on January 30, 1886, and the *San Antonio Daily Express* on January 30, 1886. More details on the Scott murder are from the *New York Times* on February 1, 1886; the *San Antonio Daily Express* on January 31, 1886, February 2, 1886, February 5, 1886, and February 27, 1886; and from the *Austin Daily Statesman* on February 2, 1886, February 5, 1886, and February 10, 1886.

The report on Austin as the healthiest city is from the *Austin Daily Statesman* on February 18, 1886.

CHAPTER EIGHTEEN

Statements from Phillips's preliminary trial were taken from previously mentioned newspapers, February 12, 1886, to February 17, 1886. Descriptions of the courthouse come from the *Austin Daily Statesman* on October 17, 1970, and June 24, 1972.

Initial rumors about Swain come from the *New York Tribune* on February 22, 1886, and the *Fort Worth Daily Gazette* on February 26, 1886, and February 27, 1886.

Swain denies charges and promises to look for originator of telegram are from the *Galveston Daily News* on February 25, 1886, and March 21, 1886; the *Fort Worth Gazette* on March 3, 1886, and March 21, 1886; and the *San Antonio Daily Express* on February 26, 1886, and February 27, 1886.

Biographical details on Ross come from Gwynne's *Empire of the Summer Moon*, pp. 180–82; Brenner's *Sul Ross: Soldier, Statesman, Educator*; DeShields's *They Sat in High Places*, pp. 331–38; Hendrickson's *The Chief Executives of Texas*; and Whiteside's "The Life of Lawrence Sullivan Ross," pp. 1–76.

Ross's lack of campaign skills comes from Brenner's *Sul Ross*, pp. 152–54. "Camp meeting drawl" is from the *Galveston Daily News*, August 12, 1886. Clark's remarks about Ross are from Clark's *A Glance Backward; or, Some Events in the Past History of My Life*, pp. 73–77 and 87.

Swain a favorite and "shoo in" in the governor's race is from the *Austin Daily Statesman*, January 24, 1886, and April 29, 1886.

Criticism of Swain is from the *San Antonio Times, Waco Daily Examiner, Balance Wheel*, and other newspapers on March 7, 1886, March 9, 1886, March 11, 1886, March 20, 1886, and March 23, 1886.

Defense of Swain is from various Texas newspapers on February 26, 1886, February 27, 1886, March 3, 1886, March 21, 1886, March 23, 1886, and March 25, 1886.

Ross opening his campaign for governor is from Brenner's *Sul Ross*, p. 175, and Jones's *The Search for Maturity*, pp. 136–37. Also see the *Dallas Morning News* on February 25, 1886, and February 26, 1886. Robertson sending the Pinkertons back to Chicago was later reported in the *Austin Daily Statesman* on March 4, 1887.

Ordinances passed by aldermen is from the *Austin Daily Statesman*, April 2, 1885.

Dr. Given committed to asylum was reported by the *Austin Daily Statesman*, the *Dallas Morning News*, and the *San Antonio Daily Express* on February 16, 1886, and February 17, 1886. Also see the same newspapers on August 27, 1886, and August 28, 1886. Given's lunacy commitment is on file at the County Court, Travis County, #1103, in which he is ordered to be "in restraints."

Jimmy Phillips's trial was covered by the newspapers named above from May 22, 1886, to June 2, 1886. The testimony was also reported in *Reports of Cases Argued and Adjudged in the Court of Appeals of Texas*, 1886, Case 2271, *James O. Phillips vs. State of Texas*.

CHAPTER NINETEEN

Reaction to the Phillips verdict was chronicled in Texas newspapers from June 5, 1886, to June 6, 1886. Lawyers' comments come from the *Austin Daily Statesman* and the *San*

Antonio Daily Express, June 6, 1886. Robertson announcing he will next try Moses Hancock also comes from June 6, 1886, editions of both newspapers.

Swain campaigning prior to the Democratic Party's state convention is from the *Austin Daily Statesman*, the *Galveston Daily News*, the *Fort Worth Gazette*, and the *San Antonio Daily Express* from June 1 to 6, 1886. Swain's stop with cheering women is from the *Galveston Daily News* on June 5, 1886. Criticism that Swain could not find the telegraph operator comes from the *Fort Worth Gazette* on May 25, 1886. Other allegations against Swain are detailed in Brenner's *Sul Ross*, p. 53. Ross beginning to rise in the polls is from the *Waco Daily Express*, July 11, 1886, and July 15, 1886.

The Democratic convention is detailed in Jones's *The Search for Maturity*, pp. 135–44; and by several Texas newspapers, most notably the *Galveston Daily News*, from August 12, 1886, to August 17, 1886. Swain returning to Austin to join a law firm is from the *Austin Daily Statesman* on December 1, 1886, and March 24, 1887.

Doc Carver's performance is from the *Austin Daily Statesman* on October 17, 1886, and the *Austin Record* (a new Austin newspaper that had just been established) on October 23, 1886. Details about Carver himself come from Thorp's *Spirit Gun of the West*.

Phillips's appeal was reported by numerous Texas newspapers on October 24, 1886, and November 11, 1886. Information also comes from *Reports of Cases Argued and Adjudged in the Court of Appeals of Texas*, 1886, Case #2271, *The State of Texas vs. James O. Phillips*.

Ross's inauguration and the Driskill ball are from Brenner's *Sul Ross*, p. 158, and the *Austin Daily Statesman*, December 28, 1888, January 1, 1888, and January 2, 1888.

Ireland promoting Texas is from the *North American Review*, December 1885, pp. 523–57.

Ireland campaigning for the U.S. Senate is from Barr's *Reconstruction to Reform: Texas Politics, 1876–1906*, pp. 100–101. The "Oxcart" nickname is from Richardson's *Texas: The Lone Star State*, pp. 246–47. Leaving the governor's office and returning to Seguin is from DeShields's *They Sat in High Places*, pp. 205–326. The Hancock trial was covered by various Texas newspapers from May 30, 1887, through June 8, 1887.

Elgin's history comes from the *Austin Daily Statesman* on July 29, 1881, and June 16, 1882.

The shooting of Elgin was covered by the *Austin Daily Statesman* from February 9, 1886, to February 12, 1886. The "false in every particular" comment ran in the *Austin Daily Statesman* on February 21, 1886. Deputy U.S. marshal White and Notary Public Thomas Wheeles testified about the footprints in the Phillips trial.

CHAPTER TWENTY

The Gainesville attacks were covered by the *Austin Daily Statesman*, *Dallas Daily Herald*, *Dallas Morning News*, *Fort Worth Gazette*, *Galveston Daily News*, *New York World*, *National Police Gazette*, *Sherman Herald*, and *Sherman Daily Register* between July 14, 1887, and August 6, 1887. The "Texas Jekyll" phrase ran in newspapers on July 2, 1887. The *New York World* article ran on August 2, 1887, and the *National Police Gazette* story was published on July 30, 1887.

People in Austin afraid the killer would return is from the *Austin Daily Statesman* on July 17, 1887.

Mayor Robertson still booming is from the *Austin Daily Statesman* on July 24, 1887, and from "Minutes of the Texas State Medical Association," p. 11.

Mayor Robertson and the "fake Pinkertons" is from the *Austin Daily Statesman,* February 22, 1887, and March 3, 1887.

Nalle winning the election is from the *Austin Daily Statesman,* December 1, 1887, December 2, 1887, December 3, 1887, December 4, 1887, and December 8, 1887; and Sevcik's "Selling the Austin Dam," pp. 215–17. Nalle putting in lights in 1888 is from Starr's *History of Travis County and Austin,* p. 250.

Dedication of the state capitol and the XIT Ranch is from the *Austin Daily Statesman* from May 18, 1888, to May 22, 1888; Jones's *The Search for Maturity,* pp. 33–36, 53–77, and 140; Barkley's *Travis County and Austin,* pp. 205–20; Haley's *Passionate Nation,* p. 383; and Davis's *Legendary Texans,* p. 17.

CHAPTER TWENTY-ONE

Among the sources that document the Jack the Ripper murders are Evans and Skinner's *The Ultimate Jack the Ripper Sourcebook;* Sugden's *The Complete History of Jack the Ripper;* Begg's *Jack the Ripper: The Facts;* and Rumbelow's *The Complete Jack the Ripper.*

The *Austin Daily Statesman*'s articles linking Jack the Ripper and the Austin killer—and the possibility that the killer was a Malay cook from Austin—ran on September 5, 1888, October 10, 1888, November 7, 1888, November 14, 1888, and November 17, 1888.

To get a sense of how big the story was in 1888, other newspapers that published articles suggesting a link between Jack the Ripper and the Austin killer were the *Dallas Morning News,* November 7, 1888; the *Fort Worth Gazette,* October 5, 1888; the *Houston Daily Post,* November 17, 1888; the *Galveston Daily News,* October, 6, 1888; the *Washington D.C. Evening Star,* November 20, 1888; the *St. Louis Post Dispatch,* November 16, 1888; the *Atlanta Constitution,* October 4, 1888; the *Chicago Tribune,* October 6, 1888; the *New York Times,* October 7, 1888; the *New York World,* October 5, 1888; the *New York Evening Post,* October 6, 1888; the *New York Tribune,* October 5, 1888; the *New York Herald,* November 13, 1888; the *London Daily News,* October 2, 1888; the *London Daily Telegraph,* October 2, 1888, October 5, 1888, and October 6, 1888; the London *Times,* September 28, 1888, October 4, 1888, and October 6, 1888; the *London Star,* October 12, 1888; the *Pall Mall Gazette,* October 1, 1888, and November 10, 1888; the *Woodford Times,* October 12, 1888; the *East London Observer,* October 20, 1888; and the *Illustrated Police News,* October 20, 1888.

The Malaysian cook connection has been studied in Newton's *The Encyclopedia of Unsolved Murders,* p. 336, and Curtis's *Jack the Ripper and the London Press,* pp. 244–45.

Buffalo Bill's trip to England is chronicled in Gallop's *Buffalo Bill's British Wild West.* The three cowboys and Black Elk being detained for questioning comes from Sugden's *The Complete History of Jack the Ripper,* p. 303.

Details on the New York Academy of Medicine come from Van Ingen's *The New York Academy of Medicine: Its First Hundred Years.*

Sources for Spitzka's biography are the *New York Times*, January 14, 1914; Wilson's *Appletons' Cyclopædia of American Biography*, p. 675; and the January 1914 issue of the *Pacific Medical Journal*, p. 91.

Coverage of Spitkza's speech was in the December 20, 1888, issue of the *Boston Medical and Surgical Journal;* the January–June 1889 issue of the *Weekly Medical Review*, pp. 154–56; and the *New York Herald*, December 14, 1888. A transcript of Spitzka's speech and his additional arguments ran in the *Journal of Nervous and Mental Diseases*, December 1888, pp. 765–78.

CHAPTER TWENTY-TWO

The Nicaragua story ran in the *Austin Daily Statesman* on February 7, 1889, and February 17, 1889. Details on the Nicaragua hoax can be found in Norder, Vanderlinden, and Evans's *Ripper Notes: Suspects and Witnesses*, p. 19.

The theory that Jack the Ripper may have read about the Austin murders is from the *New York World*, October 5, 1888.

District Attorney Robertson deciding not to retry Hancock is from the *Austin Daily Statesman*, December 31, 1888.

The Memphis detective theory is from the *Austin Daily Statesman*, October 5, 1888.

Martinez cultivating flowers is from the "State Lunatic Asylum Patient Records," p. 195, January 13, 1889.

Except for Walter Spencer, black suspects were not listed in Morrison and Fourmy's *General Directory of the City of Austin* for the years 1889–90, 1890–91, and 1903–04.

Townsend's burglary conviction is recorded in "Convict Record Texas State Penitentiary," case number 3846.

Jimmy Phillips moving to Georgetown and remarrying later in life comes from the author's interview with Donna O' Donnell, Phillips's granddaughter from his second marriage.

Information on Moses Hancock comes from his obituary in the *Waco Times Herald* on March 25, 1919, and the author's interviews with his great-grandson Richard S. Bagby.

Swain as the "Midnight Murderer" is from the *Austin Daily Statesman*, August 24, 1888. Swain's move to Houston is noted in his obituary in the *Houston Chronicle*, December 20, 1904.

Tobin's house destroyed is from the *Austin Daily Statesman* on November 30, 1888.

Nalle as boomer is from the *Austin Daily Statesman*, December 5, 1888.

Dr. Johnson's death is from the *Austin Daily Statesman* on April 10, 1889. Mrs. Johnson's death is from the *Austin Daily Statesman* on July 2, 1889.

Wooldridge's biographical information comes from Overbeck's "Alexander Penn Wooldridge" in the *Southwestern Historical Quarterly.*

Wooldridge pushing the idea of a dam in early 1888 is from the *Austin Daily Statesman* on January 1, 1888, January 4, 1888, January 6, 1888, March 7, 1888, and March 19, 1888.

Wooldridge pushing the idea again, promoting the dam as an electric plant, is from the *Austin Daily Statesman* on August 3, 1889, September 1, 1889, September 3, 1889, October 27, 1889, October 30, 1889, and November 12, 1889. More details about

Wooldridge's proposal come from Sevcik's "Selling the Austin Dam: A Disastrous Experiment in Encouraging Growth" and Suhler's "Significant Questions Relating to the History of Austin, Texas, to 1900." Information on arc lamps around the country is from Freeberg's *The Age of Edison*, pp. 47–70.

"Citizens Against Nalle" is from the *Austin Daily Statesman* on November 30, 1889. McDonald and aldermen winning their elections by a handy majority is from the *Austin Daily Statesman* on December 1, 1889.

The plan developed for the dam is from the *Austin Daily Statesman*, March 29, 1890, and March 30, 1890. The bond vote and celebration are from the *Austin Daily Statesman*, May 6, 1890.

The decision to get lights from Detroit is from the *Austin Daily Statesman*, "How Tower Lights Came to Be Here," January 1933. The size of the moon lamps and towers is from Starr's *History of Travis County and Austin*, p. 132. Trying to prevent cowboys from shooting out the lamps is from Galloway's "Moonlight Memories" in *Texas Highways*, May 1995, pp. 12–15.

The arc lamps being turned on is from the *Austin Daily Statesman*, May 4, 1895, and May 8, 1895.

CHAPTER TWENTY-THREE

Helpful sources detailing the impact of the arc lamps on Austin life were the *Austin Daily Statesman* on December 14, 1968, and March 26, 1939; Weems's *Austin: 1839–1989*, p. 25; Southwell's "A Social and Literary History of Austin from 1881 to 1896," p. 95; Jones's *Life on Waller Creek*, p. 146; the Austin Chamber of Commerce's "The Story of Austin's Famous Tower Lights"; and Humphrey's *Austin: An Illustrated History*, pp. 60, 77–76, 129–30.

"No taxes and no Negroes" is from Southwell's "A Social and Literary History of Austin from 1881 to 1896," p. 14.

Lucy retiring is from the *Austin Daily Statesman*, February 6, 1927.

Chenneville at the Merchants Police and Southern Detective Association is from the *Austin Daily Statesman*, March 1, 1904.

Details on Given's death are from the *Austin Daily Statesman* on August 26, 1886, and August 28, 1886; the *San Antonio Daily Express* on August 27, 1886, and August 18, 1886; and the 1886 *New Orleans Medical and Surgical Journal*, p. 14. Denton at the new sanitarium is from Starr's *History of Travis County and Austin*, p. 243.

Among the histories studied were Maxey's *The History of Texas to 1893*; Thrall's *A Pictorial History of Texas: From the Earliest Visits of European Adventurer to A.D. 1885*; Bancroft's *History of North Mexican States and Texas*, vol. 2, *1801–1889*; Wooten's *A Comprehensive History of Texas 1685 to 1897*; Brown's *History of Texas from 1685 to 1892*; and Pennybacker's *A New History of Texas for Schools*.

The alienists' meeting about the Midnight Assassin and "moral insanity" is from the *Dallas Morning News*, May 23, 1892, and Halttunen's *Murder Most Foul*, pp. 216–39.

Krafft-Ebing's theories are from his *Psychopathia Sexualis with Especial Reference to the Antipathic Sexual Instinct*, pp. 351–59.

The Henry Holmes information comes from Larson's *Devil in the White City*.

The Myrtle Hornsby Callan interview was conducted by the author on April 19, 2002, with follow-up telephone interviews.

Ghost references come from the Callan interview; Barkley's *History of Travis County and Austin*, p. 332; and from the *Austin Daily Statesman*, February 28, 1935.

Rebecca Ramey still wandering the streets is from the *Austin Daily Statesman*, August 28, 1888.

Jim Crow coming early is based on Humphrey's *Austin: A History of the Capital City*, pp. 35–39; Barr's *Reconstruction to Reform, Texas Politics, 1876–1906*, pp. 192–99; and Mears's *Grace Will Lead Me*, pp. 99, 138–39. After Carrington's loss, no black aldermen being elected until 1971 is from Humphrey's *Austin: A History of the Capital City*, p. 35.

Whitman details come from Colloff's "Ninety-Six Minutes" in the *Texas Monthly*, August 2001, p. 104.

EPILOGUE

Moonlight tower landmark designation comes from "City of Austin Historic Landmark Inventory," Moonlight Towers File C14h–74–028; and City of Austin, Texas, "Ordinance Designating Certain Moonlight Towers as Historic Landmarks," August 6, 1975.

The author's interview with Dorothy Larson was conducted in January 2000.

The story in *Texas Monthly* was "Capital Murder," July 2000.

The author's interviews with Peyton Abbott were conducted in September 2002 and September 2011, with follow-up phone calls.

Townsend's escape comes from "Convict Record Texas State Penitentiary," case number 3846, "Escape: July 13, 1895."

The author's interview and follow-up phone calls with Lois Douglas took place in June 2002.

The Eugene Burt information is taken from Daniell's "The Jurisprudence of Insanity, with Especial Reference to the Case and Trial of Eugene Burt," pp. 2–24.

The Black Elk information came in part from Casson's *Buffalo Bill's Wild West*, p. 190, and Neihardt's *Black Elk Speaks*.

Shirley Harrison lays out her theory in *Jack the Ripper: The American Connection*.

BIBLIOGRAPHY

Allen, Bertram Leon. *Blacks in Austin*. Published by the author, 1989.

Andreas, Theodore. *History of Chicago: From the Earliest Period to the Present Time*, vol. 3. Ann Arbor: University of Michigan Press, 1886.

Ariens, Michael. *Lone Star Law: A Legal History of Texas*. Lubbock: Texas Tech University Press, 2011.

Askins, Col. Charles. *Texans, Guns, and History*. New York: Winchester Press, 1970.

Austin History Center. "Austin Public Schools Teacher's Daily Register Primary Department Session, 1884–1885."

———. "Digest of General Ordinances of the City of Austin," for 1885–86.

Austin Police Department. "Record of Police Calls and Arrests, Oct. 21, 1879–May 31, 1885." Austin History Center.

Bancroft, Hubert Howe. *History of North Mexican States and Texas*, vol. 2: *1801–1889*. San Francisco: History Co., 1889.

Barkley, Mary Starr. *History of Travis County and Austin, 1839–1899*. Waco: Texian Press, 1963.

Barr, Alwyn. *Black Texans: A History of African Americans in Texas, 1528–1995*. Norman: University of Oklahoma Press, 1996.

———. *Reconstruction to Reform: Texas Politics, 1876–1906*. Austin: University of Texas Press, 1971.

Bartholomew, Eugene Carlos. *Diary, 1885–1900*. Austin History Center.

Beavan, Colin. *Fingerprints: The Origins of Crime Detection and the Murder Case That Launched Forensic Science*. New York: Hyperion, 2001.

Begg, Paul, Martin Fido, and Keith Skinner. *The Jack the Ripper A–Z*. London: Headline Book Publishing, 1991.

Begg, Paul. *Jack the Ripper: The Facts*. New York: Barnes and Noble, 2004.

Bellesiles, Michael A. *Arming America: The Origins of a National Gun Culture*. New York: Alfred A. Knopf, 2000.

Benedict, H. Y. *The Book of Texas*. New York: Doubleday, Page, 1916.

Benner, Judith Ann. *Sul Ross: Soldier, Statesman, Educator*. College Station: Texas A&M Press, 1983.

Berry, Margaret. *The University of Texas: A Pictorial Account of Its First Century*. Austin: University of Texas Press, 1980.

Biggerstaff, Beverly. "Austin Police Force, 1851–1962." Austin History Center.

Bolton, Paul. *Governors of Texas*. Paris, TX: Paris News, 1947.

Bopp, William J., and Donald O. Schultz. *History of American Law Enforcement*. Springfield, IL: Charles C. Thomas, 1972.

Brown, Dee. *The American West*. New York: Touchstone/Simon & Schuster, 1994.

Brown, John Henry. *History of Texas from 1685 to 1892*. St. Louis: Bechtold, 1892.

———. *Indian Wars and Pioneers of Texas*. Austin: L.E. Daniell, 1890.

Brownson, Chris. "From Curer to Custodian: A History of the Texas State Lunatic Asylum, 1857–1880." Master's thesis, University of Texas at Austin, 1992.

Burke, James. *Texas Almanac and Immigrant's Handbook for 1883*. Houston: J. Burke Publishers, 1883.

Busfield, Roger M. "History of the Austin Statesman, 1871–1956." Master's thesis, University of Texas at Austin, 1956.

Butler, Anne M. *Daughters of Joy, Sisters of Mercy: Prostitutes in the American West, 1865–90*. Urbana: University of Illinois Press, 1987.

Byrd, James W. *J. Mason Brewer: Negro Folklorist*. Southwest Writers Series. Austin: Steck-Vaughn Company, 1967.

Cameron, Deborah. "Still Going: The Quest for Jack the Ripper." *Social Text*, Fall 1994.

Campbell, Randolph B. *Gone to Texas*. London: Oxford University Press, 2012.

Cashman, Sean Dennis. *America in the Gilded Age: From the Death of Lincoln to the Rise of Theodore Roosevelt*. New York and London: New York University Press, 1984, 1988.

Cemetery Record for Oakwood Cemetery, March 1874–December 1900. Austin History Center.

Chambers, Allen. "National Register of Historic Places Inventory, Nomination Form." Washington, DC: U.S. Department of the Interior, August 14, 1974.

Chenneville, John. "Application for Appointment as Special Texas Ranger." March 11, 1889, Texas State Archives.

———. Biographical file, Austin History Center.

Clark, George. *A Glance Backward; or, Some Events in the Past History of My Life*. Houston: Rein & Sons, 1914.

Cole, Simon A. *Suspect Identities: A History of Fingerprinting and Criminal Identification*. Boston: Harvard University Press, 2002.

Colloff, Pamela. "Ninety-Six Minutes." *Texas Monthly*, August 2006.

"Compt. Swain's Administration," *Texas Review* 1/8. Austin: C. R. Johns & Sons, 1886.

Cotner, Robert C. *The Texas State Capitol*. Austin: Pemberton Press, 1968.

Cox, Heather. *West from Appomattox: The Reconstruction of America After the Civil War.* New Haven: Yale University Press, 2007.

Crunden, Robert M. *A Brief History of American Culture.* New York: North Castle Books, 1990.

Cullen, Tom: *When London Walked in Terror.* New York: Avon, 1965.

Curtis, L. Perry, Jr. *Jack the Ripper and the London Press.* New Haven and London: Yale University Press, 2001.

Custer, Elizabeth B. *Tenting on the Plains; or, General Custer in Kansas and Texas.* New York: Harper and Brothers, 1895.

Dale, Edward Everett. *The Range Cattle Industry: Ranching on the Great Plains from 1865 to 1925.* Norman: University of Oklahoma Press, 1960.

Daniell, F. E. "The Jurisprudence of Insanity, with Especial Reference to the Case and Trial of Eugene Burt." *Texas Medical Journal,* May 29, 1897.

Daniell, L. E. *Personnel of the Texas State Government.* San Antonio: Maverick Printing House, 1892.

———. *Types of Successful Men of Texas.* Austin: Eugene Von Boeckmann, 1890.

Dary, David. *Red Blood and Black Ink: Journalism in the Old West.* New York: Alfred A. Knopf, 1998.

Davis, Joe Tom. *Legendary Texans,* vol. 4. Austin: Eakin Press, 1989.

Day, James M. "Post Office Papers of the Republic of Texas, 1836–1839." Austin: Texas State Library, 1966.

Denton, A. N. *Report of the Superintendent of the Texas State Lunatic Asylum for 1884.* Austin: State Printing Office, 1884.

———. *Report of the Superintendent of the Texas State Lunatic Asylum for 1885.* Austin: State Printing Office, 1885.

DeShields, James T. *They Sat in High Places.* San Antonio: Naylor Company, 1940.

Dixon, Sam Houston, and Lewis Wiltz Kemp. *The Heroes of San Jacinto.* Austin: Anson Jones Press, 1932.

Drago, Henry Sinclair. *The Legend Makers: Tales of the Old-Time Peace Officers and Desperadoes of the Frontier.* New York: Dodd, Mead, 1975.

Dray, Philip. *At the Hands of Persons Unknown: The Lynching of Black America.* New York: Random House, 2002.

Ebert, Thomas G. A. *Social History of the Asylum: Mental Illness and Its Treatment in the Late 19th and Early 20th Century.* Bristol, UK: Wyndam Hall Press, 1999.

Enstam, Elizabeth York. *Women and the Creation of Urban Life: Dallas, Texas, 1843–1920.* College Station: Texas A&M University Press, 1998.

Evans, S. *The Ultimate Jack the Ripper Sourcebook.* London: Constable and Robinson, 2001.

Ezell, John Samuel. *The South Since 1865.* Norman: University of Oklahoma Press, 1975.

Farrell, Mary D. *First Ladies of Texas: A History.* Belton, TX: Stillhouse Hollow Publishers, 1976.

Fehrenbach, T. R. *Lone Star: A History of Texas and the Texans.* New York: Macmillan, 1968.

Fido, Martin. *A History of British Serial Killing: How Britain's Most Famous Serial Killers Were Identified, Caught and Convicted.* London: Carlton Books, 2001.

Fleming, Walter L. "Jefferson Davis, the Negroes and the Negro Problem." *Sewanee Review*, October 1908.

Fosdick, Raymond B. *American Police Systems*. New York: Century Company, 1920.

Franklin, John Hope. *From Slavery to Freedom: A History of Negro Americans*. New York: Vintage Books, 1969.

Franz, Joe B. *The Driskill Hotel*. Austin: Encino Press, 1973.

Freeberg, Ernest. *The Age of Edison: Electric Light and the Invention of Modern America*. New York: Penguin Press, 2014.

Friedman, Lawrence M. *Crime and Punishment in American History*. New York: Basic Books, 1993.

Gallegly, Joseph. *From Alamo Plaza to Jack Harris's Saloon: O. Henry and the Southwest He Knew*. The Hague: Mouton Publishers, 1970.

Gallop, Alan. *Buffalo Bill's British Wild West*. London: Sutton, 2001.

Galloway, Anne. "Moonlight Memories." *Texas Highways,* May 1995.

Galloway, J. R. *The Servant Girl Murders: Primary Source Compilation and Year of Outrage 1885*. Austin: Booklocker.com, 2010.

Gammell, Hans Peter. *Special Laws of the State of Texas, 1822–1897*, vol. 9. Austin: H.P.N. Gammell, 1898.

Gard, Wayne. *Frontier Justice*. Norman: University of Oklahoma Press, 1949.

———. *Rawhide Texas*. Norman: University of Oklahoma Press, 1965.

Gay, Geoffrey. "No Passion for Prudery: Morals Enforcement in Nineteenth-Century Houston." Master's thesis, Rice University, 1977.

Ginger, Ray. *Age of Excess: The United States from 1877 to 1914*. New York: Macmillan, 1965.

Greer, Joubert Lee. "The Building of the Texas State Capitol, 1882–1888." Master's thesis, University of Texas, 1932.

Guidebook Through the World's Cotton and Industrial Centennial Exposition at New Orleans. Harrisburg, PA: Lane S. Hart Printer, 1885.

Gwynne, S. C. *Empire of the Summer Moon: Quanah Parker and the Rise and Fall of the Comanches, the Most Powerful Indian Tribe in American History*. New York: Scribner, 2010.

Hale, Grace Elizabeth. *Making Whiteness: The Culture of Segregation in the South, 1890–1940*. New York: Pantheon Books, 1998.

Hales, Douglas. *A Southern Family in Black and White: The Cuneys of Texas*. College Station: Texas A&M University Press, 2003.

Haley, J. Evetts. *George W. Littlefield*. Norman: University of Oklahoma Press, 1943.

Haley, James L. *Passionate Nation: The Epic History of Texas*. New York: Simon & Schuster, 2006.

Halttunen, Karen. *Murder Most Foul: The Killer and the American Gothic Imagination*. Cambridge, MA, and London: Harvard University Press, 1998.

Harring, Sidney L. *Policing a Class Society: The Experiences of American Cities, 1865–1915*. New Brunswick, NJ: Rutgers University Press, 1983.

Harris, Melvin. *The True Face of Jack the Ripper*. London: Brockhampton Press, 1994.

Harrison, Shirley. *Jack the Ripper: The American Connection*. London: John Blake Publishing, 2003.

Hartsfield, Larry K. *The American Response to Professional Crime, 1870–1917.* Westport, CT: Greenwood Press, 1985.

Heintze, Michael R. *Private Black Colleges in Texas, 1865–1954.* College Station: Texas A&M University Press, 1985.

Hendricks, George D. *The Badman of the West.* San Antonio: Naylor, 1970.

Hendrickson, Kenneth E. *The Chief Executives of Texas from Stephen F. Austin to John B. Connally, Jr.* College Station: Texas A&M Press, 1995.

Henry, O. *O. Henry's Rolling Stones.* New York: Doubleday, Page and Co., 1913.

Hickey, Eric W. *Serial Murderers and Their Victims.* California: Brooks/Cole Publishing, 1991.

Holden, W. C. "Law and Lawlessness on the Texas Frontier, 1875–1890." *Southwestern Historical Quarterly* 44, October 1940.

Hollandsworth, Skip. "Capital Murder." *Texas Monthly,* July 2000.

Hood, Maurice. *Early Texas Physicians, 1830–1915.* San Antonio: State House Press, 1999.

Horan, James D. *The Pinkertons: The Detective Dynasty That Made History.* New York: Crown, 1967.

Hough, Emerson. *The Story of the Outlaw: A Study of the Western Desperado; with Historical Narratives of Famous Outlaws; the Stories of Noted Border Wars; Vigilante Movements and Armed Conflicts on the Frontier.* New York: Cooper Square Press, 2001.

Hudon, Samuel E. "Leather Apron; or, The Horrors of Whitechapel, London 1888." Philadelphia: Town Printing House, 1888.

Humphrey, David C. *Austin: A History of the Capital City.* Austin: Texas State Historical Association, 1997.

———. *Austin: An Illustrated History.* Northridge, CA: Windsor Publications, 1985.

———. "Prostitution and Public Policy in Austin, Texas, 1870–1915." *Southwestern Historical Quarterly,* April 1983.

Hunter, Marvin J. *The Trail Drivers of Texas.* Austin: University of Texas Press, 1924.

Hunter, Tera W. *To 'Joy My Freedom: Southern Black Women's Lives and Labors After the Civil War.* Cambridge, MA: Harvard University Press, 1997.

Inven, Phillip Van. *The New York Academy of Medicine: Its First Hundred Years.* New York: Columbia University Press, 1949.

Ireland, John. "An Inventory of Records, Governor John Ireland, 1879–1887." Texas State Archives.

———. "Progress of Texas." *North American Review,* December 1885.

———. Vertical Files. Dolph Briscoe Center for American History, University of Texas at Austin.

Johnson, Frank W. *History of Texas and Texans.* Chicago: American Historical Society, 1914.

Jones, Billy M. *The Search for Maturity: The Saga of Texas, 1875–1900.* Austin: Steck-Vaughn Company, 1965.

Jones, James T. "Joseph Nalle." Joseph Nalle Vertical File. Austin History Center.

Jones, Joseph. *Life on Waller Creek.* Austin: AAR/Tantalus, 1982.

Jordan, Phillip. *Frontier Law and Order.* Lincoln: University of Nebraska Press, 1970.

Juergens, George. *Joseph Pulitzer and the New York World.* Princeton: Princeton University Press, 1966.

Karolevitz, Robert F. *Newspapering in the Old West: A Pictorial History of Journalism and Printing on the Frontier.* Seattle: Superior Publishing, 1965.

Kasson, Joy S. *Buffalo Bill's Wild West: Celebrity, Memory, and Popular History.* New York: Hill and Wang, 2001.

Katz, William Loren. *The Black West: A Documentary and Pictorial History of the African American Role in the Westward Expansion of the United States.* New York: Simon & Schuster, 1996.

Kerr, Jeffrey. *Austin, Texas, Then and Now: A Photography Scrapbook.* San Antonio: Promised Land Books, 2005.

Kittrell, Norman C. *Governors Who Have Been, and Other Public Men of Texas.* Houston: Dealy-Adey-Elgin, 1921.

Krafft-Ebing, Richard von. *Psychopathia Sexualis, with Especial Reference to the Antipathic Sexual Instinct.* New York: Arcade Publishing, 1965.

Johnson, David R. *Policing the Urban Underworld: The Impact of Crime on the Development of the American Police, 1800–1887.* Philadelphia: Temple University Press, 1979.

Lack, Paul D. "Slavery and Vigilantism in Austin, Texas, 1840–1860." *Southwestern Historical Quarterly* 85/1, July 1981.

Lambert, William. "Report of the Ceremonies of Laying the Corner Stone of the New Capitol of Texas, Austin, March 2, 1885." Austin: Officer of the Commissioner of Insurance, 1885.

Lane, Roger. *Murder in America: A History.* Columbus: Ohio State University Press, 1997.

———. *Policing the City: Boston, 1822–1885.* Cambridge, MA: Harvard University Press, 1967.

Lang, Lawrence Copley. "A Study of Texas Newspapers from 1876 to 1890." Master's thesis, University of Texas at Austin, 1949.

Langford, Gerald. *Alias O. Henry: A Biography of William Sidney Porter.* New York: Macmillan, 1957.

Larson, Erik. *The Devil in the White City.* New York: Crown Publishers, 2003.

Lavender, David. *The Great West.* New York: Houghton Mifflin, 1965.

Lee, James Melvin. *History of American Journalism.* New York: Houghton Mifflin, 1917.

Legislative Council of Texas. *The Texas Capitol: Symbol of Accomplishment.* Austin, Texas, Legislative Council, 1986.

Legislative Council of Texas. *The Texas Capitol: A History of the Lone Star Statehouse.* Austin: Texas Legislative Council, 1998.

Lewis, Jon E. *The Mammoth Book of the West.* New York: Carroll & Graf Publishers, 1996.

Litwack, Leon F. *Trouble in Mind: Black Southerners in the Age of Jim Crow.* New York: Alfred A. Knopf, 1998.

Long, E. Hudson. *O. Henry: The Man and His Work.* Philadelphia: University of Pennsylvania Press, 1949.

Loughery, E. E. *Personnel of the Texas State Government for 1885.* Austin: J. M. Snyder, 1885.

Mackay, James. *Allan Pinkerton: The Eye Who Never Slept.* London: Mainstream, 1996.

Manaster, Jane. "The Ethnic Geography of Austin, Texas: 1875–1910." Master's thesis, University of Texas at Austin, May 1996.

Mann, Alfred E. *Slave Narratives.* Travis County, WPA, District no. 9, 1937.

Manry, Joe Edgar. *Curtain Call: The History of the Theatre in Austin, Texas: 1839–1905.* Austin: Waterloo Press of the Austin History Center, 1985.

Marchiafava, Louis J. *The Houston Police: 1878–1948.* Houston: William Marsh Rice University, 1977.

Maxey, Samuel B. *The History of Texas to 1893.* Originally published in *Harper's New Monthly,* September 1893, repr. Dallas: Highlands Historical Press, 1961.

McCoy, Joseph G. *Historic Sketches of the Cattle Trade of the West and Southwest.* Lincoln and London: University of Nebraska Press, 1985.

McDade, Thomas M. *The Annals of Murder.* Norman: University of Oklahoma Press, 1961.

McQueen, Clyde. *Black Churches in Texas: A Guide to Historic Congregations.* College Station: Texas A&M University Press, 2000.

Mears, Michelle M. *And Grace Will Lead Me Home: African American Freedmen Communities of Austin, Texas, 1865–1928.* Lubbock: Texas Tech University Press, 2009.

Meier, August, and Elliott Rudwick. *From Plantation to Ghetto.* New York: Hill and Wang, 1976.

Miller, Rick. *Bounty Hunter.* College Station, TX: Creative Publishing Company, 1988.

Moffat, Riley Moore. *Population History of Western U.S. Cities and Towns, 1850–1990.* Lanham, MD: Scarecrow Press, 1996.

Monkkonen, Eric H. *Police in Urban America: 1860–1920.* Cambridge, MA: Cambridge University Press, 1981.

Montejano, David. *Anglos and Mexican in the Making of Texas, 1836–1986.* Austin: University of Texas Press, 1987.

Mooney and Morrison. *General Directory of the City of Austin, Texas for 1877–88.* Austin: Eugene Von Boeckman, 1878.

Moore and Gray. *Mercantile and General City Directory for Austin, Texas, 1872–73.* Austin: S. A. Gray and Job Printer, 1872.

Moran, Frank. *The Eye That Never Sleeps: A History of the Pinkerton National Detective Agency.* Bloomington: Indiana University Press, 1982.

Morrison, C. D., and Co. *General Directory of the City of Austin for 1879–80.* Marshall, TX: Jennings Brothers Printers, 1879.

Morrison and Fourmy. *General Directory of the City of Austin, 1885–1886.* Marshall, TX: Jennings Brothers, 1886.

———. *General Directory of the City of Austin, 1889–89.* Marshall, TX: Jennings Brothers, 1889.

———. *General Directory of the City of Austin, 1903–1904.* Marshall, TX: Jennings Brothers, 1904.

Murray, John Wilson. *Memoirs of a Great Canadian Detective: Incidents in the Life of John Wilson Murray.* Toronto: Wm. Collins Sons & Co., 1977.

Nalle, Virginia. "The History of the *Austin Statesman.*" Master's thesis, University of Texas at Austin, 1935.

Neihardt, John. *Black Elk Speaks*. Albany: State University of New York Press, 1932.

Newton, Michael. *The Encyclopedia of Unsolved Murders*. New York: Facts on File, 2009.

Norder, Dan, Wolf Vanderlinden, and Stewart P. Evans. *Ripper Notes: Suspects & Witnesses*. London: Inklings Press, 2005.

Norris, Joel. *Serial Killers: The Growing Menace*. New York: Doubleday, 1988.

Nunn, W. C. *Texas Under the Carpetbaggers*. Austin: University of Texas Press, 1962.

"Obituary for Dr. E.C. Spitzka." *Pacific Medical Journal* 57, January 1914.

O'Connor, Richard. *O. Henry: The Legendary Life of William S. Porter*. New York: Doubleday, 1970.

Olds, J. W. "Texas Notes, 1885." Bancroft Library, Manuscript Collection, University of California at Berkeley.

O'Neal, Bill. *The Texas League, 1888–1987: A Century of Baseball*. Austin: Eakin Press, 1987.

O'Quinn, Truman. "O. Henry in Austin." *Southwestern Historical Quarterly* 43/2, October 1939.

Orum, Anthony. *Power, Money and the People*. Austin: Texas Monthly Press, 1987.

Overbeck, Ruth Ann. "Alexander Penn Wooldridge." *Southwestern Historical Quarterly*, January 1964.

Pennybacker, Anna. *A New History of Texas for Schools*. Tyler, TX: State Publishing, 1888.

Pinkerton, Matthew Worth. *Murder in All Ages: Being a History of Homicide from the Earliest Times, with the Most Celebrated Murder Cases Faithfully Reported, Arranged Under Controlling Motives and Utilized to Support the Theory of Homicidal Impulse*. Chicago: A. E. Pinkerton & Co., 1898.

Prassel, Frank Richard. *The Western Peace Officer: A Legacy of Law and Order*. Norman: University of Oklahoma Press, 1972.

———. *The Great American Outlaw: A Legacy of Fact and Fiction*. Norman and London: University of Oklahoma Press, 1972.

Quarles, Benjamin. *The Negro in the Making of America*. New York: Simon & Schuster, 1987.

Raine, William MacLeod. *Famous Sheriffs and Western Outlaws*. New York: Doubleday, Doran & Company, 1929.

Ramsland, Katherine. *The Human Predator: A Historical Chronicle of Serial Murder and Forensic Investigation*. New York: Berkley Books, 2005.

Reid, Sue Titus. *Crime and Criminology*, 2nd ed. New York: Holt, Rinehart and Winston, 1976.

Rice, Lawrence D. *The Negro in Texas: 1874–1900*. Baton Rouge: Louisiana State University Press, 1971.

Richardson, James F. *Urban Police in the United States*. New York and London: National University Publications, Kennikat Press, 1974.

Richardson, Rupert Norval. *Texas: The Lone Star State*. Englewood Cliffs, NJ: Prentice-Hall, 1958.

Robertson, John. *The Industries of Austin, Texas: Commercial Manufacturing Advantages and Historical, Descriptive and Biographical Facts, Figures and Illustrations. Industry and Improvement and Enterprise!* Austin: n.p., 1885.

Robertson, Margaret. "Life of James Harvey Robertson." James Robertson Vertical File. Austin History Center.

Robinson, Charles M., III. *The Men Who Wear the Star: The Story of the Texas Rangers.* New York: Random House, 2000.

Robinson, Duncan. "O. Henry's Austin." *Southwest Review* 24/4, July 1939.

Robinson, Henry Morton. *Science Catches the Criminal.* New York: Blue Ribbon Books, 1935.

Rousey, Dennis C. *Policing the Southern City: New Orleans, 1805–1889.* Baton Rouge: Louisiana State University Press, 1996.

Rumbelow, D. *The Complete Jack the Ripper.* Boston: New York Graphic Society, 1975.

Sanborn Fire Insurance Maps. *Austin, Texas.* Sanborn Map Publishing Company. Austin History Center, June 1885.

Schlereth, Thomas J. *Victorian America: Transformations in Everyday Life, 1876–1915.* New York: HarperCollins, 1991.

Schlesinger, Arthur Meier. *The Rise of the City, 1878–1898.* Columbus: Ohio State University Press, 1999 (originally published by Macmillan in 1933).

Seale, Everett Young. "John Ireland and His Times." Master's thesis, University of Houston, 1955.

Seltzer, Mark. *Serial Killers: Death and Life in America's Wound Culture.* New York and London: Routledge, 1998.

Sevcik, Edward A. "Selling the Austin Dam: A Disastrous Experiment in Encouraging Growth." *Southwestern Historical Quarterly* 96, October 1992.

Silverthorne, Elizabeth. *Ashbel Smith of Texas: Pioneer, Patriot, Statesman, 1805–1886.* College Station: Texas A&M University Press, 1982.

Simmons, Ariel W. "A Guide to the Microfilm Edition of Pinkerton's National Detective Agency." Box 9: 0618–0878, 0238–0567, and 0618–0878. Washington, DC: Library of Congress, Cataloging-in-Publication Data.

Sitton, Sarah C. *Life at the Texas State Lunatic Asylum, 1857–1997.* College Station: Texas A&M Press, 1999.

Skrabanek, D. W. *The Servant Girl Annihilators.* Wimberly, TX: S&S Press, 2014.

Smallwood, James M. *The Struggle for Equality: Blacks in Texas.* Boston: American Press, 1983.

———. *Time of Hope, Time of Despair: Black Texans During Reconstruction.* Port Washington, NY, and London: National University Publications, Kennikat Press, 1981.

Smith, C. Alphonso. *O. Henry.* Garden City, NY: Doubleday, Page & Company, 1916.

Smith, Ruie. "The Administration of Governor John Ireland, 1883–1887." Master's thesis, University of Texas at Austin, 1934.

Smyth, Frank, and Myles Ludwig. *The Detectives: Crime and Detection in Fact and Fiction.* Philadelphia and New York: J. B Lippincott Company, 1978.

Southwell, Sam Beall. "A Social and Literary History of Austin from 1881 to 1896." Master's thesis, University of Texas at Austin, 1949.

Speer, William S., and John H. Brown. *The Encyclopedia of the New West.* Marshall, TX: United States Biographical Publishing, 1881.

Spitzka, E. C. "The Whitechapel Murders: Their Medico-Legal and Historical Aspects." *Journal of Nervous and Mental Diseases* 13/12, December 1888.

State Administration of Texas. "The Twenty-seventh Legislature." Austin: Ben C. Jones, 1901.

State of Texas. *State of Texas v. James O. Phillips, Reports of Cases Argued and Adjudged in the Court of Appeals of Texas, 1886.* Vol. 22. Austin: Hutchings Printing House, 1886 and 1887.

Stevenson, Louise L. *The Victorian Homefront: American Thought and Culture, 1860–1880.* New York: Cornell University Press, 2001.

Streeter, Floyd B. *Ben Thompson: Man with a Gun.* New York: Frederick Fell, 1957.

Sugden, Philip. *The Complete History of Jack the Ripper.* New York: Carroll & Graf, 1994.

Suhler, Samuel Aaron. "Significant Questions Relating to the History of Austin, Texas, to 1900." Ph.D. diss., University of Texas at Austin, 1966.

Sutherland, Daniel E. *Americans and Their Servants: Domestic Service in the United States from 1800 to 1920.* Baton Rouge: Louisiana State University Press, 1981.

Sweet, Alex, and John Armor Knox. *On a Mexican Mustang Through Texas.* Hartford: S.S. Scranton & Co., 1883.

Swisher, Mrs. Bella French. *History of Austin, Travis County, Texas, with a Description of Its Resources.* Austin: American Sketch Book Publishing House, 1880.

Tatum, Stephen. *Inventing Billy the Kid: Visions of the Outlaw in America, 1881–1981.* Albuquerque: University of New Mexico Press, 1982.

Taylor, Quintard. *In Search of the Racial Frontier: African Americans in the American West, 1528–1990.* New York and London: W. W. Norton, 1998.

Texas State Lunatic Asylum. Martinez, Eugenio. "Patient Records, Texas State Lunatic Asylum, for January 1–December 31, 1886."

Texas State Medical Association. "Minutes of the Texas State Medical Association." Austin: Texas State Medical Association, 1887.

Texas State Penitentiary. "Convict Record for Oliver Townsend." Case no. 3846, July 13, 1895. (On file at Texas State Archives.)

Thorp, Raymond W. *Spirit Gun of the West: The Story of Doc W. F. Carver.* Glendale, CA: Arthur H. Clark, 1957.

Thorwald, Jurgan. *The Century of the Detective.* Trans. Richard and Clara Winston. New York: Harcourt, Brace & World, 1964.

Thrall, Homer. *A Pictorial History of Texas: From the Earliest Visits of European Adventurers to A.D. 1885.* St. Louis, MO: M. D. Thompson and Co., 1879.

Tillotson Institute. "Catalogue of the Tillotson Institute, 1884–1885." Austin: Swindells Printing House, 1885.

Tolbert, Frank X. *An Informal History of Texas.* New York: Harper & Brothers, 1951.

Trachtman, Paul. *The Old West: The Gunfighters.* New York: Time, Inc., 1974.

Tracy, Paul Aubrey. "A Closer Look at O. Henry's Rolling Stone." Master's thesis, University of Texas at Austin, 1949.

Travis County Court. "J. Given Lunacy Commitment, State of Texas." Case #1103. Austin, Texas, February 15, 1886.

Tucher, Andie. *Froth & Scum: Truth, Beauty, Goodness, and the Ax Murder in America's First Mass Medium.* Chapel Hill and London: University of North Carolina Press, 1994.

Twain, Mark. "An Adventure of Huckleberry Finn." *Century* 29, December 1884.

Vandal, Gilles. *Rethinking Southern Violence: Homicides in Post–Civil War Louisiana, 1866–1884.* Columbus: Ohio State University Press, 2000.

Vila, Bryan, and Cynthia Morris. *The Role of Police in American Society: A Documentary History.* Westport, CT, and London: Greenwood Press, 1999.

Waldrep, Christopher. *The Many Faces of Judge Lynch: Extralegal Violence and Punishment in America.* New York: Palgrave Macmillan, 2002.

Walker, Samuel. *A Critical History of Police Reform: The Emergence of Professionalism.* Lexington, MA: D. C. Heath and Company, 1977.

Walters, Ronald G. *Scientific Authority and Twentieth-Century America.* Baltimore: Johns Hopkins Press, 1997.

Walton, William M. *Life and Adventures of Ben Thompson: The Famous Texan.* Houston: Frontier Press of Texas, 1954.

Ward, Geoffrey C. *The West.* New York: Little, Brown, 1999.

Webb, Juanita. "The Administration of Governor L. S. Ross, 1887–1891." Master's thesis, University of Texas at Austin, 1935.

Weekly Medical Review, vol. 19, January–June 1889. St. Louis, MO: Jas. H. Chambers and Co., 1889.

Weems, John Edward. *Austin: 1839–1989.* Austin: Austin American Statesman and Hart Graphics, 1989.

Wellman, Paul I. *A Dynasty of Western Outlaws.* Lincoln: University of Nebraska Press, 1961.

West, Paul. *The Women of Whitechapel and Jack the Ripper.* Woodstock, NY: Overlook Press, 1992.

Wheeler, Kenneth W. *To Wear a City's Crown: The Beginnings of Urban Growth in Texas, 1836–1865.* Cambridge, MA: Harvard University Press, 1968.

White, Deborah Gray. *Too Heavy a Load: Black Women in Defense of Themselves, 1894–1994.* New York and London: W. W. Norton, 1999.

White, Louis. "A Pictorial History of Black Policemen Who Have Served in the Austin Police Department, 1871–1982." Austin Police File, Austin History Center.

White, Owen P. *Texas: An Informal Biography.* New York: G. P. Putnam's Sons, 1945.

Whiteside, Myrtle. "The Life of Lawrence Sullivan Ross." Master's thesis, University of Texas at Austin, 1938.

Wiebe, Robert H. *The Search for Order, 1877–1920.* American Century Series. New York: Hill & Wang, 1967.

Wilbarger, J. W. *Indian Depredations in Texas.* Austin: Hutchings Printing House, 1890.

Wilkins, Frederick. *The Law Comes to Texas: The Texas Rangers, 1870–1901.* Austin: State House Press, 1999.

Williams, David A. *Bricks Without Straw: A Comprehensive History of African Americans in Texas.* Austin: Eakin Press, 1997.

Williamson, G. R. *Texas Pistoleers: The True Story of Ben Thompson and King Fisher.* Charleston, SC: History Press, 2010.

Wilson, Colin. *The Mammoth Book of the History of Murder.* New York: Carroll & Graf, 2000.

Wilson, James Grant, and John Fiske. *Appletons' Cyclopædia of American Biography.* New York: D. Appleton, 1900.

Winegarten, Ruthe. *Black Texas Women: 150 Years of Trial and Triumph.* Austin: University of Texas Press, 1995.

———. *Black Texas Women: A Sourcebook.* Austin: University of Texas Press, 1996.

Woodward, C. Vann. *Origins of the New South, 1877–1913.* Baton Rouge: Louisiana State University Press, 1951.

Woolfolk, George Ruble. *The Free Negro in Texas, 1800–1860: A Study in Cultural Compromise.* Published for the *Journal of Mexican American History* by University Microfilm International, 1976.

Wooten, Dudley G. *A Comprehensive History of Texas, 1685 to 1897.* Dallas: William G. Scarff, 1898.

Worsmer, Richard. *The Rise and Fall of Jim Crow.* New York: St. Martin's Press, 2003.

Yadon, Laurence J., and Dan Anderson. *Ten Deadly Texans.* Gretna, LA: Pelican Publishing, 2009.

Zelade, Richard. *Guy Town by Gaslight.* Charleston: History Press, 2014.

ACKNOWLEDGMENTS

I'd like to thank Stephen Rubin, the publisher of Henry Holt and Company, and Holt senior editor Serena Jones and associate editor Allison Adler for their thoughtful guidance and insight during the writing of this book. I also would like to thank my literary agent, David Hale Smith of Inkwell Management, for his enormous patience and encouragement.

I was first told about the Midnight Assassin in 1988 by Nicole Krizak, an Austin high school teacher who was working on a novel in which the Midnight Assassin moved to London to become Jack the Ripper. She generously shared with me the 1888 pamphlet she had found, printed in England, that detailed the London police detectives' interest in the Austin killings. Steven Saylor, a well-regarded author who used the murders as the basis for his novel *A Twist at the End* (Simon & Schuster, 2000), was also more than happy to share his research with me. (Incidentally, in his novel, O. Henry solves the murders.)

Over the years, I have been influenced by the work of several

"Austinologists"—the nickname I have given to those who are as obsessed with the Austin killings as the Ripperologists in England are obsessed with the Whitechapel murders. I'd particularly like to thank researcher Allan McCormack, J. R. Galloway, a University of Texas librarian who suspects the killer was Nathan Elgin, and D. W. Skrabanek, a professor at Austin Community College who has theorized that the killer could have been John Hancock, the attorney who was on the defense teams for both the Jimmy Phillips and Moses Hancock trials.

This book would not have been possible without the assistance of the librarians and archivists of the Austin History Center, located at the Austin Public Library. Nor could it have been written without the vast collection of historical newspapers that can be found at the Dolph Briscoe Center for American History at the University of Texas. (The newspaper collection alone contains more than 4,500 titles.) I am very grateful to Christy Moilanen, the archivist for the Travis County Archives. In June 2014, when just about everyone thought there was nothing more to learn about the killings, she saw some folded pages in the bottom of an unmarked box that turned out to be the original handwritten court transcripts and inquest reports of the Susan Hancock and Eula Phillips murder cases. I am indebted to Moilanen's love of unmarked boxes.

Finally, all thanks to my wife, Shannon, who spent many years helping me go through historical collections at numerous libraries around Texas and in New York, looking for a clue—any clue—as to the Midnight Assassin's identity.

ILLUSTRATION CREDITS

page 136 Austin History Center, Austin Public Library
page 141 Courtesy of Richard S. Bagby
page 145 Courtesy of Dorothy Larson and Donna O'Donnell
page 148 *Austin Daily Statesman*
page 165 Harold Washington Library Center, Chicago Public Library
page 170 Austin History Center, Austin Public Library
page 183 Austin History Center, Austin Public Library
page 199 *Souvenirs of Austin, Texas*
page 225 Austin History Center, Austin Public Library
page 226 Austin History Center, Austin Public Library
page 249 Dolph Briscoe Center for American History, University of Texas
page 260 Austin History Center, Austin Public Library

INDEX

Page numbers in *italics* refer to illustrations.